MEXICO CITY IN CONTEMPORARY MEXICAN CINEMA

MEXICO CITY
in Contemporary Mexican Cinema

DAVID WILLIAM FOSTER

 UNIVERSITY OF TEXAS PRESS, AUSTIN

COPYRIGHT © 2002 BY THE UNIVERSITY OF TEXAS PRESS

All rights reserved

Printed in the United States of America

First edition, 2002

Requests for permission to reproduce material from this work should be sent to Permissions, University of Texas Press, Box 7819, Austin, TX 78713-7819.

♾ The paper used in this book meets the minimum requirements of ANSI/NISO Z39.48-1992 (R1997) (Permanence of Paper).

LIBRARY OF CONGRESS CATALOGING-IN-PUBLICATION DATA

Foster, David William.
    Mexico City in contemporary Mexican cinema / David William Foster. — 1st ed.
p.   cm.
Filmography: p.
Includes bibliographical references and index.
    ISBN 0-292-72541-8 (hardcover : alk. paper) — ISBN 0-292-72542-6 (pbk. : alk. paper)
    1. Motion pictures—Mexico—History.   2. Mexico City (Mexico)—In motion pictures. I. Title.
    PN1993.5.M4 F67 2002
    791.43′627253—dc21

2001005452

CONTENTS

PREFACE

It is difficult to speak about Mexico City without being hyperbolic, whether in terms that are negative (its size, its population, its pollution, its infrastructure problems) or positive (its dynamism, its variegated street life, the intensity of its cultural production, the sheer originality of so much of Mexican culture on any level). However, this study has no interest in confirming any of the standard images of Mexico City, not those of the multiplicity of guidebooks, not those of the glossy photo albums, not those of the city's array of social chroniclers, and not those of the writers of dirty realism or sociopolitical testimony.

Rather, this study examines a highly selective inventory of Mexican films of the last thirty years. Mexico City is at the height of its geometric growth in the 1970s, and it is the period, which began in the 1960s, of the emergence of a filmmaking that breaks definitively with the codes of Mexico's golden age of filmmaking, codes set in the decades following the Mexican Revolution of 1910 and the institutionalization of a unified definition of the Mexican nation. With the profound changes which begin to occur in Mexico in the 1960s, and which are too widely known to be commented on here (see Ward; Davis; Schteingatt), there is also a profound change in Mexican cultural production, including filmmaking, a change that challenges both the understanding of Mexico that institutional officialdom wishes to hold in place and the strategies of opposition that have, in a very real sense, become congealed in their own understandings of Mexican society. (The single best source of material on Mexican filmmaking is *The Mexican Cinema Project* [Noriega and Ricci].)

The majority of the films selected are drawn from the decade of the 1990s, and I include only a few films from the previous two decades. There are many reasons for this, but the most obvious one is that there is confluence in the 1990s of an intense social preoccupation with the Mexican capital, the consequence, in part, of the 1985 earthquake but also of the geometric demographic explosion of the city, a preoccupation that quite understandably finds its reflex in the country's cultural production and the notable increase in the quality of Mexican filmmaking. The international recognition that has been coming to Mexican filmmaking, especially since Alfonso Arau's 1992 megahit, *Como agua para chocolate,* inaugurates a decade in which Mexican independent filmmaking actually begins to compete with commercial products and foreign imports. As Maciel points out in his study on the last two decades in Mexican filmmaking, production in the 1980s, in terms of artistic merit and interpretive content, is nothing short of dreadful, and few products from the period hold more than passing interest for in-depth analysis. Thus, the films I have included prior to the 1990s stand out as exceptions to a very poor harvest, which is even more the reason that the films I have included are either something like cult classics (Arturo Ripstein's 1973 *El castillo de la pureza* and Luis Alcoriza's 1971 *Mecánica nacional*) or outstanding exemplars of other sociocultural issues: Jorge Fons's 1989 *Rojo amanecer* is the only full-length narrative film on the 1968 Tlatelolco massacre, while Paul Leduc's 1984 *Frida, naturaleza viva* corresponded to the international rise of fascination with the life and work of Frida Kahlo.

The contestatorial voices of the New Left in Mexico, the internationalism of the Onda writers, and the emergence of a host of subaltern voices have been extensively detailed (for an excellent analysis of Mexican counterculture of the 1960s, see Zolov). But there is one thing that they had in common that merits underscoring here: almost all of them had Mexico City as their point of reference. This is because of the meteoric growth of the metropolis and its conversion into a postmodern megalopolis; it is because of the ways in which new forms of political opposition, inspired in part by international student and protest movements, necessarily addressed themselves to the seat of national government; and it is a consequence of how subaltern identities (women, lesbians and gays, slum dwellers, sex-trade workers, ethnic groups, to mention only a few that have come to prominence in recent Mexican culture), while they may not be confined to metropolitan centers, have fundamentally seen themselves identified in relation to those centers, whether it be because of the opportunities for visibility, the possibility of appropriated spaces, the contact with international points of reference through tourism and world trade, or the opportunities for social action those centers have to offer. Precisely, the sensation that Mexican cultural production is all over the map, is so variegated in its dimensions and manifestations, so dynamic in its alternative constructions to the interpretation of life in Mexico, and so insistently urban is what contributes to the complexity of studying contemporary Mexican culture: it is often, quite simply, impossible to know where to begin.

I do not know what an inventory of images of Mexico City in contemporary Mexican cultural production might look like. Certainly, one can think of the novels of Carlos Fuentes, the essays of Elena Poniatowska and Carlos Monsiváis, and the theater of Vicente Leñero as some places in the recognized canon with which to begin constructing such an inventory. Nor do I know what such an inventory might look like if we limit attention to filmmaking. To be sure, during the golden age of film in Mexico, so much effort was concentrated on an allegedly authentic rural Mexico that Mexico City did not get much attention, and when it did at the hands of Luis Buñuel with *Los olvidados* (1950), unquestionably the founding text of a Mexican urban filmmaking, it was only to generate intense criticism because of the deviation—and, moreover, at the hands of a foreigner, an invited guest in Mexico—from official myths: Buñuel's images of lost and forgotten youths who become part of the rubbish of urban landscape could hardly have set well with ideas of beneficent paternalism held by the ruling party (see Buñuel's comments in Colina and Pérez Turrent [60–63] on the controversies his films provoked; for an overview of Buñuel's Mexican films, see Wood; also Mahieu).

However, in the same way that contemporary Mexican cultural production in general makes insistent reference to the city, the same can be said of contemporary filmmaking. While films that do not reference the megalopolis continue to be made in Mexico, the vast majority do take place in Mexico City, describe the relationship that individuals enjoy with the city, provide a slice of urban life, or establish some measure of pathetic fallacy between the city and the lives of its inhabitants. It is not so much a matter of the way in which the city is a protagonist of these films, but rather of how the city is a locus for human lives and how those lives necessarily involve interaction with the dimensions, parameters, and convolutions of the city in whatever literal and metaphoric ways such terms may be understood.

The films that have been chosen for this study are all independent texts that have received some degree of critical acclaim, distribution, and notoriety; in a few cases, they can even be said to constitute classics or paradigms of contemporary Mexican filmmaking; many of them have won national

and international prizes and have been distributed internationally: *Danzón,
La tarea, Frida, El Callejón de los Milagros, Rojo amanecer,* all fall into one
or more of these categories. While I have not chosen the dozen or so films
to be analyzed in depth, from among the several hundred available for the
thirty-year period in question, for particularly idiosyncratic reasons, there
are a number of special reasons having to do with some outstanding feature
concerning how Mexico City is represented. My goal has not been simply
to talk about an "image" of the city being conveyed in/by the film. On the
contrary, eschewing the facile notion that the city already exists as a given,
awaiting only to be "reflected" in the cultural text, my interest lies with how
the city is created, enacted, and interpreted as part of the process of producing cultural meaning through semiotic texts (it should be clear that I am
taking my cue from concepts of human geography as formulated by Edward
Soja and developed by Doreen Massey, Steve Pile, and Rob Shields, and
from my own work on the city of Buenos Aires, *Buenos Aires: Perspectives
on the City and Cultural Production;* and I have found useful collections of
essays on the body and the city, such as *Mapping Desire,* edited by Bell and
Valentine).

In this sense, then, the city is an integral part of these films, not just someplace for the narrative of the film to take place. The city is not a setting, but
part of the overall effect of meaning for the film, and as such it is brought
into being as much as the characters and plots. Of course, there is a real
Mexico City, but that real Mexico City has no meaning in and of itself. It
has meaning only to the extent that its materiality is inserted into a semiotic
process for the substantiation of meaning. As Julio Cortázar said about
Buenos Aires, "Buenos Aires, como toda ciudad, es una metáfora" (Buenos
Aires, like all cities, is a metaphor).

For this reason, there is no foretelling what that meaning will look like
in any one of the films examined here: there is a different and very particular Mexico City to be found in each one of these films. In some cases, it may
be the more directly verifiable Mexico City that one can identify in conjunction with other established paradigms, such as tourist images, official
paragons, or, generally speaking, overdetermined sites of cultural interpretation (such as provided by a glossy but nevertheless extremely valuable
tourist guide like the *Insight Guides* volume on Mexico City [Schütz]). In
Danzón, for example, some basic primes of Mexico City are surveyed, in order to establish the juxtaposition with Veracruz, in the interplay between
traditional and commercial culture in Mexico. In *El Callejón de los Milagros,* a tiny segment of the vast megalopolis stages the complex interactions
between individuals thrown together by the circumstances of urban

dwellings. And in *Rojo amanecer* the city is never seen, but rather the life that it generates—the social, political, and economic conflicts played out in the city—irrupts into the refuge of family life.

In most of the cases of the films examined here, there is not the sweeping view of the city one might associate with films in which the narrative is the pretext to showcase a city, as in the countless films made about New York or Paris, nor is what is involved here a slice of urban life, the portrayal of melodramatic urban lives, or an object lesson in how to survive in the belly of the megalopolitan monster: television soap operas and sitcoms do pretty much the trite and superficial work with which such views of the city are content to satisfy themselves. Indeed, in many of these films, those who may already have seen them may wonder what there is to say about the city in their regard: the city is there, but that is only a function of the way in which the greatest interest in Mexico now lies with life in the city; and for that reason, so much cultural production, therefore, simply takes place in the city. The challenge, then, becomes the demonstration of how individuals create the city through their lives and how their lives are circumscribed in significant and often violent ways by the city: this is particularly true in interpretations of how the city impacts minority groups or the defenseless, such as young people (*Lolo, El castillo de la pureza*) or women (*Lola, Frida*). The result is not necessarily a greater understanding of the nature of Mexico City, and no pretense is made that these films constitute in any way a secondary bibliography that would contribute to a social science knowledge, properly understood, of the city. Of course, information is there obliquely, and it is possible to obtain a sense of the size of the city and some of the ways in which people live in the city through viewing the films analyzed here and the larger filmography they represent. Yet, the understanding that this study wishes to provide of Mexican filmmaking and Mexico City is how film is a cultural genre that can privilege, through its visual nature, encodements of the city in personal lives and narratives. Lived human experience takes place in places (hence the possibility of this verbal redundancy), and vast segments of modern lives take place in cities, while vast segments of Latin American lives—and, notably, Mexican lives—take place in large metropolitan centers. But how those lives take shape and assume meaning as a consequence of their interaction with and mutual imbrication in the city is the task that so-called urban human geography has set for itself. To view that process as it is interpreted through Mexican cultural production—specifically, one set of contemporary films—is the interest of this study.

No attempt is made to provide a history of Mexican filmmaking: this has been well covered by others (Carl Mora; Ayala Blanco, *Búsqueda del cine mexicano;* Ayala Blanco, *La aventura del cine mexicano;* Ayala Blanco, *La condición del cine mexicano;* Paranaguá; García Riera; García and Aviña's scrapbook on the golden age of Mexican filmmaking is of particular interest). Yet many of them provide little more than a name-and-title catalog and some brief comments on theme or production history, with little, if any, in the way of interpretive analysis of either film language or the ideology of the filmic text. And since my emphasis lies with close readings of the ideological structure of each film (my inspiration in this and previous studies on Argentine and Brazilian filmmaking continues to be the work of Zavarzadeh), in the attempt to bring out the ways in which the city is interpreted through the medium of film, no attempt is made to survey the film career of any particular director, actress, or cameraman. Although there is some good specialized research on Mexican films (e.g., Julia Tuñón's and Joanne Hershfield's monographs on the representation of women during Mexico's golden age of film; Berg's work on the independent films from the 1960s on), there is still a dearth of scholarly bibliography on what is, without question, the largest national filmmaking enterprise in Latin America.

The following intellectual principles sustain this study:

1. Contemporary independent filmmaking in Mexico has directed a sustained gaze on Mexico City, as Mexican life becomes more and more an urban phenomenon with the geometric growth of the Mexican capital and other major Mexican metropolises. After decades of continuing to emphasize the alleged greater authenticity of a rural or provincial Mexican life, as promoted by a dominant ideological stand of postrevolutionary culture, Mexican culture—and, along with it, filmmaking—began slowly to place greater emphasis on the city, until, at the present, the city is virtually the dominant venue of independent filmmaking. It is this emphasis on the city in recent Mexican filmmaking, especially evident in the production of the 1990s, that this study wishes to represent.

2. Mexico City has been insistently studied from any number of historical, sociological, and anthropological perspectives, and there is no dearth of research publications on the city, whether as the center of Mexican society or as a laboratory of urban development. This study neither intends to duplicate the knowledge provided by such studies nor pretends to illustrate them by confirming images drawn from film. Cultural production is, if not an independent domain of knowledge, a significantly different formulation of it: culture constitutes a practice of the interpretation of lived human experience, an interpretation that may supplement or enhance other forms of knowledge, but it conforms to its own principles of internal coherence and

verification, and it cannot be surprising, to any important degree, that the interpretations provided by cultural products do not always conform to those available in other domains of knowledge. Because of its emphasis on the visual, film has an immediacy that may give the impression that it is more verisimilar and less mediated than other forms of interpretive analysis or, indeed, other forms of culture. However, as the analyses put forth by this study wish to demonstrate, film is a highly complex genre that requires careful and detailed scrutiny in order to grasp (in the case of these films focusing on Mexico City) exactly what dimensions of the city are being presented, how they correlate with the human lives enacted in them, and how those dimensions are part of an interpretive project rather than just a backdrop for human events.

3. Many of the sources on Mexican filmmaking are essentially historical accounts, or they are surveys of prominent themes in film; rarely do they constitute ideological analyses of how meaning is created in the filmic text. My goal here is to model how such ideological analyses may be undertaken with regard to films dealing with the city. It is for this reason that I will emphasize repeatedly, if only by implication, that such analyses must concern themselves with much more than what aspect of the city is represented and what social or historical theme is being covered. Human lives take place within specific geographic spaces, and the events of those lives characteristically have meaning in terms of the interaction with the spaces that enclose them. If one of the features of contemporary Mexican filmmaking is what life is like for the contemporary citizen of Mexico City, one proper ideological analysis of how a film creates meaning with respect to that life will necessarily involve a detailed examination of how one lives in and through the city and how the material qualities of urban life circumscribe and intersect with individual and collective stories of the urban experience.

4. For this reason, Mexico City cannot be taken as an unanalyzed given. To be sure, there are some statistical and demographic givens that can be consulted in various sources regarding the city: its extension, its population, its political divisions, its services and infrastructure, and its political conflicts. Lived human experiences interact with these givens (which, to begin with, are neither stable nor unimpeachably ascertained). It is in this interaction that the city becomes a human geography, an interpretation of which underlies, sustains, and gives dense texture to texts of cultural production about those experiences. As film is one such genre of cultural production, film becomes available for examination in terms of how it serves to create unique or particular meanings through its visualized portrayal of the interaction between individuals and their urban spaces.

ACKNOWLEDGMENTS

As always, I must first acknowledge the pleasure of the company of my students: dialogue with them is what makes my research on Latin America so meaningful to me. I also acknowledge the support, over a period of almost four decades, of various programs of Arizona State University.

Particular students and colleagues have made special contributions to the integrity of this study: first and foremost, Cecilia Rosales, who obtained several of the films for me and who closely invigilated my comments on Mexican society, as did also Francisco Manzo Robledo. Mikel Imaz, David R. Miller, Kanishka Sen, and Juan Antonio Serna all saw and commented on portions of this manuscript. Mónica Castillo and Ricardo Szmetan assisted in finding material on specific films. Daniel Enrique Pérez assisted in the preparation of the index.

MEXICO CITY IN CONTEMPORARY MEXICAN CINEMA

ONE   # Politics of the City

The texts analyzed in this chapter relate to how sociopolitical processes are played out within the confines of the city, with reference to the urban landscape of the city and as specific responses to conditions of life imposed by the various dimensions of Mexico City during the latter part of the twentieth century.

For example, the demographic evolution of Mexico City brought with it a series of demands for structural reforms in government and politics. Taking its cue from the international May 1968 movement, Mexico City youth and their allies sought educational and social reforms that led, ultimately, to the student massacre in the Plaza de las Tres Culturas (Tlatelolco) on October 2, 1968. While this event had a profound impact on Mexican cultural life as a whole, one of its notable features is the way in which it involved a specific urban space that became invested with multiple, determined ideological resonances. Although Mexico City is never directly seen in Jorge Fons's *Rojo amanecer* (1989), it is omnipresent as the dominant axis for the construction of meaning in the film.

Guita Schyfter's *Novia que te vea* (1993), in addition to being an important entry in an inventory of feminist filmmaking in Mexico, is notable as the first Mexican film to deal directly with the Jewish community of Mexico City. As such, it exemplifies the postmodern concern in Mexico—in contrast to the modernist synthesis of the culture of the State following the Revolution of 1910—to break with a homogeneous national culture and to promote the identity of subaltern groups, groups whose primary existence, especially in the case of contemporary Jews in Latin America, is a phenomenon of urban social life.

Paul Leduc's *Frida, naturaleza viva* (1984), while attaining an international recognition for its intelligent and probing interpretation of the great Mexican artist Frida Kahlo, may be read with an emphasis on the way in which Kahlo's artistic interests and her particular relationship to Mexican society involved a commitment to the development of Mexico City cultural and social life during the highly ideologically charged period of the consolidation of Mexican society following the end of the Revolution of 1910. Although it is not immediately apparent that Kahlo dealt with urban themes in her paintings and other artwork, Leduc's film makes constant use, in creating an interpretation of Kahlo's career, of her involvement with life in Mexico City in the 1930s and 1940s.

Finally, Antonio Serrano's *Sexo, pudor y lágrimas* (1999), portrays a fully postmodern Mexico City—or, at least, the postmodern city its protagonists would strive to experience, a city in which their often frantic efforts to create and recreate their personal lives are only made possible by their urban experience, while at the same time those efforts are conditioned by that experience. It is inconceivable for Serrano's characters to have a meaning beyond their condition as self-absorbed urban sophisticates; and by setting his film in the wealthy district of Polanco, Serrano underscores a comfortable space that allows for so much self-absorption, self-analysis, and self-fulfillment that the film would appear to have completely left behind the trappings of traditional concepts of a collective national life, trappings that continue to color the urban experiences of the characters of the other films discussed in this chapter: the panorama of urban Mexico City as the scenario for experiences that transcend the personal has been replaced by the micropolitical hysterics of privileged end-of-the-millennium high-rise apartment dwellers. Where there is a political dimension in all of this, although highly attenuated by personalist concerns, is in the relevance of issues of gender equality as part of a project of personal self-fulfillment in modern city life. While all of this customarily comes under the heading of the so-called Americanization of Mexican national, and particularly urban, life, it is, unquestionably, a sociohistorical reality that is as much deserving of serious filmmaking as less middle-class themes are.

Rojo amanecer (Red Dawn)

Jorge Fons's *Rojo amanecer* (1989) occupies a unique place in Mexican filmography: it is the only film dealing directly with the massacre of students in

Tlatelolco, the Plaza de las Tres Culturas (Plaza of the Three Cultures), on the evening of October 2, 1968 (concerning the representation of Mexican social history in the film, see Múñoz). Although there is extensive literary and sociohistorical material on the Tlatelolco massacre, the problems of re-creating such an event on film have discouraged—or prevented—other film-makers from undertaking such a project; there are, however, some films that deal with the consequences of the massacre, especially Felipe Cazals's *Canoa* (1975)[1] and Leobardo López Arteche's short *El grito* (1968), which Pérez Turrent identifies as "the best available record of the 1968 student move-ment" (98). The massacre involved students who had been protesting a wide range of alleged injustices in Mexican political life since the early summer of 1968, issues that the government refused to address. When school resumed in the fall, protests over these issues increased, including public demonstrations.

The government, anxious to suppress any form of social unrest because of Mexico's hosting of the international Olympic games in October, under-took to repress such protests. Faced with a massive demonstration in one of the most symbolically important plazas in Mexico City—Tlatelolco's alter-nate name as the Plaza de las Tres Culturas commemorates how Catholic culture was literally built over Aztec culture and how the culture of Mexi-can nationalism had forged a third, mestizo culture—President Gustavo Díaz Ordaz ordered a military operation against the protesters (see the 1998 documentary *Gustavo Díaz Ordaz y el 68*, part of the *México siglo XX: el poder* series; I have not been able to obtain Oscar Martínez's documentary *1968*).

The result of this operation was considerable carnage in the plaza and in the low-rent housing projects, built for government employees, that tower over the square. There has never been an accurate accounting of how many people were injured or lost their lives in the plaza and in the buildings (the buildings themselves were seriously damaged, and it is probable that scars from the strafing by overflying helicopters still remain).

Perhaps the most memorable text on this event is Elena Poniatowska's *La noche de Tlatelolco* (1971; published in English as *Massacre in Mexico;* see Foster, "Latin American Documentary Narrative," for an examination of the documentary nature of this narrative). Poniatowska interviewed dozens of individuals, including protesters, bystanders, government officials, jour-nalists, and political commentators, and the result is a very striking testi-monial documentary that is something of a standard for such works in Latin America, although it should be noted that she has had her detractors as re-gards the quality of her document (see especially the comments of González de Alba and the reply by Álvarez Garín).

Tlatelolco was, to a great degree, a loss of innocence for Mexico, and the historical reputation of Díaz Ordaz is likely always to be haunted by the fact that he ordered the massacre. His government was under intense pressure to make sure the Olympics, which were being held for the first time in Mexico, went well: the Olympics are always a publicity-propaganda event for the host country, but Mexico's perceived need to convince the world that it had "arrived" as a nation to be reckoned with—1968 was the fiftieth anniversary of the end of the Mexican Revolution; in 1918 the new Mexican constitution was promulgated—appears to have had the judgments of otherwise extremely astute political powers. Mexico had prided itself, because of the solid social and economic bases that derived from the triumph of the revolutionary project of 1910, on escaping from the cycle of personalist dictatorships that plagued many Latin American countries in the twentieth century and, beginning in 1964, the neofascist tyrannies that took hold in the southern cone of the South American continent.

Although Mexico officially supported the Cuban revolution of 1959 and the subsequent Castro government—as it would the 1978 revolution in Nicaragua and insurgency activities in other parts of Latin America against dictatorships—the ruling Institutional Revolutionary Party, the PRI (Partido Revolucionario Institucional), made it quite clear that social unrest in Mexico of any sort would not be tolerated. To be sure, throughout Mexico there had been acts of official violence against peasant protests, along with stories of police corruption and mistreatment at the hands of the police. But such phenomena were socially tolerated as both business as usual and the cost of carrying out the project of creating a modern state under the aegis of a long-lasting revolutionary process. However, what happened at Tlatelolco was substantially different in nature.

In the first place, it was a massive attack against individuals with highly prominent supporters, such as journalist and novelist Elena Poniatowska and television personality and novelist María Luisa (La China) Mendoza. Secondly, the attack took place in a highly visible place: it is one thing to massacre peasants in a village that most people may never have even heard about, but it was quite something else to fire on students in the Plaza de las Tres Culturas, in full view of TV cameras, photographers' cameras, and the residents of the high-rise buildings in the neighborhood (it is important to note that TV coverage was delayed, as film was at first confiscated and then only released several days afterward). And, finally, the massacre at Tlatelolco took place in the context of the Olympic games, when many prominent international personalities were present in the country. In fact, the famous Italian journalist Oriana Fallaci was present at Tlatelolco and was wounded by police agents; Fallaci went on to make sure that her readers knew about the events in Mexico (indeed, she is quoted by Poniatowska in terms that, under other circumstances, would never be permitted a visitor to Mexico, as commentary in Mexico on internal affairs by non-Mexicans is strictly prohibited). Tlatelolco, then, marks a dividing line in Mexico's socio-historical consciousness; and in many ways the enormous changes in Mexican society in past decades, including considerable erosion of the PRI's political authority and symbolic stature, are a consequence, if not directly of what happened in the plaza, of fault lines in Mexican society that became brutally evident with those events.

Fons's film is a skillful and eloquent record of the massacre (therefore, I disagree with Luna's comment that "The film is pathetically obvious and influenced by mainstream Mexican films of the 70s: the plot invariably leads to a final cathartic slaughter" [177]—as though the "final cathartic slaughter" were fiction and not based on historical fact). The narrative time covers the period of a day, from one morning, that of October 2 (at the beginning we see someone exposing that date on a daily calendar by tearing off the sheet for October 1), to the next. The story is told completely from the point of view of one family: a father, Humberto, who is employed in a high government agency; a mother, Alicia; two adolescent sons involved in the protest movement; a young daughter; a little boy; and a grandfather, Don Roque, who was an army officer. At the breakfast table, the father warns his sons about the foolhardiness of challenging government authority, while the grandfather glowers in anger at the thought of questioning institutional authority. The mother attempts to play the role of peacemaker and, as everyone goes off to work and school, is left with anguished concern over the possible danger to her loved ones.

Her premonition turns out to be correct. As the situation deteriorates in the plaza (which the spectator never sees: events are at first only displayed obliquely through the eyes of the actors as they look out the windows of the apartment), the mother's anguish grows. There are a number of objective correlatives to the impending events: the telephone stops working, the electricity goes off, ominous noises are heard. At one point, as the grandfather and the little boy are reenacting military battles with toy soldiers on the building's roof, the grandfather looks over the ledge in concern at the growing mass of people in the plaza.

As the massacre occurs, panic begins to set in at the apartment. The father does not return home from work, and the sons show up suddenly

FIGURE 1   María Rojo (as Alicia) serving breakfast on the fateful morning of
October 2, 1968.

with fellow protesters who have been attacked by special agents, the Hal-
cones (Falcons). One protester has been wounded seriously and is bleeding
profusely. The father finally makes it home as the mother and the others are
attempting to help the wounded student. As everyone tries to go to sleep, despite the noise that continues to come from outside, police agents—apparently from a death squad—burst into the apartment. The family attempts
to keep the wounded student from view. However, when he is discovered,
the assault troops go berserk and end up killing everyone in sight, except for
the little boy, who has hidden under a bed. In the final sequence, the little
boy comes out from hiding, clearly in shock, steps over the bodies of his
dead family, and walks down the stairs of the apartment building to the entrance way. In what is the only exterior shot of the film, we see him wan-
dering around, treading the debris of the massacre, the lone survivor, the
child of the Mexico that will emerge as a consequence of the events of October 2, 1968.

 Rojo amanecer is clearly neither a documentary nor a testimony to the
events at Tlatelolco, but a work of fictional narrative; and, as such, it pro-

motes a particularly ideological posture toward the massacre, as evidenced in the violence of the assault troops, the panic and hysteria that finally take hold of the family, and the pathos of the closing sequence. What is particularly notable about the film is the way in which the family contemplates with horrified astonishment the collapse of the illusions of social and political security of the Mexico within whose revolutionary myth they have been raised. This is particularly the case of the grandfather, as a retired military officer, the father, as a government employee, and the mother, as the guardian of the prototypic Mexican household over which she presides. The point is that, too late, they discover that the sons who are involved in the protest movement are right after all about the degree to which Mexico under Díaz Ordaz, and under the PRI's hold on the government, has drifted toward the same sort of police tactics that Mexico officially deplored with reference to the military dictatorships elsewhere in Latin America. The next administration, that of Luis Echeverría, emerged as the most "leftist" Mexico had seen since that of the legendary Lázaro Cárdenas in the late 1930s. However, the fact is that, despite his attempts to court intellectuals, artists, and writers who had become disaffected from the great Mexican political family, Echeverría was always to be remembered as Díaz Ordaz's Minister of the Interior and, thus, the one who was directly responsible for giving the orders to carry out the operation against the students in Tlatelolco. In sum, *Rojo amanecer* offers a very strongly articulated lesson in Mexican political history, one offensive to many sectors of official Mexico, but also one that constitutes an unquestionably crucial segment of contemporary cultural production in that country.

One of the singular characteristics of *Rojo amanecer* is the fact that the film is shot almost entirely within the confines of Humberto and Alicia's apartment; only at the end of the film does the camera move outside of the apartment and the hall and stairs leading to it, and then only minimally. Although Mexico City is only present by implication (i.e., not directly photographed), this does not mean that the film does not construct a sense of the city and of lived human experience in it. Quite the contrary.

It is important to note, first of all, that it is unlikely that the film could have been made in any other way, not in 1989 and probably not today, more than thirty years after the events related. Unlike the Greek director Costa-Gavras (Konstantinos Gavras), Fons cannot have had the opportunity to film acts of state terrorism outside of Mexico. In 1973 Costa-Gavras made *State of Siege* in Chile on the repression of the Tupamaro urban guerrilla movement in Uruguay, and in 1982 he made *Missing*, in which the 1973 overthrow of Salvador Allende and the ensuing repression and disappear-ance of Allende supporters are graphically detailed. But if the Mexican au-thorities were willing to allow Costa-Gavras to use sites in Mexico City to film violent political unrest, scenes of a military coup, and the torture and murder of individuals, it is impossible to contemplate that they might have supported a similar request from Fons, particularly since neither the State nor those who exercised its power in 1968 have ever acknowledged guilt or responsibility for the massacre at Tlatelolco. Indeed, there are those who continue to insist that there has been a massive cover-up of the details of the whole event.

It is unnecessary to make much of an issue out of how Humberto and Ali-cia's modest apartment is a microcosm of Mexico City; this can be said es-sentially about any living space, and the apartment would only be more gen-erally representative here because the family is representative of the lower end of the middle class that constitutes the bulk of the city's population and because Humberto is employed as a minor government bureaucrat, the most solid and secure employment available in the city. Far more important is the specific way in which the apartment is representative. For example, it sum-marizes some of the most important demographics of the city: a married couple with several children (three sons and a daughter), an employed hus-band and a wife who is the homemaker, and the widowed parent of one of them. Their clothes, their demeanor, and the decor of the apartment are all typical of life in Mexico City in ways that would permit one to focus on them to extrapolate features of life in the city. For example, note the inter-action between the grandfather and his grade-school-age grandson (who will become the only survivor of the family in the subsequent massacre). Since the child only goes to school half a day, the grandfather exercises an important role in providing attention to the child. Since Don Roque served in the Mexican Army (a detail of some irony, since he believes that this will oblige the invading shock troops to pay attention to his attempts at expla-nation), he can share newspaper clippings and anecdotes with the child, which he does as a way of imparting circumstantial civics lessons; and he can take time to play war with the boy's set of tin soldiers on the roof of the building, where they just happen to make out signs of ominous movements in the plaza below.

With this family, Fons strives for a degree of typicalness that will serve to underscore the way in which the massacre reached deep into the center of the city's workaday middle class, and how, rather than suppressing an il-legitimate student protest movement, it impacted a broad spectrum of the society of the city. This is a point Poniatowska attempted to make with her interviews, which went well beyond the immediate protagonists. The typicalness of Humberto and Alicia's family is particularly evident because of the wealth of details of everyday life and the commonness of everything about this family, things the film is able to include in its visual frame. Even the details of a measure of privilege are in reality details of commonness. Humberto's bureaucratic job provides him with a measure of credibility and authority, as he attempts, in vain, to convince his two older sons that they are very foolish to believe that the government will continue to tolerate the way in which the protest movement is upping the ante with its public demonstrations. And Don Roque, as a son of the Republic from the halcyon years following the Mexican Revolution and the affirmation of the ideology of the great State's benevolent treatment of its citizens, decries the protest movement and seconds his son-in-law's admonitions to the two sons while finding it difficult to believe that the State, in the person of the armed forces in which he once served, will engage in violence against its own citizens.

If Humberto and Alicia's household stands in for domestic life in the city as a whole, the locale and structural integration of their household also are paradigmatic. Their apartment is in a multifamily high-rise, and that building in turn is only one of a series of massive structures that make up one (lower) middle-class residential district in the city. These are buildings that have been built by the State for specific groups of citizens, in this case, low-level government bureaucrats. While they do not quite have the grimness that characterizes Soviet-style mass residences, they do have the sort of overwhelming presence that bespeaks the presence of the State in disposing the circumstances of residence of its citizens and employees. While the buildings are grouped around an important central plaza, Tlatelolco/Plaza de las Tres Culturas, the refuge of the plaza (that is, the visual relief provided by its openness and the oxygen provided by its greenery, not to mention the way in which the plaza is a recreational extension—albeit a rather grim one— of the cramped living quarters of the residential building) becomes a dead end, in which the army, deploying sharpshooters from the roof and helicopters overhead, is able to pick off the protesters, like shooting fish in a barrel. And if the protesters are cornered in the plaza, the families are cornered in their apartments, underscoring the way in which there is no chance of escaping the power of the State or of countering its decision to exercise violence. There is a geometric progression from street to plaza to building to apartment to room, and the protesters (and along with them, other members of the family) that we see murdered by the shock troops in the closing

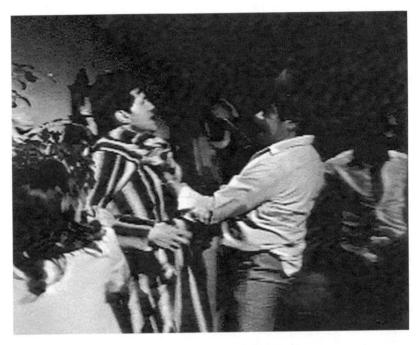

FIGURE 2   The incursion into the apartment of federal shock troops.

sequences of the film are exemplars of one fundamental aspect of life in Mexico City in the late 1960s: the public display of dissatisfaction over the delivery of education. Thus, what the family's children, their friends, their parents, and Don Roque bring to the enclosed space of the apartment, to the sanctity of the home, is the harsh reality of life out on the streets of the city, an importation of urban reality that is tragically trumped by the invasion of the shock troops into the apartment and the ensuing massacre.

When the youngest child of Humberto and Alicia's family emerges from under the bed where he has taken refuge, he is enacting the trajectory of street-to-home in reverse. We see him emerge from under the bed in one of the rooms, wander down the hall (in the process, stepping over the bodies of his dead family), out into the building and down the stairs, and out into the plaza. While Fons does not (cannot?) show the plaza as a whole, it is the tip of the public realm into which the boy will now presumably wander, the urban monster, the terrorist State, and an inhospitable society such that the spectator can only wonder at how he will be able to survive. Of course, one can speculate on how the boy will eventually be taken in, how relatives might care for him and raise him. But this form of survival is not what is at issue here. Rather, it is what the Tlatelolco massacre means for the collective Mexican psyche and what it says about the dimensions of life in the capital.

The incursion of the life of the city into the family's apartment occurs in an incremental fashion. Surely, this is part of the buildup of suspense in the film, but it is also a calculated dose of the increasingly violent incursion of public life into private life. An American film might stress this in the form of uncontrolled random crime: thus, Hollywood movies of the sort where a family, believing that it is protected by the sanctity of the home, falls victim to invading criminals. The classical example is William Wyler's 1955 *The Desperate Hours* (starring Humphrey Bogart), in which three escaped convicts terrorize a suburban household; part of the sense of the film is the challenge to the 1950s mystique of the suburb as a particularly protected space, removed from the terror of the urban jungle. However, in Latin America State terrorism is frequently perceived as more of a threat than random violence, and even when a film may deal with the crime of individuals, it is likely to be tied in some way to the violence of the State.[2]

In the case of *Rojo amanecer*, the initial vehicle of invasion is the information brought into the home by the two eldest sons, who are involved in the student protest movement; the information they bring into the home is supplemented by the comments of their father, Humberto, in his advice to them to mind the consequences of what is taking place. Subsequently, as the movement begins to group in the Tlatelolco plaza, and as armed forces elements also begin ominously to concentrate, other members of the family comment on the events: I have already mentioned what Don Roque and his grandson see from their building's rooftop, and both Alicia and her father, who has gone to get her at the home of a friend, will comment on the course events are taking as they come from the street. Later, when both the telephone and the lights go out, there is the material manifestation in the household that something serious is about to take place.

Television and radio are significant ways in which so-called outside reality makes incursions into the private space of one's home, and television is so omnipresent now in Mexican society that, although the camera cannot leave the apartment, it can capture images on the television screen that are coming into the apartment, at least as long as the electricity is still on. However, the displaced images of the television screen become palpable reality when Humberto and Alicia's sons return with companions, one of whom is seriously wounded: both the protest movement and the State violence it has engendered are now directly visible within the household and, consequently, within the frame of the film. It is in pursuit of these protesters (and anyone else they can catch) that the shock troops will eventually invade the apartment. Before this happens, however, not only do we see the family looking out the windows of their apartment and commenting on what is going on below, but gunfire directed against the protesters on one occasion actually smashes through the apartment windows; the gunfire is at first thought to be fireworks. This detail is important, in that it reminds the spectator of how one permanent trace of the massacre is the scarring of the buildings by the blankets of gunfire coming from the helicopters deployed above. This physical evidence is similar to damage to other buildings as the result of military coups in other parts of Latin America, the most spectacular being the gutting by air fire of La Moneda, the Chilean executive seat in downtown Santiago, during the September 11, 1973, overthrow of Salvador Allende. Even though Mexico has survived the twentieth century without the military coups of virtually every other country in Latin America, the Tlatelolco massacre has often been likened, at least in the way in which it was conducted and in the psychological scars it has left, to a military operation amounting to a coup. This is certainly very much the impression given by Elena Poniatowska in her documentary narrative *La noche de Tlatelolco* (1971), reinforced by the photographs of military personnel and corpses in the morgue (see also Juan Miguel de Mora's best-selling *Tlatelolco 1968: por fin toda la verdad*).

The invasion of the shock troops involves the direct representation of horrendous physical violence. We see it first in terms of a woman, perhaps a neighbor, who becomes hysterical over her missing son, whom she thinks has been killed by the forces. Then we see the shock troops pursue one protester down the staircase, leaving him to die stretched out on the cement stairs. Finally, they burst into Humberto and Alicia's apartment, and the ensuing pandemonium is played to the hilt, with yelling and shouting, pummeling and throwing around, and finally the methodical elimination of all of the family members and their children's friends, with the exception of the youngest child, who has hidden under a bed. The way in which Fons is able to exploit maximally the details of this violent home invasion by the State breaks down the multiple walls (apartment, floor, building) that separate the apartment from the world outside. The image is one, so to speak, of jack-booted soldiers raging through the home, barking orders at its occupants and throwing them around, and then eventually pumping rounds of bullets in them, leaving them to bleed to death on the floor of their own home. I have written this to sound rather clichéd, because the circumstance, unfortunately, is: Fons had little work to do plotting this scene, since there were so many prior cinematographic and television images on which he could rely.

Yet what is of considerable importance is the context into which this cliché is inserted, which is, of course, the uniqueness in Mexican history of the Tlatelolco massacre — or, at least, the uniqueness in Mexico City's history. And what is also of considerable importance is the fact that Fons's film remains the only feature-length narrative made that directly involves the State violence of that massacre.[3] Thus, while spectators may be seeing a series of clichés, what they are understanding is worthy of Greek tragedy: the inexorable denouement of a circumstance of urban life as it invades a domestic realm and, quite literally, blots it out in a bloodbath.

Novia que te vea (I Want to See You a Bride)

"México ya no existe." With this declaration, Carlos Monsiváis underscored how the Mexico of a hegemonic postrevolutionary society, predicated on the assumption of a glorious shared identity that needed to be defended at all costs for all Mexicans against the invasion of foreign cultures, had, approximately seven decades after its invention, ceased to exist (Ramírez 29). It is debatable to what extent all Mexicans, or, specifically, which Mexicans, subscribed, or were convinced to subscribe, to such an ideology. Certainly, the availability of foreign products and culture for those able to pay for them has always been high, and the international commerce and connections of the ruling and financial elite have always been beyond dispute.

Although strong remnants of a mythical, authentic Mexico, whose symbolic center is the legendary Museo de Antropología, continue to exist, its ideological efficaciousness has yielded in many quarters to globalization and the now stronger impetus for Mexico to participate in a worldwide neoliberal economy that makes it difficult to sustain allegiance to a single identity and to a single definition of national existence.[4] The Americanization of the country has always been the bugaboo of hegemonic postrevolutionary Mexico, but the defense of hegemony now takes second place to the imperative to participate in the global economy, and one must accept the changes that that participation will bring.

Under the aegis of hegemonic postrevolutionary Mexico, all inhabitants of Mexico were welcome to subscribe to the national identity, but only those who could fulfill adequately its requisites could be Mexicans. This not only meant that most inhabitants born outside of Mexico would never acquire Mexican citizenship, but meant more profoundly that many individuals born within Mexico would never come to be considered fully Mexican. Thus, for example, the hegemonic identity could make much of the indigenous roots of the nation, but indigenous Mexicans, unless they were willing to give up tribal identity and ancient forms of social and cultural autonomy—such as speaking their pre-Columbian languages rather than Spanish or adhering to tribal sociopolitical organization rather than becoming a part of the PRI-dominated system—would never come to be considered fully Mexican. That is, they would be as foreigners in their native land. Indeed, one must understand the Chiapas rebellion as in large measure the revolt of an unrecognized and unacknowledged autonomy, excluded from the full rights of citizenship, against a central government that was viewed as an imperial oppressor.

Given the profoundly symbolic value of indigenous culture in Mexico and the intensely felt significance of the Chiapas rebellion, the relationship between indigenous groups and the central government in Mexico has been particularly symbolic of the rending of the fabric of a nation unified around a hard core of identity ideology. Yet the paradigm shift implied by Monsiváis's words has brought to the fore elements of Mexican society previously excluded from the "banquet" of full national identity: women, ethnic minorities other than the indigenous population, lesbians and gays, and other disenfranchised groups that perhaps still remain to be fully identified and represented by Mexico's cultural production. This is not the place to go into the demographics of such subaltern identities nor to discuss the bases of the ways in which they did not enjoy participation in the plenitude of Mexicanness, nor what all of the circumstances have been that have allowed for them to vie for a place of dignity in the national imagination. Nevertheless, it is unquestionable, when one examines the record of cultural production in Mexico during the past three decades—that is, since the beginnings of the collapse of the symbolic hegemony, a collapse that, in a very real sense, began with the student massacre at Tlatelolco in 1968—that there has been a significant addition of new constituents to the categories of Mexican culture.

Although there has always been a measure of writing by women in Mexico, there has been a quantum leap in the amount of woman-marked and feminist-marked production. While there has always been a degree of representation of homoeroticism (more often in the form of the representation of gender transgression) in Mexican culture, usually tinged with a seriously homophobic stance, one can now speak of a gay and lesbian tradition, at least as regards major urban areas (see Schaefer). Ethnic identities have been more problematical, and in the case of Jewish culture, which will concern us here, the record of cultural production has been quite slight (see Cortina's recent monograph on Mexican Jewish women writers, including Nissán). This is a rather curious fact, since Jews are really quite prominent in Mexican society, and Daniel Goldberg's 1995 film documentary, *Un beso a esta tierra*, testifies to the enormous presence of the Jewish community in broad sectors of Mexico's public life. Note should also be taken of Alejandro Pelayo's 1993 film *Miroslava*, on the Czech immigrant Miroslava Stern (originally Sternova), who committed suicide in Mexico in 1955 right after her thirty-first birthday; she appeared in something like thirty films, assuming very much of a Marilyn Monroe–like persona.

Yet there is a strong component of Jewish culture in Mexico City and in other urban areas, such as Monterrey, from both Sephardic Jews, who were part of Hispanic culture from the first (as *conversos* or as crypto-Jews), and East-European Jews, who arrived as part of what little immigrant policy Mexico has had. Lázaro Cárdenas was particularly open toward refugees from the 1936–1939 Spanish Civil War, as part of his Mexican foreign policy to support the victims of tyranny, particularly fascism, in Europe. Others have reviewed this history, and others have reviewed this nascent cultural production. Rosa Nissán is part of a cluster of Mexican Jewish writers and is fortunate to have had her first novel, *Novia que te vea*, made into a film of the same name by Guita Schyfter in 1992 in a full commercial production (concerning the relationship, and divergences, between film and novel, see Mennell). *Novia que te vea* (the title means something like "I want to see you a bride" in Ladino, the Spanish spoken by Sephardic Jews at the time they were expelled from Spain in 1492 [Sephardic, of course, means Spanish]) is the story of two young women and their struggle for cultural identity in Mexico in the 1960s; the film turns on the occasion of their reunion several decades later, and in that meeting they recall their separate and intertwined stories, as told by Nissán's novel and Schyfter's film.

Novia que te vea is notable for a number of reasons. It is part of a growing number of films being made by women in Mexico: the legendary Paz Alicia Garciadiego waited years to be allowed to direct a film despite working with others for decades, and women only began to direct films in earnest in that country in the early 1990s. Not only is *Novia que te vea* one of the handful of films directed by women, but it is also the first Jewish-marked film in Mexico. While Argentina has a long tradition of Jewish filmmaking, filmmaking in Mexico has been no different from other genres of cultural production in acknowledging the existence of Jewish ethnicity. Finally, *Novia que te vea* is unique in its representation of linguistic diversity; I will have more to say about this below.

Jewish culture in Latin America is not necessarily an urban phenomenon; specifically in Argentina and Brazil, there were attempts to locate Jews in rural areas, particularly in the case of the former, as part of the official ideology of "gobernar es poblar" (to govern is to populate): this gave rise in that country to the cultural icon of the Gaucho Judío (Jewish Gaucho). No similar icon exists for Mexico, although very eloquent photographic and other graphic material is presented regarding the intersection between Creole Mexican life and that of Jewish immigrants in sources such as *Imágenes de un encuentro* (Bokser de Liwerant; for an overview of Jews in Mexico, see Elkin; Cimet; Krause; for Jews as a historical curiosity, see Lerner). Note should be taken of a pioneering Mexican woman filmmaker of Jewish descent, Matilde Ladeneta (1910–1999), who did not, however, make reference to Jewish themes in her work. Yet the simple fact is that Jewish immigrants to Latin America have tended to cluster in major metropolitan areas, repeating the ghetto and quasi-ghetto experience of the cities of their provenance and paralleling the experience of Jewish immigrants to the United States. And, as in the United States, those Jews who did settle in the countryside often resettled in metropolitan areas or saw their children do so (see Irving Howe's account of this for the United States and Eli Cohen's documentary on Argentina, *Argentina's Jews: Days of Awe* [1980]). The result is that Jewish society and institutions remain predominantly urban throughout Latin America. Whether or not they are pronouncedly visible is another matter. Certainly synagogues and other buildings that may be explicitly identified as Jewish by signs in Hebrew or Jewish cultural icons are visible, unless constructed in such a way so as not to call the attention of passersby. Questions of assimilation have affected the degree to which the use of yarmulkes and black fedoras by men, traditional facial hair, dark clothing, and the like are visible in public, whether during the period of the Sabbath or every day; and assimilation has affected Jewish communities differently from one country to another in Latin America.

In the case of Mexico, historically there has been a very rigid distinction between what occurs in private and what occurs in public. Since most Latin American Jewry tend to be conservative, observation of Jewish custom has been important for daily life. Yet, in Mexico—unlike Argentina or Brazil, where visibility is very high—the need to manifest as much as possible a canonical Mexicanness in order to be accepted in daily life and to enjoy the financial and political benefits of being taken fully as a Mexican has meant that the door of the home is a threshold that demarcates very carefully the inside realm of Jewishness and the outside realm of Mexicanness. Thus, at least for the universe of Schyfter's film, being a Jew in Mexico has meant being a Jew in the privacy of the home, a circumstance that very much evokes the metaphor of the closet.[5] Now, it is debatable if the image of Jewish life in Mexico provided by Schyfter's film corresponds, strictly speaking, to actual social realities. While Mexico City is hardly New York or Buenos Aires, Jews have, at least since the middle of the twentieth century, enjoyed considerable visibility, prosperity, and accommodation in Mexican society, and while the Mexico of American and international tourism does not easily accommodate Mexican Jewry, it does not take much effort to discern the place that they have made for themselves in urban culture.

Yet Schyfter's film, which, to be sure, reaches back to the beginnings of a modern Jewish presence in Mexico (as opposed to the slight Sephardic presence that can be traced back to the time of the Spanish conquest), prefers, for rhetorical purposes, to suggest a universe of Jewish life that remains essentially isolated from the dominant non-Jewish mainstream. Of course, one could argue that the degree of Jewish assimilation in Mexico does, in fact, constitute a form of oppression of Jewish society, since the pressure to assimilate brings with it the need to be like everyone else and/or to conceal the ways in which one is different; non-Jews (and this is only one instance of a larger issue of assimilation that goes beyond only ethnic identity) may often find it difficult to perceive the ways in which any suggestion of assimilation is, in fact, a form of oppression, a form of anti-Semitism. The Mexican writer Ilan Stavans speaks of his own experiences in this regard:

> After graduating from [Jewish] high school, most of my friends, members of richer families, were sent abroad, to the U.S. or Israel, to study. Those that remained, including me, were forced to go to college at home to face Mexico tête-à-tête. The shock was tremendous. Suddenly, I (we) recognized the artificiality of our oasis. What to do? I, for one, rejected my background, I felt Judaism made me a pariah. I wanted to be an authentic Mexican. ("Lost in Translation" 229)

Where Stavans speaks of the isolation and artificiality of the Jewish "oasis," Schyfter's film more dramatically promotes the image of the closet. The

closet has traditionally been a metaphor that has served to designate the se-
crecy of the private lives of queers, those whose sexual preferences trans-
gress what is allowed by patriarchal heteronormativity. However, contemporary theoretical writing on the concept of the closet underscores how
similar strategies of concealment (and the parallel phenomenon known to
homosexuals as homophobia: the right of others to out you and then to
punish you for your transgressions) function just as powerfully for other social subalternities. Since one of the prevailing forms of racism in Latin
America has been to believe that one cannot be a practicing Jew and be a
patriotic national at the same time, at places and in times of intense nationalism (Mexico since the 1910 revolution, Argentina at the time of the Cen-
tennial in 1910 and during periods of fascist influence in the 1930s and
1940s and neofascism during the military dictatorships of 1967–1973 and
1976–1983), the importance of concealing one's observation of Judaism
can be a matter not only of acceding to the benefits of assimilation, but of
simply keeping oneself from being the victim of racial slurs or protecting
one's physical integrity. Schyfter's film has one long sequence in which Oshinica is dating the son of an influential family. Oshinica is invited to eat
with the family and an invited friend, equally an influential man. The conversation quickly turns on the two motifs, so useful in constructing an entire monologue of racial put-down, "Some of my best friends are Jews" and
"You Jews are the problem, because you do not want to assimilate." Oshinica's essential silence in the face of a densely woven, if delivered in friendly
tones, slur is a restaging of the effect of the closet: the structure of the monologue is such that there is virtually no way to mount an effective counterdiscourse without violating the social past of amiability. Such feigned amiability is, of course, monstrously effective in impeding a public discourse on
the social legitimacy of being Jewish as well as forestalling any attempt to
explain the effect of the closet in terms of the psychological and emotional
toll it takes on its inhabitants. (Obviously, throughout this paragraph, I am
relying on the metaphor of the closet as developed by Eve Kosofsky Sedgwick: although Sedgwick's work refers specifically to homosexuals, she is
careful to show how it refers to any double bind of having to remain in the
closet to avoid persecution, which rarely is an effective option, and of only
being able to defend oneself from persecution by coming out of the closet,
which often only provides the opportunity to intensify persecution. Sedgwick discusses Jews and the closet [75–82].)

Because of the long-standing stigma of being Jewish in Mexico—or, at
least, of being a Jew who resists the lure, or the imperative, of assimilation—

FIGURE 3   Oshinica and her family arrive by train in Mexico City.

Schyfter's film is of crucial importance to Mexican culture because of the images of being Jewish that it contains, and ever more so against the backdrop
of Mexico City in the 1940s. Thus, the film is significant for the presence of
the city and for the interplay between the public and the private, an interplay best understood in terms of the metaphor of the closet. Oshinica and
her family arrive in Mexico City at the central train station, from Turkey
during the Second World War, as refugees from the expanding Holocaust.
They are Mediterranean or Sephardic Jews, and thus the Ladino they speak
enables them to take a place in Mexican society with greater ease than the
German or Ashkenazi Jews who made up the bulk of the immigration to
Argentina and Brazil, whose Yiddish and other East European languages
made Spanish for them a completely foreign language. Oshinica's family is
fortunate enough to meet a man at the train station who is also a Sephardic
Jew. He takes them to his home, and thanks to his generosity, they are soon
installed in the centrally located Lagunilla district, where they join the le-
gion of Jewish tradesmen concentrated in that area; Oshinica's father has a
storefront business selling clothes.

The opening sequences of the film are highly charged, and they are tinged with the circumstances of the closet, as Oshinica and her family make their way through the first spaces of a new and daunting environment. It is significant that the man at the train station recognizes them by their language, a badge of identity that saves them from the vortex of people swirling around them at the train station. The foreground-background contrast underscores the problematical inside-outside status of the social alien: one is outside the social situation in which one is inescapably caught, being on the inside. The recognition of the shared Ladino language serves to forge a strategic link that provides a protective isolation from a situation of threatening isolation (that is, not being able to negotiate the arrival in Mexico City).

As their newfound friend leads them through the streets of Mexico City, the family observes the displayed artifacts of traditional Mexican culture. This is a rather conventional sequence as such: the new arrival impressed by unfamiliar sights and sounds. However, in the context of the particularly heightened sense of the outsider in Mexico, especially in the 1940s, the decade which is the apogee of postrevolutionary nationalism, Schyfter (who was actually born in Costa Rica, but identifies as a Mexican) is asking the primary audience—her fellow Mexicans—to grasp the sense of alienism of these immigrants. Mexico, to be sure, receives hundreds of thousands of outsiders every year in the form of foreign tourists, for whom the artifacts of traditional Mexican culture are virtually cultural—and, often, erotic—fetishes: Mexico's difference is its greatest tourist asset. However, Mexico has, throughout the twentieth century, never been a country of immigration, and the immigration of the period at issue was exceptional as part of Lázaro Cárdenas's leftist policies of articulating a defiance to capitalist-generated Nazism: indeed, Cárdenas's sympathy for the refugees from fascism was as much a deviation from the rampant cultural nationalism of the period as it was an effective ideological ploy to internationally affirm Mexican greatness.

The opening sequence concludes with the family arriving at the home of their newfound friend, and as the door closes on them as they enter this safe zone, they have stepped out of the public space of the overpowering culture of the land to which they have come: the effectiveness of their arrival depends on suspending reference to how, actually, they have already traversed half of the country, which is therefore not quite so alien to them, since their arrival by ship in Veracruz. And in stepping out of the public space into the private space of the home, they are stepping out of Mexico's generalized Catholicism and (back) into Judaism, out of Spanish and into Ladino. Certainly, it is this refuge that enables the family to eventually begin to become an integral part of public life; and the following sequence of the film focuses on growing up in the Lagunilla area, the shops of friends and family, and the tight-knit quality of a Ladino-speaking, Sephardic Jewish family against the common denominators that serve as reference points of Mexican public life for this one story of the process of accommodation and varying degrees and levels of assimilation.

One of the most notable aspects of *Novia que te vea* is the presence of Ladino, beginning with the title itself. Ladino is fifteenth-century Spanish, and it is different from contemporary Spanish in general because it preserves phonetic and grammatical features that have remained frozen in time: this is not uncommon for offshoots that become separated from their base language of origin. In the latter, the language continues to evolve, and much evolution is likely to take place in almost five hundred years. By contrast, offshoots are often limited in their usage, such as in the home, since the subjects of the Sephardic diaspora went on to acquire the language spoken by the inhabitants of the place where they came to settle; and by the second generation, the children were native speakers of that language and heritage speakers of Ladino. Unless heritage languages are renewed by some form of (re)contact with the native base, they are likely to become fossilized, which explains the lack of far-reaching evolution in Ladino by contrast to that of the Spanish of the Peninsula from which it came. Part of that evolution, in addition to internal features of phonology, morphology, and syntax, included, in the case of Spanish, the consequence of Castilian becoming the language of Empire and the creation of a classic norm, along with, over time, the Latinate influence of the Renaissance, the French influence of the Enlightenment and Romanticism, and the contemporary influence of English. In short, Ladino is pretty much the reflex of a proto-Castilian Spanish; and the fact that, for the majority of the diaspora, it was more written than spoken, is also a characteristic of a heritage language: speakers of native languages have written and oral fluency, while speakers of heritage languages tend to have only oral fluency. In all of this, there are many ways in which Ladino and Chicano Spanish are alike. Moreover, in the case of Ladino, the Jewish tradition whereby learning is the province of only some men serves to maintain Ladino as essentially a "kitchen" language.

In the case of Mexican Spanish, there are other differences. Since Spanish has been spoken throughout both American continents for five hundred years, not only has it diverged in significant ways from Peninsular Spanish, but dialects of one nation, and even one region, have diverged from each other. In this sense, Spanish is like English: a vast world language spoken as

FIGURE 4   The clan matriarchs playing cards and speaking Ladino.

a native language in many countries with many dimensions to the relationship between oral and written norms and in which there is no one official or
academic standard, despite the efforts of some to retain a common ground
norma culta. The divergences are along many axes, not the most insignificant one being the degree to which any one national standard has been influenced by the indigenous languages over which Spanish was laid by the
conquerors and colonists; these indigenous languages continue to exist in
usually complex, uneasy ways alongside Spanish. Since Spanish is univer-
sally the official language of the Latin American republics, not to speak
Spanish—and, particularly, to speak instead, especially monolingually, an
indigenous language—is virtually to be a social outcast, as again witnessed
in the case of the sociolinguistic dimensions of the Chiapas rebellion. Some
countries have had periods marked by an attempt to restore, at least in part,
the indigenous language (Quechua in Peru, Guaraní in Paraguay) or to re-
value it romantically (Nahuatl in Mexico), but there can be little challenge
to the hegemony of Spanish, no matter how many government-sponsored
programs of bilingual education there may be in the indigenous communities.

Thus, when Schyfter's characters persist in speaking Ladino, it becomes a vivid marker in the film of their difference within the urban setting, since Mexico City Spanish establishes the norm for the country and marks the beat of its changes and developments. It is not significant that arriving immigrants speak a foreign language, but it becomes socioculturally significant when they persist in doing it. There is an important sequence in the movie in which Oshinica's mother is entertaining other female family members and friends. The women, all elegantly dressed, are playing canasta and speaking Ladino. On the one hand, they are served by Oshinica's mother's maid, who serves them silently but whose face betrays her sense of estrangement from these florid women speaking what she may take to be an incomprehensible version of Spanish, virtually another language, in the bosom of her own country. On the other hand, they are surrounded by the children speaking Spanish. Spanish here is the urban reality of Mexico brought into the household by the children, who have become inhabitants of Mexico in profound ways that their parents cannot. This is particularly demonstrated when Oshinica announces that she wants to be an artist and has no intention of getting married, thereby defying the legislative sense, in patriarchal terms, of the title of the film: it may be grammatically subjunctive, but despite the politeness of the use of a predicate of volition, the pragmatic force is imperative.

Schyfter's use of Ladino in the film points in two directions. First of all, it serves to continue to mark the Sephardic family as outsiders, as immigrants and as Jews, no matter how much they make it in Mexico and, in the end, how comfortable they have become: the reunion that we see at the end of the film between Oshinica and Rifka—with the entire film being the remembrances of conversation that takes place at that reunion—shows how much they, their husbands, and their children are now, decades later, solidly and unimpeachably Mexican. But the differences are still there, and if they were not, there would be no need for the depth and vividness of the recollections in which Oshinica and Rifka engage nor the eloquence with which they are recreated in the film. Precisely, the originality and the impact of Schyfter's film come from the bringing to the fore a dimension of Mexico City's urban culture that has to date very little record in cultural production and the degree to which the Jewish culture is, in the heart of Mexico City, so noticeably different from the traditional markers of Mexicanness. Ladino here has, therefore, an extratextual function as a synecdoche of difference.

The second direction in which the use of Ladino in the film is extratextual is in the way in which it is a challenge to the spectator, whether the native speaker of Mexican Spanish or of any other variety of modern Spanish, to understand Ladino as a marker of difference. While only those trained in Ladino will catch everything that is said, most of the dialogues are intelligible to the modern speaker of Spanish. Thus, Ladino is not really a foreign language. But the alien quality of the phonology of Ladino, which in its use of fifteenth-century palatals is reminiscent of modern Portuguese, the use of grammatical constructions that sound "wrong" (as in the case of the title of the film), and the use of words, whether from Old Spanish or Hebrew or some other language, that are unrecognizable to the untrained spectator contribute to creating a distancing effect that provides the texture of the linguistic—and, along with it, the cultural and religious—difference that is at issue here. What is doubly notable about the use of spoken Ladino in the film is that no subtitles are provided. This is virtually an outrageous decision on Schyfter's part, since Mexican cultural nationalism has attempted to create a fissureless image of Spanish within the country, one in which foreign words and phrases, not to mention foreign languages in their entirety, are considered with disfavor, and one in which the particular genius of Mexican Spanish must assert itself triumphantly.

True, the particular enemy of the integrity of Spanish in Mexico is American English, and the degree to which English is studied in Mexico at the present time and the degree to which English-language cultural products have penetrated the Mexican marketplace are significant challenges to any anti-English mentality in the country: it is no exaggeration to say that 90 percent of films shown in Mexico and a similar amount of music heard are American in origin. Yet the importance of U.S. tourism and the imperative of global neoliberalism provide English with important revisions of historic attitudes toward the language in Mexico. Ladino can hardly be seen as a challenge to the cultural integrity, especially Mexican Spanish. Yet Schyfter uses it effectively in the film as a marker of difference in a society that, since the 1910 revolution and until relatively recently, has long insisted that difference give way to assimilation—or be radically marginalized. Moreover, this detail of difference—and one must recall that questions regarding language trigger profoundly emotional reactions in most people, and many consider foreign languages to be tongues of the Devil—only serves to enhance the really very radical difference of Jewishness in Mexico City in the moment between the high cultural nationalism of the postrevolutionary period and the still very much premodern quality of life in Mexico City in the 1940s. Mexico City may not be, strictly speaking, a provincial backwater in the 1940s. Hardly. But it has yet to embark on the vast project of modernity that will begin to take place in the 1950s, a transformation that is reflected in the Oshinica and Rifka of the end of the film, now prosperous and urbane middle-age sophisticates.

The Mexico City of *Novia que te vea* is a fragmentary one: the central train station, the Lagunilla market place, some scenes of student life in the 1960s, and an upper-middle-class household. But the story the film tells cannot belong anywhere else but in urban history; and the interaction between the public and the private, of which language is a dominant synecdoche, speaks to the ideological transformations that have taken place in Mexico City regarding culture during the fifty years covered by the film.

Frida, naturaleza viva (Frida, Living Nature)

Paul Leduc's *Frida* (1984) is perhaps one of the most famous Mexican productions of the century. In it he provides a singularly creative interpretation of the life and work of Frida Kahlo (1907–1954), and *Frida*'s enormous international success is unquestionably due in large measure to the so-called Fridamania that has come to characterize interest in her work, making prices for her work some of the highest in Latin American art and the highest for any woman artist (on the commodification of Frida Kahlo, see Lindauer). The artist who plays the part of Frida, Ofelia Medina, is so cleverly made up that the spectator needs to make no leap of faith (as is necessary in the case of Juan José Gurrola's representation of the muralist Diego Rivera) to believe that it is, indeed, Frida who is there on the screen (the nature of the creation of subjectivity in Leduc's film is discussed by Valdés). Max Kerlow also does a very credible representation of Leon Trotsky, who was a close friend of Frida and her husband, Diego Rivera, and, it is suggested, a lover of Frida's; Trotsky's assassination in Mexico City by orders of Stalin in 1940 is one of the major events in the film.

The film is constructed as a flashback of her life as Frida lies bed-ridden, close to death as the consequence of the many ailments that plagued her body throughout her life and, indeed, constituted the principal subject of her paintings. Surrounded by mirrors, Frida studies herself and her body and, in an apparent stream-of-consciousness fashion, recalls key events of her life that are then enacted as the film's narrative. The film concludes with Frida's casket on display in the foyer of the Palacio de Bellas Artes in downtown Mexico City, where just before her death the first general exhibit of her works was held in Mexico. Her casket is draped with the Soviet flag, as a reminder that Frida and Diego were long supporters of the Communist

Party (of which Rivera was the secretary general). The film ends with Diego Rivera shouting his wife's name out of despair over her death, and the film credits roll over the image of her lying in state in the greatest official establishment to art in Mexico (the relationship between Frida and Mexican history is discussed by Pick).

Frida is essentially a silent film. There are only a handful of dialogue exchanges, making it possible to view it profitably without the distraction of subtitles. By contrast, Leduc underscores other sensorial and conceptual elements. In the first place, many of Frida's paintings are on display through the film, which takes place mostly in her studio in Coyoacán, in Mexico City, which is now a museum to her work. We see Frida working on her paintings and other pieces of art, and we see some of the creative techniques she used, such as studying herself in the mirror and seeking correlations between her body and elements of Mexican culture, both in its modern and pre-Columbian versions. Because of the intense use of color in Mexican folk art, which so influenced Frida, color is a primary vehicle of expression in the film as well. The sounds of art being made are heard, such as the sawing and hammering of frames and easels, which in one scene Frida correlates painfully with the amputation of one of her limbs as a young girl after a streetcar accident. Music is also very much present, both Mexican music and other popular airs, reinforcing the continuity between the artist's work and her sources and parallel contacts. The noises of the street are present in the form of the protest marches in which Frida participated, pushed along in her wheelchair by Diego. These were marches to protest both national and international events of the day, such as the persecution of peasants, the war, the bombings of Japan. These marches assembled many people in downtown Mexico City, and on occasion the protesters were hassled by the police. In one segment, Frida and her group join peasants holding a vigil, and we see her armed against possible violence. In another, they join a vigil for peasants who have been killed demanding land reform, and the only sound is the chorused repetition of each peasant's name and the phrase "Es de Dios" (he now belongs to God). Even dialogue such as this is more phatic than communicative, and it merges with the overall texture of sounds that take the place of spoken dialogue so intimately associated with most filmmaking. Finally, the film portrays the bodily interactions that replace spoken communication between characters. People touch and caress each other, and eye contact becomes an important form of direct physical interaction.

One of the important dimensions of the film involves Frida's erotic life, and without actually depicting scenes of sexual activities, Leduc is forthright in depicting Frida's pansexuality as both a dimension of her understanding of life as a material experience grounded in the body and her utilization of sexuality as a legitimate compensation for the unusual level of pain she experienced with her body. In the first place, Frida and Diego Rivera had an intense physical and emotional commitment to each other, and the film portrays Frida's exasperation at Diego's frequent affairs with other women: it is, however, apparent that Frida was not only jealous of the other women as objects of the sexual interest of her husband (and it is important to note that Frida and Rivera were divorced on one occasion because of his philandering). Rather, Frida resented the contrast of the perfection of their bodies, at least by comparison to her own body, deformed by disease and surgery. In one significant scene, she becomes infuriated with Diego, whom she discovers with her sister. However, Diego is not making love, at least not in any conventionally understood fashion, with the woman, but instead he is painting her in the nude, something he would not likely have done with Frida.

More significant are the representations of Frida's interests in other individuals: it is obvious that, from a conventionally bourgeois point of view, she had no cause to be jealous of Rivera's affairs, because she herself was erotically involved with others; of course, from a more profoundly human point of view, one is left to speculate on the dynamics of the stormy Kahlo-Rivera relationship. I have already mentioned her relationship with Trotsky, with whom she exchanged love letters. In another scene, we see her going to his library, where he is lost in intellectual endeavors, to show him examples of highly erotic pre-Columbian art, a veritable Aztec Kama Sutra. Much more intriguing, however, were Frida's lesbian relations. Mexico is arguably a very homoerotic country, although it is debatable the extent to which the homoerotic elements that can be perceived, elements that are decidedly "queer" by contrast to the sobriety associated with an Anglo heterosexist norm that serves as one controversial model for Mexican modernity, actually result in same-sex couplings to any more notable degree than in other societies (concerning varieties of homoeroticism in Mexico, both modern and premodern, see Lumsden, Murray, Núñez Noriega). There are three lesbian instances in *Frida*. Each one is substantially different from the other, and they serve to enrich immeasurably the figure of Frida in terms of her commitment to an intimate relationship with the body. The first involves a friend with whom she and Diego have dined in Paredes, the famous restaurant in downtown Mexico City frequented by Frida and her group, including the gay-centered literary movement of Los Contemporáneos, and for which Frida painted a mural that is still a feature of the place's decor. After dinner, the group continues to drink, and at one point they begin to sing "Soy un pobre venadito." Frida begins to flirt openly with one of the other women and begins to play with her earring. As far as the other members of the group are concerned, there is nothing unusual about this behavior (it is important to note, in regards to the sexual dissidence of Leduc's film, that he enjoyed the collaboration on the script of gay novelist and essayist José Joaquín Blanco).

The second instance involves another close friend with whom Frida is preparing a meal in the kitchen of the house in Coyoacán. As they begin to sing Agustín Lara's "Solamente una vez" (I only fell in love once), the two women begin to play with each other's body, with the friend displaying a leek of a clearly phallic appearance; the friend ends up pushing Frida over the work counter in a passionate embrace. What is particularly striking about this scene is, in addition to the reinforcing effect of the song, the use of color and the luxurious presence of the ingredients of Mexican cooking, which the spectator can virtually smell and taste, as sensuous accompaniments; the scene is also notable for taking place in the privileged women's space of the kitchen. The final scene involves the now very sick Frida, swaying in a hammock in her garden. As she begs a nurse for "just a little jab" of morphine, she begins to make seductive gestures toward the nurse, although it is not apparent from the sequence if the nurse responds at all to her advances. The nurse's strikingly beautiful indigenous features underscore Frida's abiding interest in Mexican folk culture, which she appears even to eroticize in a fetishistic fashion.

The most significant feature of Frida Kahlo's art is central to Leduc's film; it is her need to chronicle her own body and to do so in a way that breaks with the typical idealizations of the female body by Western art. Not only is Western art an overwhelmingly masculine and masculinist—and heterosexist—undertaking, but male artists, while they do not engage in grotesque sexist repudiations of the female body, customarily represent the female in idealized forms as synthesized in the tradition of the Virgin Mary/Madonna or the Mona Lisa. Not only does Frida, as a woman artist, break with these two abstract extremes of the female, but she undertakes to represent material and symbolic dimensions of the female body, dimensions that, except for anatomical representations, especially gynecological ones (which are not themselves exempt from misrepresentation), virtually never appear in the work of male artists.

Frida's representation of the body is two-fold on two levels. On one level, it is the representation of the female body as a woman experiences it (itself a proposal not necessarily free from misrepresentation, although one might argue that any misrepresentations are substantially different), while at the same time it is the representation of one specific body, that of Frida Kahlo, with an emphasis on the depiction of her own biography as "written" on that body: her polio, her accidents, her operations, her miscarriages, and one doctor-ordered abortion. On a second level, the representation of the materiality of the feminine body is mediated by an array of surrealistic and abstract codes of representation that provide specific visual interpretations of that materiality. The result is works of art of considerable layered subtlety and complexity. What Leduc has attempted to do in his film is to transfer to the filmic medium that layered and dense texture of representation. The result is an intriguing film that has been effective in engaging the interests of U.S. audiences not only because of the historical figure of Frida herself, but because of the way in which the film models several current contemporary cultural interests, such as the queering of sexual ideologies, an interest in bodily representations (especially "dismembered" bodies), and enactments of the erotic outside of the conventions of pornography.

An extremely significant aspect of *Frida* is the way in which it takes to the streets of Mexico City. In general terms, although Kahlo's paintings are associated with the surrealism and expressionism of the early part of this century, they are also very much associated with contemporary urban culture; it is also possible to read into them the sorts of social and political commitments that Kahlo, Diego Rivera, and their circle of associates maintained, without seeing in her paintings the sort of propagandistic art that was also prevalent at the time, associated in general terms with social realism—indeed, some of Kahlo's last, unfinished paintings were in the propagandistic vein of social realism. It is, therefore, possible to relate Kahlo's work in a number of ways with urban life and with the relationship of urban life to social and political movements that passed through Mexico City (such as the presence of Trotsky and his eventual assassination in 1940, which is an important segment of the film); and in turn Leduc's film captures important dimensions of Mexico City.

In the first place, Mexico City is quite present in Leduc's film because of Kahlo's and Rivera's political activism. We see them participating in public rallies, in a public prayer vigil for slain peasants demanding land reform, in a protest against the repression by the government of political parties that opposed the former's policies (Rivera was at this time secretary general of the Mexican Communist Party, which was persecuted: the official line was that its goals were already a part of the programs of Mexico's Institutional

Revolutionary Party, the PRI), and protesting against the development of nuclear bombs: in one eloquent scene in the film, we see Kahlo become extremely distraught while seeing on television images of U.S. nuclear testing in the Pacific. This interior duplication—the TV film footage within Leduc's film—underscores how the creation of a uniquely Mexican autochthonous culture in the years following the consolidation of national society after the Revolution of 1910, a project with which Kahlo and Rivera collaborated (this is the period in which Rivera is executing his monumental murals commissioned by the government, despite the obvious contradiction of belonging to the Communist Party), cannot be removed from international forces that Kahlo sees as one more manifestation of the patriarchal violence with which her own production is as a whole a confrontation. It is particularly telling, as we see her dressed in and surrounded by the vibrant colors of her beloved Mexican culture, that Kahlo contemplates with a terrified look on her face the black-and-white images of the TV screen: it is the life of immediate and tangible color versus the death of the removed and flat TV images. Along another axis, it is this death, made possible by U.S. armament technology versus the folkloric images of death in Mexican society, which is also captured in dazzling color. Kahlo confronts death throughout the film—recall that it is told as a flashback as she lies dying—but the images of this death are put forth as integral to her culture, while the TV broadcast captures the remote, yet all too real, death that threatened by nuclear holocaust during the Cold War years in which Leduc's film takes place.

The film underscores the public participation of Kahlo throughout her life in movements of political protest that involved taking to the streets; Kahlo was involved in the public nature of art as it emerged during the heyday of the Mexican postrevolutionary period. While Kahlo herself was never involved in the sort of highly politicized mural art that made Diego Rivera an international figure, she was very much involved in his world, in that of the artists who were working to forge a new national art for Mexico based on traditional and indigenous materials, as well as with those artists, particularly the Contemporáneos, whose perspectives were more cosmopolitan and internationalist. These two groups were never as separate as cultural controversies have made them out to be, and Frida Kahlo was, among others, very much of a bridge between them during a period in which the internationalism of some national writers combined with the international fervor over the nationalism of others to create a very dynamic environment in which Kahlo moved with ease. When she was dying, Kahlo had her first major exposition at the Palacio de Bellas Artes, the most important official forum for contemporary Mexican culture; and after her death, her coffin, covered by the Soviet flag to which she remained loyal, is placed on display; this display, and Rivera's despair over the death of Kahlo, make up the final sequence of the film. To the extent that the Palacio de Bellas Artes is such an integral part of the public presence of official Mexican culture, located as it is in the administrative corridor of downtown Mexico City, Kahlo's exhibition and her subsequent lying in state underscore an integration into Mexican urban life that is contrasted semiotically with the reclusion in suburban Coyoacán that marked the majority of the events covered in Leduc's film.

Of course, the spectator will know that Kahlo's house is now a museum (and Coyoacán is no longer the tranquil suburb it was forty years ago), and this official status is juxtaposed with the public space of the Palacio de Bellas Artes, both in the sense of the contrast between Kahlo's private life as an artist and her public life as a political militant and in the sense of the countercultural emphasis of much of her work as opposed to the public co-option of her work that has taken place since her death. Indeed, much of Kahlo's work has become commercialized and kitschified, to the extent that images that are specifically hers are to be found all over the urban space that is involved in Mexico City's very important tourist trade as well as a style of tourist art that can be called Frida kitsch; the latter, in turn, is continuous with a number of other images of tourist art, images that draw their quality as kitsch from other sources, such as Mexican charro culture, versions of the country's pre-Columbian civilizations, and Virgin-of-Guadalupe Catholicism, among others (on Frida as tourist kitsch, see Stavans, "Frida and Betina"; Lindauer).

These are details of urban reality on the level of narrative exposition in Leduc's film. However, there is in the film an even more profound level of urban presence that belongs to the details of Kahlo's life as they made constituent parts of her paintings. Both the paintings and those details are narrated in the film and, thus, are in a sense continuous with the elements I have already described. Yet in a very real sense, they belong to a deeper lived experience in Kahlo's life and are, therefore, of greater significance in depicting her relationship with urban Mexico City. Kahlo grew up in Mexico City during the period of enormous transformations provoked by the Revolution of 1910 and its aftermath. Her most important work was executed during the postrevolutionary period that saw the city begin to emerge as a vast megalopolis. The intersection between the life of modern society and the lived experiences of the individual human subject are integral to Kahlo's art, and it is some of these elements that are used as structuring principles in Leduc's film.

Kahlo never represented urban life in the sort of direct social-realist way that one can associate, say, with some of the fiction of the period (e.g., Luis Spota), the filmmaking of the period (e.g., Luis Buñuel, whose 1950 *Los olvidados* became the first great film of Mexico City and is only one of an impressive inventory of films Buñuel made in Mexico), or one dimension of the photography of the period by both Mexicans (e.g., Luis Álvarez Bravo) and non-Mexicans (e.g., the Italian-American Tina Modotti or the American Helen Levitt). Rather, Kahlo's representational codes lay in the direction of the expressionistic recreations of the violence experienced by the individual in society in general and modern society in particular. Many have commented on the feminist dimension of Kahlo's works and the way in which the cynical record of her gynecological sufferings are the basis of many of her canvases. This is not an unrelated issue, since the demands placed on women to be reproductive are as central to modern society as they are to the society of all women throughout history (Zamora's monograph is the best feminist analysis of the body in Kahlo's work). The difference lies in the intrusion of medical science into the body, whether with specific reference to her reproductive history or to other problems of the body that are indirectly or directly related to gynecology. Part of the grim fascination of many of Kahlo's paintings has to do with the imprisonment of the female body by the technical apparatuses of medical science (e.g., *Hospital Henry Ford* [1932] or *La columna rota* [1944]), a science that is, of course, principally urban: urban women are treated by male physicians who are part of the interdependent structures of urban life and its understanding of the human body, whereas rural women continue customarily to be treated by *curanderas* and *parteras* who are members of a separate feminine culture. It is interesting to note that it is not unreasonable to see a link between the evocation of modern death through nuclear holocaust and the immediate trappings of modernity in the urban realm as related metonymically by Kahlo's medical history.

One of the most wrenching segments of the film is the urban accident Kahlo suffered as a youngster, and it is generally held that this accident, along with polio (a very modern affliction of the day), weakened her body to the point of making it impossible for her to have a successful pregnancy (the film does not include reference to Kahlo's unsuccessful attempts to seek medical treatment in the United States). The urban accident described in the film happens in traffic: a bus and a car collide, and Kahlo, who is riding the bus, has a metal rod thrust through her pelvis. This event is very graphically displayed in the film, including the first attempts to pull the rod free. The result is to confirm in an unmistakable way the impingement of urban life, of which traffic accidents are everyday occurrences, on the body of the individual. Equally graphically portrayed is Kahlo's loss of a leg, which will confine her to a wheelchair. This event is represented both by her pitiful pleading to be spared the amputation and by how that event is reevoked for her by the whine of the carpenter's table saw in her studio. Scenes and sequences like this underscore how the circumstances of Kahlo's body are imbricated with the violence of urban life in ways that are particularly vivid.

It is important to note that Leduc does not appear to be particularly interested in seeing Kahlo as a figure of urban Mexico City. Because the film is constructed as a flashback, the emphasis is on the cinematographic representation of psychological states of mind: Kahlo remembers and evokes, and the film accompanies the convolutions of memory, whose complexity increases exponentially with the number of different aspects of postrevolutionary Mexican society in which the artist was involved, by reenacting them in the form of narrative stagings that are to one degree or another verisimilar and to one degree or another explicit—that is, many events are alluded to in rather elliptic ways, and many of the recreations have a fantasy or dreamlike quality about them. Indeed, many of the recreations are themselves expressionistic, such as the famous kitchen scene in which Kahlo and a close woman friend segue from making a salad to playing with the vegetables in erotically evocative ways to initiating lovemaking on the cooking bench.

Because of the highly foregrounded filmic texture of the film, it is not surprising that, except for scenes of political protest that move through the streets of the city (the most effective sequence being Kahlo being pushed along in her wheelchair by Rivera, all the while waving a sign on a stick), the dirty realism of urban space is not present. And, as I have already indicated, the Arcadian tranquillity of Coyoacán and Kahlo and Rivera's home and studio are featured in the film as privileged domains of some of the most internationally famous artistic production of contemporary Mexico, so much so that the film at times seems to take on qualities of a documentary. Yet this would be a simplistic understanding of the way in which the complexity of life takes place. The individual does not just move through urban space, picking up here and there elements from it.

Rather, urban life inscribes itself on the body in multiple and complex ways, such that those inscriptions become a part of the body and are transported with it wherever it goes. This is vividly the case with the traffic accident of which Kahlo was a victim, and it is also the case with the polio she acquires by living in the city at a time in which it is pandemic. These are very specific elements whose materiality is immediately evident. *Frida* captures less tangible, but no less material, elements in a number of plot lines throughout the movie. For example, the sequence dealing with bomb testing is not just a remote event associated with the foreign menace to the north that might impinge upon Mexico in the event of a nuclear holocaust. Rather, this is the period in the early 1950s in which, placing the more extreme nationalistic rhetoric of the early postrevolutionary period behind it, official Mexico is seeking an economic and commercial rapprochement with the United States that will result, beyond the time frame of the film, in the creation of the megalopolis that is Mexico City today and whose urban problems exercise such an immediate impact on the urban dweller (e.g., through the air pollution that has come with the unchecked growth in the city, growth directly related to the development of industrial and financial Mexico as initially sought in the 1950s). And, urban life is there in the institutions of the modern city in the specific form of modern (patriarchal) medicine with which Kahlo had such a long and conflict-filled relationship. In this sense, Leduc's film is very much imbricated with the urban reality of mid-twentieth-century Mexico City, even though it may not be immediately apparent in the specific details of the film.

Sexo, pudor y lágrimas (Sex, Shame, and Tears)

Antonio Serrano's *Sexo, pudor y lágrimas* (1999; filmed in 1998) is an excellent example of an urbane sex farce set in a neoliberal fantasy land of contemporary Mexico City, one in which the urban landscape is carefully and severely limited to a particular social class (upper or upper-middle professional) without any other details of life in the megalopolis intruding to dilute the features chosen to portray that class, and one in which these features equally carefully and severely are limited to establishing continuities between that class and an international class of moneyed, professional sophisticates. Serrano wrote and directed this film adaptation of his successful stage play, and the witty panache with which the film is executed makes it clear that it is intended by Serrano and Producciones Titán to compete on the foreign market in a way in which several other Mexican films of the past decade have intended to (e.g., Alfonso Arau's *Como agua para chocolate* [1992], María Novaro's *Danzón* [1991], and Jorge Fons's *El Callejón de los*

Milagros [1995]) without quite making it triumphantly: *Como agua para chocolate* may have been one of the largest grossing foreign films, but it did not win the critical acclaim that would have established it as a great foreign film. In the American market for Spanish-language films, this recognition seems to have gone to the Spaniard Pedro Almodóvar, whose apparently inexhaustible creativity and absolutely unprejudiced and magnanimous eye—as far as the modalities, especially sexual, of contemporary urban life—no one else in the Spanish world has come close to touching, not, at least, since the prime of Luis Buñuel. Yet Serrano's film is a good film and makes an honest, if not always satisfactory, attempt to capture the texture of Mexican social elements that are changing the urban landscape. Many spectators might perhaps object that most of the first half of the film is spent with the characters screaming at each other, which may be an index of the hysterical intensity of life in Mexico City for the current generation of go-getters, but it does get a bit annoying after a while.

Perhaps the best way of approaching *Sexo, pudor y lágrimas* is as soap opera; moreover, Serrano and the production personnel of the film were involved in the soap operas *Nada personal (Nothing Personal)* and *Mirada de mujer (A Woman's Look)*. If the original play is best understood as involving the formulas of melodrama, this is even more so in the case of the film, since it is able to make productive use of the carefully controlled visual image that is crucial to soap-opera television (concerning melodrama in Serrano's play and in contemporary Mexican theater, see García Arteaga). That is, while live theater involves the visual, it reduplicates, albeit not without its own stylization, the sensation of lived human life; and through the fourth wall of the realist theater to which Serrano's play corresponds, we see verisimilar images of our own daily existence. The difference with film is the fact that camera manipulation creates a carefully measured field of vision, all the while playing with the depth of vision provided by the mobility of angle and focus, such that an artificiality promotes a putatively heightened realism that is crucial to the superficial gloss with which soap opera customarily works: by being so selective, the eye of the camera is able to exclude what is inconvenient to the "realism" of the image that is being promoted. This is all standard filmmaking fair (with its concomitant version in the television camera), but it is important to recall it here in order to understand the intense level of artificiality that in reality lurks behind the surface of everyday life Serrano handles in his film.

Like soap opera, *Sexo, pudor y lágrimas* engages in a process of circumscription in which everything is eliminated that does not contribute to the sense of a particular lifestyle. Certainly, all films that do not propose to be a slice of life manipulate the images of reality, and all slices of life are as much ideological interpretations of the life at issue as any other text of cultural production. The difference is that, in a very substantial way, soap opera plays, disingenuously one would dare to say, rather extensively with the contradictory forces of providing a slice of life, while at the same time editing that slice of life to sell or promote a particular image of the texture of social existence. It is not so much that soap operas engage in falsifications, but rather that the clash between an apparent urgency to providing a reflection of a ground-zero reality (and reflection is a proper choice here, since transparent imaging is of considerable rhetorical importance) and the need to engage in calculated maneuvers of the frame of vision lends, at least to the critical observer, a patina of artificiality that resists interpretive analysis beyond characterizations like "phoney," "exaggerated," or "contrived."

In the case of *Sexo, pudor y lágrimas* the soap opera elements may be enumerated as follows. In the first place, the stories of several individuals are woven together, often in ways that seem more like an exercise in narrative geometry than a strategy for providing complementarity and contrast to profoundly complex human lives; often such an interweaving is based on unexplained motivation and unexamined consequences, such that the interest of the text lies in what is being immediately portrayed rather than in any subsequent reflection it may pretend to encourage. Moreover, the human lives portrayed belong to a fairly circumscribed social stratum: these are urban individuals; they are roughly in their late twenties or early thirties; they are, generally speaking, highly successful professionals with sophisticated tastes and wide experiential horizons; they move in large circles of equally sophisticated urban professionals who have extensive international connections or, at the least, extensive international perspectives; they live comfortably and with a notable degree of ostentatious splendor (apartments, clothes, cars, food and liquor, and leisure activities), certainly by comparison with the majority of their compatriots; and they adhere to a U.S. comfortable middle-class norm, disporting themselves in ways that minimize national specificity, such that, details of national dialect aside, they may be as much Argentine, Chilean, Venezuelan, Puerto Rican, or Brazilian as Mexican.

The problems of the lives of these individuals tend to limit themselves to those of sexual intimacy, expressed in varying degrees in terms of traditional romantic love as much as in terms of sophisticated quests of heightened erotic experience. Finally, sexual intimacy is played out against the back-drop of their privileged lives and involves the resources of those lives; e.g., a feuding couple can easily separate and survive independently. In this sense, the "tears" of their damaged or failed intimacies are played out against what is otherwise the background of a perfect world, as the title of a famous Mexican soap opera of the eighties claimed, *Los ricos también lloran (The Rich Also Weep)*, forgetting to point out, however, that usually problems of intimacy are the only reason the well-off have to cry. The details of urban re-ality are coextensive with the private world the characters inhabit, so much so that public realms become an extension of the former, whereas for most individuals in society the private realm is an extension of the public because one cannot count on the resources necessary to create a significant excep-tion between the two. Yet, for these individuals, public reality becomes re-duced to their reality, and if they move in the world—which is, to be sure, not completely free of its dangers and intrusions—it is notably a world that always looks like the one they inhabit in their realms of privileged life (the home, the club, the workplace, the store), and in any way in which they may step out of these privileged realms (which never occurs in *Sexo, pudor y lá-grimas*) the contrast is dramatic and usually portends some sort of disaster.

But I do not want to make too much of the soap-opera dimensions of Se-rrano's film. Unquestionably they are there, and unquestionably they point toward a merger between television programming and serious filmmaking (or between television programming and commercial theater, to refer back to the film script's origins as a successful play), not so much because it means an effective appeal to audiences between cultural genres that some might want to maintain as separate (especially in Latin America, where serious filmmaking is often viewed as fulfilling a crucial role lost to both television programming and dominant Hollywood imports—indeed, there is a refer-ence in *Sexo* to how one of the protagonists has exchanged his youthful project, a serious film, for work in an ad agency). It is, rather, because such a merger means a unification in the imagining of social reality between those genres. If television, with rare exceptions, sells a social reality that is an ex-tension of the commercials that support it, so much so that it often appears, in Latin America even more than in the United States, that television is com-mercials with some programming rather than programming punctuated by some commercials, the expectation remains, for an audience committed to the potential of national art films, that such films will engage in a level of in-terpretive analysis greater than what is allowed to television.

However, where *Sexo, pudor y lágrimas* most demonstrates the difficulty of maintaining this distinction is in the representation of Mexico City, and I would like to devote some space to a commentary on how the city is encoded in Serrano's film. *Sexo, pudor y lágrimas* is set in the upscale section of Polanco, just northwest of the Reforma-Insurgentes axis that constitutes the central core of the city. Polanco is not the most elegant area of the city: residential areas like the Pedregal and San Ángel or the artistic suburb— really now more of a semi-suburb, with the phenomenal growth of the city—of Coyoacán overshadow Polanco. However, the area is characterized by broad boulevards, high-rise apartment and commercial buildings, fine shops and restaurants, and abundant greenery; and in these details it vies for comparison with upscale near-town residential and business neighborhoods throughout Latin America. Polanco is associated with the city's prosperous Jewish middle class, and it is an area in which professionals and young business entrepreneurs have preferred to live and play. Guadalupe Loaeza's 1989 chronicle of life in Polanco, *Las reinas de Polanco (The Queens of Polanco)*, which emphasizes its women, has given it a particular prominence in contemporary Mexican writing. Polanco indicates, rather than a historical identity, a particular lifestyle, one of economic privilege that affords a certain isolation from a consciousness of the city as a demographic black hole, as portrayed in many of the chronicles of Carlos Monsiváis, the essays about marginal urban life by Elena Poniatowska, or the in-depth exposés of Alma Guillermoprieto, especially in the wake of the 1985 earthquake that served to bring to the fore serious and extensive problems with the city's infrastructure of services and utilities.

It is not that Polanco is completely isolated from the rest of the city, since if nothing else it is equally enveloped by the smog that plagues the urban valley. Yet the difficulties of surviving in postmodern Mexico City are not an issue in Serrano's film. The only detail that does appear as a leitmotif is the perennial failure of the elevator in the building where part of the action takes place, forcing residents and visitors to hike five stories up to the elegant apartment of one of the couples featured in the film. The only real black-humor detail of the film, one in which the fate of the individual is taken over by a manifestation of the urban monster, comes when the couple's wacky friend Tomás ends up committing suicide by throwing himself down the elevator shaft, which has been left exposed by the nonfunctioning system. This event comes close to the end of the film, and it is in part a catalyst for the two couples whose relationship is given prominence in *Sexo, pudor y lágrimas* to get on, in one case, with their relationship, and, in the other, with their separate lives. Tomás's suicide is a culmination of the

FIGURE 5　The action of private lives moves out into the streets of Polanco.

high intensity emotional positionings of the characters in the film, and although the exact reason for his suicide is never expressed and comes as a shock to his friends (although he does state at one point that he has blown off ten years of his life), his behavior throughout the film is as an outsider. Literally, at the beginning of the film, he returns to Mexico after years bumming around the world as a form of confrontational resistance to the bourgeois stability of his friends, all of whom apparently went to school together. Tomás, the doubting Thomas of the group, is the one to take wry and wacky exception to what he sees as the dehumanizing quality of bourgeois life as represented in the attempts of his friends to make it financially and professionally in an urban center in which the plastic niceties of Polanco cover over the grotesque forces that drive them in the business world they inhabit and its social derivations. Significantly, what Tomás perceives are these grotesque forces of dehumanizing behavior, as exemplified by a party, at a business titan's palatial home, that degenerates into a stereotypic Roman orgy, rather than the alienating characteristics of the travails of megalopolitan life, where the simplest task for survival requires a life-and-death struggle against pollution, traffic, crime, and collapsing infrastructures. The sort of image of Mexico City itself as a malevolent force, as found in Carlos García Agraz's 1964 *Días de combate (Days of Combat)* or even as far back as Luis Buñuel's 1950 *Los olvidados (The Forgotten*, released in English as *The Young and the Damned)*, is simply not present in Serrano's film, which is why Tomás's suicide, through availing himself of the open elevator shaft, is the one allusion in the film toward something that does not work right in an otherwise flawless urban enclave.

The fact that the physical opportunity for Tomás to commit suicide in such a dramatic fashion is the only flaw in the landscape of these individuals would seem to indicate that it is an opportunistic plot element rather than one that can be developed as somehow significant in terms of the relationship between individuals and their urban environment: what is otherwise an incidental opportunity for some comic effect—the need to climb so many flights of stairs to get to an elegant apartment because the elevator is never working—is suddenly given a new meaning without any context being provided for it that would make that event resonate with the rest of the text. Of course, it does resonate as the culmination of the strains of so much high-pitched emotional negotiation between these characters, and it does underscore how, in the final analysis, what Tomás represents can never be accommodated in their lives: their concerns for personal awareness and fulfillment, for freedom from the stultifying existence of bourgeois conformity, are, after all, never going to go anywhere important. But, in terms of the urban texture of the film, this, the most dramatic occurrence in the film, is simply dropped there circumstantially.

Yet the urban landscape is not circumstantial to the film; rather it is integral to it. The manipulation of the spacious interiors of the two apartments featured allows for the opportunity to underscore the multifaceted personalities and activities of each of the characters, since the spaces that they enjoy as their own and that they share in common point to the diverse texture of their personal and interpersonal lives: these are very successful and accomplished individuals, and the living space that they have within the overall confines, so restrictive for most individuals, is a sign of the privilege they enjoy. One of the privileged details of their lifestyle is not only to occupy apartments that have spacious rooms, but also to have an extensive balcony, one that wraps around the entire exterior of the apartment and not just a small walk-out space limited to a portion of the living room. Such a balcony functions as a promenade, giving access to a panoramic view of the city, with the effect of "owning" or "controlling" the city as an important correlative to the financial status of the apartment's residents.

Moreover, such a balcony provides for visual control of the immediate space of one's residence, and if spectators are able, because they know Polanco, to place the apartment building immediately, it is because the line of sight of the camera follows the conversations of the characters as they relate to the world around them in terms of the ways in which that world en-ters into the private human drama they are living. This is the case for an advertisement featuring the stereotype of a gorgeous model decorating the windowless facade of a neighboring building: she advertises a Wonderbra, with the slogan "¿Entiendes ahora lo que es la realidad virtual?"[6] That woman becomes an integral part of the negotiations of the men between themselves and with their female partners (with some exchanging of partners at issue) with respect to sexual roles and gender differences. Apartments with such balconies and their accompanying glass facades not only command a view of the city (the verbal metaphor here is not insignificant), but also make the boundaries between the residence and the city porous: one does not live in an apartment in Polanco, but rather one lives Polanco and all of the upscale details of its community life, thus confirming the importance of one's own personal life.

There is a lot to see and comment on from these balconies, not because life is more diverse in Polanco—in fact, it is probably more heterogeneous there than elsewhere in the city—but because what one sees, and hears, from the balcony is so coextensive with what one senses herself or himself to be all about, which is living the life of privilege such that one has the time and the monetary resources to engage in the sort of extensive emotional negotiations, over human and sexual relationships, that the film is really all about. It would be useful to think about the difference between *Danzón*, which also deals with agendas of intimate sexual fulfillment, and *Sexo, pudor y lágrimas:* there is no yelling and screaming in the former, and while the movement between Mexico City and Veracruz does mark a degree of pathetic fallacy in the film, whereby the vagaries of individual human sentiment are mirrored in inanimate nature (as in the way in which many ships in the harbor of Veracruz bear the names of the boleros that Julia lives by), there is nowhere the degree of unexamined symbiosis that is featured in Serrano's film between the privileges of individuals and the support services of their environment.

The apartment balconies play another crucial role in the film: as the invisible fourth walls of facing stages of gender theatrics. At one point in the film, the two couples split up, and the husbands join Tomás in one of the apartments, while the two wives join a third woman, an old friend who is an anthropologist and has also returned briefly to Mexico, in the apartment of the other couple. Each side of this gender divide enacts gender-specific spectacles for the other. The men, despite Tomás's interest in attempting to move beyond conventional gender performance, lapse into paradigmatic macho boorishness, while the women, two of whom (Ana and Andrea) in one way or another are sexual partners with the unconventional Tomás, engage in displays that are alternative girls-nights-out and feminist psychodramas. Each side studies the other and provides reactions to it, in a way sort of reminiscent of spectator involvement in an open theater performance. Much of this ends up as rather dull stuff, except for some notable displays of the body, particularly that of Jorge Salinas, who is known to his fans for his career in soap opera. One supposes that such body display is of passing interest, especially since it confirms once again the urban privilege of these individuals, who are able to eat properly and to work out enough in a gym to have bodies deserving of prominent display.

Actually, Salinas's display of his hunky attributes is not a totally extraneous exploitation of the visual dimension of film, especially since his stereotypical hypermasculinity is at odds with the many ways in which his sex life with his wife is in shambles. Rather conventionally, he is portrayed as a sexual oaf, while, rather trendily, she is allowed to speak her sexual dysfunction: thus, she is not much interested in sex, while one begins to suspect that he, despite his spectacular body, is not very good with women. Miguel, who is the character Salinas plays, is an advertising executive, and his buffed body and expensive clothes are themselves high quality products of the sort he sells. By contrast, Tomás, played by the leprechaunish Demián Bichir, displays his considerably more "natural"—i.e., unconstructed—body throughout the film, including one memorable dropped-pants sequence in the middle of the street in front of the apartment building; and when he first arrives at his friends' house (Carlos and Ana), he suddenly appears totally naked to plop down on the couch between them and say something like "¿Dónde me puedo dar un baño?"[7] This is not so much a sexual innuendo as it is a marker of the conventionality that the couple Carlos and Ana are now living; and where Miguel's brief bodily display shows how his body is of a whole with this privileged lifestyle, his gleaming apartment, his fancy car, and his executive suite at the ad agency, Tomás's is a constant challenge to bourgeois decency. Thus, while Polanco sophisticates are hardly models of reserve in their lovemaking (remember the orgy party mentioned above), the sort of randy sexuality that Tomás exudes, as part of his liberationist values, is hardly appropriate to the boardroom mentality of Miguel's set.

While the film is pursuing the theatrics of the sex wars through the facing proscenium arches of the two apartments (the film excludes any reference as to what inhabitants of surrounding apartments or passersby in the street might have to comment on the six performances), it pulls back from much of any allusion to the realignments of sexual preference that may result from an inquiry into sex and gender roles. Although there is much talk about sexual dysfunction, as we observe it through Tomás's critical eyes, it is the consequence of bourgeois stultification rather than the possibility of the limited range imposed by heterosexual normativity. Alternatives to such patriarchal heteronormativity are suggested elsewhere in contemporary Mexican filmmaking (e.g., Jaime Humberto Hermosillo's famous 1985 gay film, *Doña Herlinda y su hijo [Doña Herlinda and Her Son]*), but Serrano's glimpse into the world of these privileged individuals does not, except for some throw-away references to the homosexual possibilities of the men living together and the women living together, involve any enactment of the homoerotic potential of the sexual realignments that take place or acknowledge that the sexual dysfunction—for example, Miguel's impossible relations with women—may be the consequence of the need to explore such realignments. It may not be inverisimilar for this not to have occurred, but it is indeed odd that this Mexican version of Neil Simon's 1966 *The Odd Couple* (made into a 1968 film by Gene Saks, with a television series in the early 1970s and various subsequent film sequels) remains as arch about such matters as Simon's rather disingenuous play. In this sense, of course, Serrano's text is suddenly discontinuous with the urban reality in which it takes place, not just because of the notable gay visibility of Mexico City, but specifically because of the privileging of that visibility in the venues of sophisticated Polanco. This does not mean that Serrano's play and its film version should have moved in this direction, but what it does mean is that the analysis of sex and gender roles in an urban setting where homoeroticism is part of the analytical restructuring of such roles (see Armando Ramírez's 1980 novel, *Violación en Polanco [Rape in Polanco]*, set in Polanco) affords the film, despite everything else, a conventional sexuality that does not seem quite interesting enough, given the urban sophistication involved. If Tomás or one of the other characters, perhaps one of the women, had turned out to be bisexual or gay, the analysis of sex and gender roles would have assumed a more biting or harder edge. As it stands, men and women yelling at each other and Tomás's promoting sex on the dining-room floor as an antidote to bourgeois doldrums are not quite as interesting as they might be in the context of contemporary Mexico City and hip Polanco. (It should be noted that, while Mexico has a highly successful gay film in the form of Jaime Humberto Hermosillo's 1985 *Doña Herlinda y su hijo,* the only Mexican film that raises the question of lesbianism is Arturo Ripstein's 1993 *La reina de la noche [The Queen of the Night]*, on the popular singer Lucha Reyes [born in 1908], who committed suicide in 1944.)

Yet, having said this, it is important to note that there is another way of understanding the heterosexual situations in *Sexo* as, while conventional in the sense of being heterosexual, unconventional in terms of Mexican film-making or Mexican cultural production as a whole. The way in which women's sexual needs, especially Andrea's sexual frustration (Ana, likewise, is frustrated by her overly intellectual husband, Carlos), are explored is notable, as is the questioning of the sexuality of the superstud, Miguel. Andrea's sterility is displaced in terms of a collection of porcelain dolls she collects, and the mismatch between her and her husband is explored on occasion with brutal frankness. In particular, the film, like other recent films such as Alfonso Cuarón's 1991 *Sólo con tu pareja (Only with Your Spouse)* and Rafael Montero's 1995 *Cilantro y perejil (Cilantro and Parsley)*, is important for exploring the dynamics of middle-class marriage in contemporary Mexico, particularly how the fault lines of that marriage are brought out in the revolt of the women against the men, a revolt that is viewed as essentially legitimate if only of limited efficacy. The two couples' friend, María, a respected zoologist, shows up championing ideals of women's liberation from the tyranny of sexual and emotional dependence on men. Yet her pseudofeminism, despite the revolt against their husbands she has engineered for Ana and Andrea, comes to naught when she is reduced to tears on the telephone with her estranged lover in London, whom she begs to take her back.

Yet *Sexo, pudor y lágrimas* comes up short in terms of what it might have done to represent Polanco as one area of the human geography of contemporary Mexico City. The city, in the form of the highly influential Polanco area, is very much present in this film, not only as a sign of a privileged lifestyle of a group of prosperous thirty-something adults, but also in terms of the ways in which features of life in Polanco are essential to the characterization of the human conflicts involved. Unfortunately, unlike the majority of the films examined in this study, Serrano's film is unable, in the final analysis, to make the correlation between the private and the public into a profoundly engaging story.

TWO   Human Geographies

A series of films that examine the human geography of Mexico City are
examined in this chapter—that is, films that examine the ways in which
individuals relate to the specific social and physical dimensions of their
urban spaces and how their urban lives are shaped by the material and
emotional conditions of their lives in the city. *El Callejón de los Milagros*
(1994), which is based on Nobel prize–winner Najib Mahfouz's *Midaq
Alley* (1995), which is centered on his native Cairo, explores the interrelationship of individuals' lives as imposed by their occupation of a residential
cul-de-sac in downtown Mexico City. *Mecánica nacional* (1971), one of the
first independent films to engage in a critical parody of Mexico City life, beyond the slapstick potboilers of Cantinflas, is organized around the crucial
juxtaposition between the growing congestion of urban traffic and the
artificiality of a Grand Prix–style stock car race through the Mexican countryside: in both cases, the automobile is an icon for the organization of human society and the horizon of knowledge for individual identity and meaning. *El castillo de la pureza* is also from the 1970s, specifically 1973, but,
where *Mecánica nacional* addresses itself forthrightly to the onslaught of life
in the city, the former is a Gothic meditation on the consequences of an attempt to withdraw from the monstrosity of that onslaught. If the city is
overwhelmingly present in *Mecánica nacional* by direct display, it is indirectly present in *El castillo de la pureza* in the guise of the efforts made to
staunch its implacable incursion into the daily lives of individuals who find
it threatening and repugnant to their dignity as human beings. That they

cannot stave off that invasion in the end speaks less to the futility of any attempt to withdraw from the alleged impurities of life than it does to the way in which the life of the city pardons no one. The individual's attempt to come to terms with and even to defy the implacable texture of life in the city is the basis of *Todo el poder* (1999), where power here refers not to any group of individuals, but rather to the unyielding might of urban life, such that the citizen of a megalopolis like Mexico City has no choice but to be swept along by forces far beyond personal will or control. Finally, by contrast to the urban sophisticates that populate the urban comedy *Todo el poder*, *Lolo* (1992) focuses on an individual representative of one of the most striking demographic features of Mexico City: young adolescents for whom the urban economy has virtually nothing else to offer but despair, alienation, and a life of crime and early death.

El Callejón de los Milagros (Alley of the Miracles)

El Callejón de los Milagros (1994), by Jorge Fons, is one of the most exemplary contemporary Mexican movies as regards the attempt to capture the texture of life in the largest city in the world. The winner of more than thirty national and international prizes, it is also one of the most important Mexican films of the nineties. Eschewing the sort of panoramic contextualization of Carlos García Agraz's *Días de combate* (1994), Fons's movie opts for a strategy of synecdoche, whereby the vast human frieze of the city is extracted in terms of one residential neighborhood as defined by an "alley" of interconnected businesses, multiple-family dwellings, and public spaces.

Mexico City is a city that is intensely defined in terms of its neighborhoods. While there are traditional neighborhoods in the city, including officially designated administrative districts and satellite towns that have become incorporated into the vertiginously expanding megalopolis, residents of the city maintain abiding roots in the area in which they grew up. Many may be members of the young urban poor, and many people identified with the city are among those who daily flood into the capital seeking the sort of survival livelihood that may be more possible there than anywhere else in the republic, and perhaps these individuals identify with urban space much less in terms of the meaning of an overarching neighborhood identity than is the case with those with generational roots in a particular part of the city. Some areas of the city, such as the Zona Rosa, known as one of the city's principal tourist centers, Coyoacán, a legendary center of artistic activity, or the Zócalo, the vast main square where the Municipal Cathedral and the palaces of both the national and the municipal government are located, are part of Mexico City's imagery. Yet they mark more as points of reference for the city's enormous tourist industry than they do as coordinates for urban spatial identity on the part of the millions who live in Mexico City, those for whom the barrio may be little more than a wedge of the city bounded by major thoroughfares.

Fons's decision to provide an interpretation of Mexican urban life through the synecdoche of a microcosmic neighborhood defined in terms of one short dead-end street is inspired by a novel by Egyptian author Najib Mahfouz, translated into English as *Midaq Alley* (another of Mahfouz's novels was made into *Principio y fin [Beginning and End]* in 1993 by Arturo Ripstein, whose father, Alfredo Ripstein Jr., produced Fons's film). Mahfouz's novel belongs to a fictional genre that can best be described as the "city as a beehive," a denomination I take from the novel *La colmena* (1951; translated as *The Hive*), by the Spanish Nobel prize–winner Camilo José Cela, where an apartment building in Madrid becomes the microcosm of post–Civil War, Franquista society. In the case of Mahfouz's novel and Fons's film, the slice of urban life is located in the dead-end street as a more variegated self-contained space than Cela's apartment building. Certainly, it is more typical of urban life in Mexico City.

Although El Callejón de los Milagros is a nonexistent street in Mexico, it is an unmistakably authentic Mexico City space. There is every indication that it is located in the heart of the city, close to the Zócalo, which is the megalopolis's ground zero, and there are several scenes in which one can make out buildings that are apparently from this administrative core. This is Mexico City's *primer cuadro,* first block: the original site of both the Aztec capital Tenochtitlán and the beginnings of this one center of Spanish domination in what is today central Mexico. Thus, the buildings are a mixture of administrative edifices, both historic and modern, multifamily dwellings that are likely to have originated in nineteenth-century palaces or convents, and small businesses that occupy the ground floors of these dwellings. The following are the principal specific spaces that appear in Fons's film. (1) Various apartments in one building in/on the Callejón (the instability of the preposition here will be treated below). There are three apartments in particular: that of Susana, who is the owner of the building and whose apartment is particularly well appointed; that of Don Rutilio, cantina owner, and his wife, Doña Eusebia, comfortably decorated; and that of Doña Cata, a fortune-teller and provider of home remedies, and her daughter Alma, which is rather modestly furnished. Thus, the effect is that of a cross-section of the Mexican petite bourgeoisie. (2) Don Rutilio's cantina, which, in typical Mexican homosocial fashion, is the locale in which the majority of masculine life in the neighborhood takes place, which means that it is the principal site of all-man social commerce. Güicho is the all-purpose barman in Don Rutilio's establishment, and in the course of the film he will marry the much older Susana as a form of socioeconomic advancement. (3) The neighborhood barbershop, where young Abel works, who will briefly court Alma, but run off to the United States with Don Rutilio's estranged son, Chava, only to return to find that Alma has disappeared. This shop is a typical hole-in-the-wall neighborhood operation. (4) The public space of the Callejón itself, where Zacarías, one of the denizens of Don Rutilio's cantina who meets with other men to play dominos, administers (i.e., shakes down in return for protection against the police) a host of street persons: fire-eaters, mimes, shoe-shine boys, and the like. (5) Various minor locales, such as a food stand, a bookstore, and a jewelry store. A men's shirt store, which appears to actually be off the Callejón itself and in a more open area (i.e., on a thoroughfare), also figures briefly in the movie, as does a traditional bathhouse of the sort that supplements, in older neighborhoods of Mexico, the inadequacy of bathing installations in the older dwellings like the one featured in the film; these bathhouses may or may not (although they are now more likely to than not) be brothels or sites of male homoerotic activity, as this one in fact is for one narrative thread of the film.

In *El Callejón de los Milagros,* Fons reinforces the sense not only of connected human lives, but, more significantly, of connected human lives as a consequence of cohabitation in porous spaces. It is not so much that the lives these individuals live create these porous spaces, although that is in part what does in effect take place: the enormous sociality of Hispanic life, particularly on the social level of the inhabitants of the Callejón, is unquestionably a communitarian one of diverse historical origins, such that the personal is collective, everyone has a stake in everyone else's life, and, most importantly, there is a tendency for everyone to share significant details of his or her life with those with whom almost daily, and often hourly, contact is maintained. Certainly, such commingling of individual stories, centering often on the socially vital discourse genre of gossip, and abetted by institutionalized forms of confession or revelation as found in fortune-telling, barbershop confidences, and the sort of male boasting that occurs in places like the local cantina, requires access by individuals to each other, access that promotes a shared physicality that lends itself especially well to filmic portrayal: in a movie such as *El Callejón de los Milagros,* there is very much of the sense of the texture of lives in which formal boundaries are often abstract and the crossing of those boundaries is less a transgression of the private space of the other than it is a quid pro quo driven by the principle that everyone is in this life together and that life is more defined by the collective than by the individual (see Dealy for an interesting interpretation on the public nature of individual life in Latin America).

Yet such porous sharing of space is also the direct consequence of the design for living of the buildings available for occupancy in/on the Callejón. These buildings have, in the first place, evolved over a period of several centuries, although the majority of them probably date from the period of Porfirio Díaz (president of Mexico, 1877–1911), when the city underwent, in what is now the central core, a major expansion as the consequence of the liberal modernism of the regime. Mexico City construction continues to be in the form of relatively low buildings, and the landscape of the city is dominated, with the notable exception of relatively recent high-rises and skyscrapers, by buildings that are rarely more than three or four stories. As in the case of the utilization of older buildings, in which shopping galleries have historically been constructed in what were originally porte cocheres, the ground floor tends to be utilized by small businesses of the sort described above for the Callejón. Yet the interpenetrability of these spaces is affirmed not only by their opening out onto the public space of sidewalk and street, but by the fact that they may group around the inner space of a gallery, which may also typically have, to the side or in the back, a staircase that leads up to the apartments serving as individual residences, or may open out onto alleys and back (or, often, inner) courtyards—open, covered, or semi-sheltered—that are as much storage spaces as they are meetings spaces and avenues of access. In the case of the sort of apartment building presided over by Susana, the apartments may open out onto a common space, be constructed along a semi-open gallery, or simply be interconnected in the Latin American version of the railroad or shotgun house. It should be stressed that these are not tenement houses, nor are they pensions, although they may be used for that purpose. However, the residents depicted in *El Callejón de los Milagros* are economically stable, and their household circumstances, while not those of the city's prosperous professional and commercial class, are hardly to be confused with those of the impoverished, such as the urban poor of the first great film on the city, Luis Buñuel's *Los olvidados* (1950).

The circumstances described above are evident in Fons's film in terms of the way in which individuals move from one space to another, from their own to other's private spaces, and commingle in the many public spaces that occur in pockets between those private spaces. Doors, windows, archways, and staircases mark spatial transitions, but not in the way in which this customarily takes place as the conventional punctuation of architectural structures. Rather, it takes place, as the movement of the camera insistently underscores, in ways that show how these details of construction serve to facilitate transition rather than to fix boundaries: characters burst in on one another through closed doors, spy on one another through open doors and windows, use windows as doorways, and, in general, overhear one another because of the indeterminacy of architectural barriers. This does not mean that there is no privacy or that everyone's life is open to public view. But what it does mean is that Fons's film emphasizes the porousness of shared spaces in the sort of *vecindad* modeled in the film.

The indeterminacy of architectural barriers is, thus, as much the consequence of the interpenetrability of public and private in traditional Hispanic culture as it is the result of the history of the structures that make up the Callejón, so much so that it would be difficult to establish a cause-and-effect relationship between one and the other. The consequence, from the point of view of both narrative content and the discourse strategy of Fons's use of the perspective of the camera, is to promote the image of a group of human beings whose stories—whose lives, and therefore whose living circumstances—are irremediably intertwined, such that "individual," "independent," "autonomous" and "private" are only some of the qualifiers that are inappropriate to this slice of Mexico City life being portrayed.

Fons's interest in representing such a slice of late twentieth-century urban life in the world's largest city primarily makes use of the tangible interconnectedness of physical, lived, material space that the camera is able to capture so well in its fluid movements along various planes that make up the domain of the Callejón and its extensions out into the immediate environs of Mexico City. Moreover, from the point of view of spatial distribution, the film exploits the ambiguity surrounding the proper prepositional choice to refer to location; and it is difficult to know whether one should speak of the Callejón in the metaphoric mode as a container, a realm *within* which this human microsociety lives out its drama, or as a place *at* which that drama takes place. Of course, the Callejón is both things at once. In appropriate synecdochal fashion, there is a hierarchical chaining of spaces, such that rooms make up apartments and in turn make up buildings. These buildings are spread out along the Callejón, with various degrees of remove from the actual space of the street to one room or another, one habitational unit or another, the imagined space, which captures in part the fact that not every space is in direct physical contact with the street that carries the name Callejón de los Milagros, but rather some lie on receding planes from it. Yet it is as though the Callejón actually circumscribed a particular space rather than traversed it. That is, in the manner of an abstract geometry, the Callejón is not the straight line that appears on the (here fictional) map of Mexico City, but is imagined to be a multidimensional sphere that envelopes this fragment of the city. It is one thing to know with certainty that one is or is not *on* the Callejón, as concretely marked by the street signs provided by the city, and it is quite something else to be able to sense when one is or is not within the sphere of the Callejón, in a movement that is perpendicular to it, through the maze of amassed, overlapping, and conjoined constructions that are like the archeological sedimentation of the historical development of the city, away from the officially designated passage.

There are two other principal ways in which literal and figurative interconnectedness is displayed in the film, ways that are as much a part of narrated account as they are part of the ocular strategies of the camera. The first concerns the organization of the film around four stories, titled "Rutilio," "Alma," "Susana," and "El regreso." The first three concern erotic affairs, while the last one concerns the return to the Callejón of two characters who left for the United States as a consequence, in one way or another, of those affairs. Rutilio's story is that of a middle-aged man who embarks on an affair with a young man; his son, Chava, bursts in on Rutilio and Jaime in the shower of the local baths, batters Jaime seriously, and decides to flee to the United States until the scandal of his violence has subsided. Alma's story is that of the daughter of the fortune-teller; although she has her sights set on larger fish, Alma accepts the advances of the Callejón's barber, Abel. When Chava flees to the United States, he begs Abel to accompany him, and Abel, his *compadre* (buddy, in the Mexican system of close same-sex bonding), agrees to accompany him. Although Alma has agreed to wait for Abel, she is seduced by the local hotshot, José Luis, and ends up disappearing to work in the brothel he owns (or administers; it is not quite clear), leaving her mother, Doña Cata, devastated at Alma's disappearance.

In the case of Susana, although she has flirted with Chava and agrees to lend him money to go to the United States, she successfully woos Güicho and marries him in a wedding celebration that is the one occasion in which all of the residents of the Callejón come together on screen (except for Chava and Abel, who are already in the United States); although Güicho

FIGURE 6   Abel dies in Alma's arms in the middle of the street.

steals from her, this is the one erotic relationship in the film that seems more or less to work. Finally, in "El regreso," Chava returns from the United States with a woman and child in tow; although his father initially rebuffs him because he is not married, he is eventually won over by the fact that the child has been given his name. Abel returns separately, and discovering that Alma is in José Luis's hands, he tries to win her back, although José Luis intimidates her into staying with him, whereupon Abel returns to the brothel and essentially commits suicide in front of Alma by slashing José Luis's face with a straight razor, only to be subdued by José Luis's bodyguards while José Luis eviscerates Abel with his own razor and throws him into the street. Alma runs out after him, and Abel dies in her arms in a replay of the Pietà. No further word is heard of Jaime.

Each of these four stories exemplifies some dimension of the ideology of love in contemporary Mexican society, and each involves the values of the residents of the Callejón in some systematic way. As a consequence, not only do all of the main characters play a role in each of these love stories, but the structural organization of the film is such that all four are going on at the same time, and as a consequence, a particular sequence may be repeated from a different point of view. For example, one of the most notable involves Abel's first attempt to attract Alma's attention, and it is notable because it involves the framework of the window of her room as an example of a porous architectural marker that permits narrative exchange between two spaces. The scene in which Alma catches sight of Abel, with Chava at his side, outside her bedroom window as she dries her hair, is repeated in the segments dealing with each of the three love stories; and this sort of repetition of events serves to provide the film with the sense of a dense human drama in which individual stories cannot be separated out: Rutilio's, Alma's, and Susana's attempts to find erotic fulfillment do not occur independently of each other, nor is it simply a question of them occurring simultaneously. Rather, they are imbricated within one another, so that, for example, while Chava observes with disgust the homoerotic adventure of his father, he is encouraging Abel in his soap-opera story-line pursuit of Alma, and at the same time he is evading the clumsy flirtations of the sex-starved Susana.

In a larger sense, however, these stories are imbricated with each other because they bring into play society as a whole as represented by the microcosm of the Callejón. For example, in the case of Rutilio's affair with Jaime—it is important to note that the representation of his story is legitimated in the film not only in terms of the growing visibility of homoerotic life in Mexico City, but in terms of the way in which there is a long human, and, therefore, Mexican history of older men seeking the company of younger, sexually, emotionally, and economically dependent men—although Rutilio, in the best tradition of the Mexican macho, makes vociferous claims to his right to a personal life and, as a consequence, his right to refuse to provide any explanation to his wife (whom at one point he roughs up for even raising the subject) or anyone else for his sexual exploits, the film makes it clear that not only does it impinge on the lives of his immediate family, but it has a bearing on the lives of all of the members of the Callejón and his cantina patrons as well, not so much for moral reasons but because it has become public knowledge.

While Chava discusses his father's homoerotic philandering with Abel—Chava will later silently confront Jaime in a magnificent cameo of the dynamic of Mexican homophobia—the cantina patrons comment, with the broad and biting humor of the Mexican double entendre (the *albur*), on their host's new sexual proclivities, and Doña Eusebia, his wife, tearfully consults with Doña Cata. Susana overhears this consultation, thereby ensuring that everyone else in the Callejón will know about it. Of course, there are no real private lives for any of us as social subjects, and gossip is certainly a primal narrative that binds us all together. But Fons's film underscores the way that, beyond society in general, beyond Hispanic and Latin America and Mexican social narratives, in the sort of urban collective existence as modeled by the Callejón, no narrative can really function if it does not contain a structural role for each one of the members of the collective to fill.

This brings us back again to the way in which Fons's film does not simply tell four stories, but rather implies something like an allegorical interrelationship between them, which is also why "El regreso" is a coda that brings the stories all together into one image of life in the Callejón. *El Callejón de los Milagros* offers none of these love stories as a model, but neither does it denounce any of them as politically, socially, or morally inappropriate. Rutilio's affair is not problematical because it involves a homoerotic relationship, but rather because he conducts it in such a way that it impacts negatively on his family and neighbors: this may be as much a question of Mexican machismo (the "I'll be damned if I care what you think I do as a man" attitude) as it is a fact of the growing visibility of homoerotic relationships in contemporary Mexico City. Alma's restlessness would appear to be less a matter of poor object choice or even the betrayal of Abel—who, in the end, places his loyalty to Chava above his professed love for Alma— than it is a matter of dead-end lives for women of her social class in Mexico. After all, she hardly has in Eusebia (who spends more time in church than at home), her mother, Cata (a fortune-teller), or Susana (a sexually unsatisfied landlady) any viable feminine role model. And too, while she may be attracted to Abel's simple and sincere charms, José Luis suggests to her the possibility of living the good life offered by the city's vast popular-culture industry. Finally, Susana only seems to get the best of the bargain because she has economic security to offer Güicho, and her own needs for affection and sexual fulfillment appear in the end to outweigh her husband's thievery.

If there is any judgment rendered by the film of these various love stories, it may be in the way in which male homosociality must always trump every other narrative: Abel's failed courting of Alma in the end is something between him and the man who stole her from him; Rutilio's philandering is played out in the confrontation, and eventual reconciliation, between him and his son; Güicho steals from Susana to be able to have some indepen-

FIGURE 7   The all-male homosocial world of Don Rutilio's cantina.

dence in his social life with men outside her home; the inviolable bond of compadres requires that Abel abandon Alma to go to the United States with Chava; and the affairs of the Callejón are repeatedly the principal concern of the men who gather in Rutilio's cantina to play dominoes.

The domino game is, cinematographically, the principal way in which the four narrative segments are tied together, and it is the second device of reduplication referred to above. The same opening moves of the domino game are repeated at the beginning of each of the first three segments; this appears in a somewhat changed fashion in the fourth segment. This sequence is not an exact duplication from one segment to the other, but its essential reenactment in four virtually identical versions confirms the interrelatedness of the three love stories and the value of the final segment as a coda to all three of them. More important, the function of this sequence as an introduction to each of the four segments confirms the overarching homosociality of life on the Callejón. The homosocial environment of the cantina dominates the Callejón: on one occasion in which Susana accompanies Güicho to the cantina, she remarks that she has never been there before; and at no time does Eusebia, Cata, or Alma, or any other woman, enter the space of the cantina. Moreover, the fact that influential men from the Callejón gather there to drink, play dominoes, and, most significantly, engage in boisterous and often brutal commentary on events in the neighborhood underscores how the "life and miracles" of the residents are primarily the concern of men in concert with one another. None of the narratives of the women in this sense matter, not Eusebia's prayers, not Cata's fortune-telling, and not Susana's gossip. Or, if they do matter, they are superseded by the homosocial narrative of the council of men in the cantina. Numerous Mexican feminine texts have made a point of offering images of the validity and power of women's counternarratives in the face of the primacy of Mexican homosociality: Elena Poniatowska's 1969 testimonial novel, *Hasta no verte, Jesús mío (Here's Looking at You, Sweet Jesus),* comes to mind, as do feminist films such as María Navaro's 1991 *Danzón* and Sabina Berman and Isabelle Tardán's 1995 *Entre Pancho Villa y una mujer desnuda (Between Pancho Villa and a Naked Woman).* The fact that *El Callejón de los Milagros* does not provide such a counternarrative is less likely because its director is a man than because the point of the film is the verist texture of this slice of contemporary urban society in which, unquestionably, the homosocial imperative continues to dominate.

The closing scene of the film is worth commenting on in some detail: under the nighttime sky near the Callejón, Alma holds the dying body of Abel. Susana's love story seems to have worked more or less; and since Chava does not actually kill Jaime (a welcome respite from the customary denouement of homophobic violence), there is always the lingering possibility of resumption of Rutilo's and his relationship or a similar one for Don Rutilio. Moreover, the relationship between Alma and Abel never expresses itself in any way that could be said to deviate from soap-opera formulas. Nevertheless, they are the youngest couple, and it is difficult for the spectator to overlook the resonance of a story told about the so-called next generation and a renewed promise for a better life for them. Fons may close his film with the tender moment of the embrace between the two lovers who have become separated by the ugly realities of life, but it is those realities that end up holding sway: Abel dies as a consequence of evisceration at the hands of a cynical ponce, and there is no doubt that Alma has little choice but to return to pursue her career in the brothel. One supposes that Chava will support the mother of their child (despite the rapidity with which he promptly has an affair with a friend of Alma's soon after returning home) and take over his father's cantina, but this prosaic matrimony is lost in the background of the allegorical force of what happens to Abel and Alma (whose names are rather transparent flags for the way in which they should be viewed as allegorical figures).

Fons's *El Callejón de los Milagros* is a particularly successful film because it is notable cinematographically and, thanks to the discursive properties of the camera, narratively. By providing such a complex representation of a slice of life in a paradigmatic Mexico City neighborhood in which the lives of individuals are closely linked with their tie to the barrio, Fons has produced one of the most important examples of urban filmmaking in contemporary Mexico.

Mecánica nacional (National Mechanics)

Produced only a handful of years after the student massacre in Tlatelolco in October 1968, Luis Alcoriza's *Mecánica nacional* (1971) belongs to the emergence in Mexican filmmaking of a critical attitude toward Mexican society, one that has continued to the present day (regarding the new direction taken by the filmmaking of the 1970s, see Costa). To be sure, criticism of Mexican society had been present in many films prior to Alcoriza's, but it had been cast, first of all, in a pathetic mode, and, second, it tended to emphasize historical injustices prior to the 1910 revolution, segments of Mexican society that had yet to be incorporated into the dominant ideology of the ruling party that came to power subsequent to the revolution, or those elements of society that assumed a dissident or "dissolvent" stance vis-à-vis the promises and guarantees of the revolution. Moreover, Mexican filmmaking (like narrative fiction) tended to focus on the rural context. One exception was Luis Buñuel's *Los olvidados* (1950), which is a classic of urban filmmaking, and it is memorable for the way in which it charts the radical alienation of young adults in the second generation of postrevolutionary Mexico. The fact that Buñuel was not a Mexican and that he chose (despite having received official support for his film) to attack by implication and in an unsentimentalizing fashion the social programs of the government led to his film being dealt with harshly by audiences and critics; and it has on occasion been excluded from treatments of Mexican filmmaking (Carl Mora, for example, only mentions it once in passing).

However, in addition to representing a harshly critical stance toward Mexican society, Alcoriza's film turns away from the pathetic mode that characterizes so many films from the golden age of Mexican cinema.

Mecánica nacional, reflecting the director's long apprenticeship as Buñuel's assistant, relies instead on parody, slapstick, and the grotesque to ridicule sacred myths and traditional mores of Mexico, while at the same time focusing on the life of lower-middle-class individuals in Mexico City (while he does not discuss the film in any detail, Pérez Turrent acutely observes the influence on Alcoriza of "the Italian model [which] used comedy as a tool to uncover social ills" [102]). The film makes use of a plot that is basically a pretext to engage in a burlesque of modern Mexico, since the plot in and of itself is of little interest: Eufemio and his family (wife, daughter, and mother) pile in the family car to travel to a point, on the outskirts of Mexico City, through which the contestants in a Grand Prix–style car-racing event will pass.

Thousands gather at this point in the thoroughfare, and, to begin with, as a parody of the growing culture of the automobile in the modest but general prosperity of Mexico in the late 1960s and early 1970s, there are massive traffic jams at the site where people gather to see contestants whiz by briefly. The place becomes an enormous campground and a microcosm of Mexican society: people bring food and drink and spend the night in order to have a good vantage point for the time in the morning when the race cars will pass by. They eat and drink, sing, flirt, make love, talk, argue, fight, threaten each other with violence, all in a ship-of-fools atmosphere that does little to connect with the loving images of Mexican types long perpetuated in national filmmaking. That is not to say that there are not films prior to *Mecánica nacional* that engage in parody, the grotesque, and the ridiculous. But they do so in a way that always resolves what otherwise might be a mockery of Mexican society by explaining away conflicts in terms of individuals who are basically good, generous, and loving, as is the case throughout Cantinflas's entire production. Cantinflas may often represent grotesque types, but the display of picaresque behavior at the service of the survival of an essentially decent sort drains his films, in the final reel, of any really coherent criticism of Mexican society, anything that could be dangerous in terms of the hegemonic ruling power and its programs (regarding the crucial importance of Cantinflas, see Stavans, "The Riddle of Cantinflas" 31–52).

Alcoriza's choice of actors to portray his grotesque view of contemporary Mexican society establishes from the outset the degree to which he is willing to mock established paradigms. For example, he casts in the role of Eufemio, the patriarchal guardian of his family's honor, Manolo Fábregas, whose film and stage career had consisted mainly of roles as suave and sophisticated types, thoroughly at home in drawing rooms and elegant boudoirs. But as Eufemio, Fábregas plays the part of a loud and crass automobile repair shop owner, used to barking orders at his family, swilling beer with his buddies, and swaggering on the street in a never-ending display of his self-confident masculinity. Fábregas's role throughout the film is to present a rhetorically heightened version of the performance of Mexican masculinity, both in the management of his family and in his confirmation of patriarchal structures in his relations with other men and women, including, of course, in particularly hilarious ways, doing things, in conformance with his rights as a man, that he expressly forbids his wife and daughter to do.

Eufemio, as a grotesque parody of a certain class and type of Mexican manhood, serves Alcoriza for a number of reasons: he exemplifies life lived to the zero degree of self-reflection; he embodies dimensions of Mexican popular culture that are driven by unquestioned presuppositions; he contradicts, overtly and implicitly, prevailing national beliefs having to do with modesty, discretion, respect, and kindness; and, finally, the extent of his self-absorption is such that the only possible basis of his interpersonal relations has to do with how much others may confirm his self-image. Fábregas is funny enough, but in somewhat of a grim fashion, because Alcoriza is charting the appalling depredations wrought on human character by the ways in which urban life produces an alienation in the individual, particularly in the hard-scrabble life of the lower middle class, for whom a measure of comfort and stability remains always tantalizing beyond their immediate grasp: it is there in the advertising, but never in their experience of reality.

Much funnier in a less mediated fashion is that part played by Sara García, known as the quintessential long-suffering mother and grandmother. The enumeration of the films in which García played such roles is indeed vast, so much so that her image, dressed in black, touched off by a cameo or something similar, wearing gold-rim glasses, her white hair piled around her ears, and alternately smiling benevolently or sighing with the pain of human suffering, came to be used commercially beyond her films. One suspects that reality imitated art, to such a degree that women felt constrained to be like Sara García in order to properly be the paradigmatic, revered Mexican maternal figure. However, in *Mecánica nacional,* García enacts a mordant parody of her canonical roles. While she recreates her much venerated image, the grandmother of Alcoriza's film is foul-mouthed, acid-tongued, and an unrestrained glutton, so much so that, as the others drink, flirt, and fight around her, she eats everything in sight, suffers from an *empacho* (something like an acute case of bloat), and dies at the campsite. At first, everyone

FIGURE 8   The grandmother's laid-out body is abandoned by everyone: the big-city auto race takes precedence over traditional family ties.

gathers round to pay her homage, weeping and wailing over the disappearance of their beloved *mamacita/abuelita*. She is laid out on the ground, surrounded by candles, bedecked with flowers, and someone initiates a rosary for the salvation of her soul. Just then the shout goes up that the race cars are coming into view. At first torn between duty and fun, but then with excited abandon, onlookers, friends, family peel away until Doña Lolita is left abandoned; the only one still interested in her is a dog, who undoubtedly is attracted by the odor of the massive amounts of food she has consumed. When the camp is broken after the race cars have disappeared, Eufemio and family pack Doña Lolita up with the rest of the stuff and make their way back to Mexico City. In the midst of the massive traffic jam, they use the dead woman's propped up body as a way to gain enough sympathy from the other drivers to cut their way through the stalled cars in a hilarious parody of a funeral cortege.

Finally, the singer Lucha Villa plays Fábregas's wife, Chavela. Her part does not require much inventiveness, as it requires her to do little more than be a doormat to her husband's cretinous manhood. However, at one part in the film, some people start singing, and Chavela takes up the guitar to do her part for the festivities. Needless to say, Villa has no choice but to play this part also as a parody, as she masterfully sings so badly that it is unlikely that she hits a single note correctly.

Alcoriza is so skillful in finding just the right level of parody to represent this menagerie of social types that the viewer, particularly the one able to identify the parameters of urban Mexican reality being represented, is kept laughing throughout the film. And, indeed, it is not necessary to have profound sociological analysis, since so much is going on at any one time in the film that the spectator is entertained enough by getting only a small percentage of all of the allusions at play. Moreover, the film necessarily parodies the spectators themselves, since in all parody one always is witnessing one's own life being represented, and the comic response is in fact a measure of how much one accepts the accuracy of such a portrayal.

Mecánica nacional is not the first film to deal with a sense of the mushrooming megalopolis, it is not the first to provide a comedic interpretation of Mexico City's lower middle class, nor is it the first to provide a biting analysis of urban life. But it is the first to adopt a carnivalesque stance toward these three parameters. The carnivalesque—understood here as a narrative modality whereby competing stories, and the languages and characters of the stories, are densely intertwined and involve a contrasting and overlapping switching, back and forth, between them—is present in the film in many dimensions. Certainly, the very idea of a broad cross-section of Mexico City life is provided by the jumble of spectators that converge on the site through which the automobile race will pass; and the clash of their stories, suspended for the ludicrously few moments in which the cars roar by, is a model of the life that they live every day and every hour in an urban space. It is assumed that they think the excitement of the automobile race will provide them with a respite from that life.

Alcoriza's carnival of a car jam is in striking contrast to Julio Cortázar's utopian "La autopista del sur" (1966, from his short-story collection, *Todos los fuegos el fuego*). Cortázar's story is utopian in the sense that the massive traffic jam on the highway carrying weekenders from the south of France back to Paris becomes the opportunity to create a new society among the victims of the traffic jam. This new society, sort of a spontaneous global village, is founded on interdependency, a sense for the welfare of others, and a trust in one's neighbor that are meant to reverse the sense of the dystopian narrative as found in the microcosm of survivors of a shipwreck or cast-aways on a deserted island (see William Golding's 1954 novel, *Lord of the Flies,* or Alfred Hitchcock's classic 1944 film, *Lifeboat*). In Cortázar's story, when the traffic jam breaks up, so does the spontaneous new society that had been forged, and life returns to normal.

In *Mecánica nacional,* life also returns to normal, but one of the points of the film is that the microcosms brought into play—Eufemio's family, his circle of friends, his wife's circle of friends, his children's circle of friends, the campsite they set up to watch the automobile race roar by, the city they traverse to return to home and work—are all structural images of the same way of life. The various high-volume languages of the film are all translations of one another: verbal interactions between the characters, body language, the language of dress and personal display, and the language of traffic (especially the chorus of horns). It is for this reason that Alcoriza's film in no way gives a panoramic sense of Mexico City. Quite the contrary; the city is portrayed in terms of three locales and three locales only: Eufemio's household, garage, and immediate environs; the site of the highway-side encampment; and the congested thoroughfare leading the family, with the dead grandmother, Doña Lolita, propped up with her jaw tied shut, in the front seat of the car. No tourist views of Mexico City are provided, none of the images of the majesty of the capital and the glories of Aztec-Hispanic-postrevolutionary Mexican culture, none of the details of the vast cultural and social sophistication for which the city is legendary: only the cramped and inhospitable residence; the dusty, makeshift campsite; the car, noise, and presumably exhaust-choked thoroughfare.

The closing sequence of the film centers on the thoroughfare and the struggle to get Doña Lolita's body back to Mexico City (and here there is at least some gesture of solidarity, as the other drivers, when they learn that Eufemio is transporting his dead mother, are willing to let his car pass through their ranks). By making this the final image of the film, the closing sequence establishes a basic juxtaposition between the clogged Mexico City thoroughfare and the racetrack (which is a national highway set aside for this ad hoc purpose) that is a basic metaphor for life in the city. The official designation of the national highway as a racetrack, the utilization of the resources of the country's infrastructure in order to bring the race off, the attention received from national television, and the unanimous and enthusiastic endorsement of the whole affair by the citizenry promotes this local Grand Prix into a metaphor of something that transcends daily life. Perhaps it is unimportant to understand what it might be a metaphor of: it is more important that it is a metaphor of something transcendent that these people do not have in their daily lives—such as, for example, the uninhibited camaraderie that the encampment permits, including some significant examples of social leveling. The fantasies and illusions of popular culture, whether advertising or programming itself (and really the two are the same thing), are less about something specific than they are about lack: they model the love, the economic success, the sense of living life with meaning, and perhaps even the tranquillity that this all brings, that does not exist in the everyday lives of the spectators. *Los ricos también lloran* may have served as something like a conciliatory title for a soap opera of the 1980s of the sort "the lives of these people on television are no different from the lives of you the spectators." But of course, it was: the tears of the soap-opera characters were spilled on marble and parquet floors and wiped away by silk and linen handkerchiefs, in stark and, one might add, rather cynical response to a film like Pedro Infante's *Nosotros los pobres* (1948; directed by Ismael Rodríguez).

Yet there is a way in which the automobile race does address a specific lack that is more (Marxian) material than (Lacanian) specific. Eufemio and his family and friends live in Mexico City in a lower-middle-class *colonia* in which it is virtually impossible to conceive of a street scene free of the visual, auditory, and olfactory signs of incessant traffic. They adjourn to a campsite through streets of incessant traffic, and the campsite is transformed into not only a vast parking lot, but also a congested site in which the accumulation of cars makes the movement of cars impossible. This is evident both in the way in which it is impossible for an ambulance to get to the place where Doña Lolita is dying and in the way in which it at first appears there will be no way that all of these cars will negotiate their exodus from the campsite once the reason for the assemblage has passed. And, finally, this is evident in the closing sequence, which is possibly the most sustained image of a traffic jam in Mexico's film history.

The incessant images of traffic jams, composed mostly of aging and beat-up cars, is juxtaposed, if only fleetingly and more by insinuation, with the sleek race cars, which have been given free and open access to the highway. These cars not only do not face any of the impediments to their flow faced in the daily lives of Eufemio and company, but also represent a potential way of life far beyond the ken of the Mexican common folk. In this sense, the race is less a sports event than the image of an unattainable lack—but, then, it is likely that this is the case with sports events in general as well as much of the popular culture of which they are a part. But the symbolic specificity that I wish to underline here is how, beyond a general symbolic meaning the automobile race may represent—the fact that it is so fleeting is one eloquent way of underscoring how unattainable its essence is—this race is a very literal correlative, in the sense of being a powerful counterimage, of the traffic congestion that even thirty years ago had already come to characterize the texture of daily life in the Mexican megalopolis. The traffic jam, with all of its layered annoyances that lead to frustration, anger, verbal abuse, and physical violence is both a synecdoche and a metonymy of life in the urban jungle.

It is a synecdoche in the way in which it is one of a cluster of experiences that characterize urban life: the lack of services (imaged in a passing way by the vain appeal to the paramedics on the scene when Doña Lolita has her attack), bureaucratic indifference, and an overarching sense of alienation in personal and collective life are all images that have been repeated in films on the Mexican urban core. And it is a metonymy in the sense that the phenomena of traffic is a social sign that speaks to the emergence of the modern city in Mexico, where the system of social mobility, commerce, and the sort of public-display popular culture evidenced by the automobile race all involve the massive displacement of individuals by car as an integral aspect of their functioning.

One of the recurring motifs of the film is a couple that is entirely out of place among Eufemio and his associates. A man and a woman apparently in their mid- to late twenties, they are both dressed chicly from head to toe in white. With sleek and well tended bodies, they set out for themselves the sort of picnic one usually only sees in fancy advertising: sipping wine and eating delicacies, they settle in to await, along with Eufemio and the others, the passing of the race cars. They are clearly out of place here, and while no one seems much to bother them or bother with them, they cannot remain entirely separate from their fellow citizens. Thus, as the evening progresses, they become covered with dust, splattered with whatever, and hounded by the first rather disorderly and then quite noticeably drunken comings and goings of the others. By the time the race cars have whizzed by and everyone rushes to break camp, they are forlorn and much the worse for wear.

In their minor travails, Alcoriza makes them stand-ins for a number of different social dimensions. In the first place, they represent the other Mexico that is not directly present in the film but is yet there by implication, since it is their social class (i.e., if not upper class specifically, at least comfortable professional or financial middle class) that is directly involved in something like a costly automobile race and the infrastructure that supports it—i.e., the infrastructure is directly responsible to people like them. In the second place, the degree they are out of place indicates the extent to which, nevertheless, a popular-culture event such as the one at issue here necessarily appeals to individuals like Eufemio, if for no other reason than perhaps the fact that the utilization of the public infrastructure must court at least some minimal support of the "people." Yet the interplay of class distinctions, which remain strong in Mexico, and even more so in the often life-and-death competitive struggle for access to resources in the megalopolis, is present in events like the automobile race. This is less because the race might not appeal to spectators across a broad class spectrum than because the class of individuals like Eufemio will only have the sort of limited and primitive access that is depicted in the film. The incursion into Eufemio's space for whatever reason (no explanations are given) of spectators from a different social class only serves to reinforce the nature of Eufemio's class and, by implication, the existence of a completely different social class that is, except for these two interlopers, off someplace else, presumably at a well-equipped vantage point where they will have more than a fleeting glimpse of the race cars.

Finally, this couple has an abstract meaning that is also part of their being out of place at the campsite. Their dress is so abstract, especially in contrast to the typical Mexican use of abundant and often clashing colors, that they almost appear to be otherworldly. This other worldliness, I would suggest, points toward a level of social, economic, and class attainment that is so remote for Eufemio and his family and friends that one way to understand why they barely see them is that what they represent is so alien to their daily lives it is as if they were not even there, as if they were, in effect, extraterrestrials. In turn, the extent to which this couple ignores their fellow citizens as though the latter weren't even there, despite the way in which the presence of those fellow citizens will impinge on them by dirtying their clothes with their rough comings and goings, signals the way in which the lower classes simply do not exist in the eyes of the privileged. Thus, when all of the others have sped off, the couple is left, dirty and forlorn, but wrapped in the cloak of their privileged distance from the masses.

Alcoriza's film, although it is part of the development in Mexico of an urban consciousness that began with the writings of Luis Spota in the 1950s, with the turn-of-the-decade writings of Carlos Fuentes (especially *La región más transparente* [1958]), and the writings of La Onda in the 1960s only hints at the monstrous urban problems that will begin to emerge in the city in the 1980s and 1990s, in particular after the severe earthquake of September 21, 1985. And something like a definitive interpretation of the dysfunction of Mexico City will occur with Carlos García Agraz's *Días de combate* (1993), in which violence taking place in the city is in part attributable to the collapse of the urban infrastructure. Yet it is obvious that those problems are suggested here. The title of the film does not evoke a local-color interest in the tics and foibles of a people: there is a long tradition in Mexico of writing about the charming and not-so-charming ways in which people behave—that is, the way in which the country functions as a consequence of these collective and self-perpetuating ways. Rather, Alcoriza's title evokes the automobile, both that of the race, that of Eufemio's article of transportation, and his work with automobiles in his garage. The automobile is a symbol of modernity and, for the subaltern individual, a displayable sign of attaining a certain economic and social level. Yet the automobile is the bane of Mexico City, as in so many other congested and ailing urban concentrations, and it is important to note that one of the things that Mexico City has done has been to attempt to control, with limited success, the circulation of automobiles in the city during the workweek. In this sense, then, *Mecánica nacional* is not just a clever fable in which the automobile race and the traffic jam point, in antonymic ways, to particular details of megalopolitan life. Rather, the movie focuses on one key element of the dynamic of that life, an element that does not allegorize but, rather, represents materially, specifically the texture of contemporary life in the city.[1]

El castillo de la pureza (The Castle of Purity)

Arturo Ripstein released *El castillo de la pureza* in 1973, and it has come to be recognized as one of his signature films (on Ripstein's career, see Agustín). Based on a true story (and with a screenplay by the noted novelist José Emilio Pacheco), Ripstein's film takes place entirely within the confines of a large, dilapidated house in downtown Mexico City, one of the kind of dwellings for large and extended families that were built at the turn of the century and that later came to be used as apartment houses, boarding houses, cheap hotels (often housing prostitutes), and, in general, for marginal functions, only subsequently to be torn down in the continued development of modern Mexico City. It is the type of dwelling that serves as the basis for Fons's *El Callejón de los Milagros*, examined elsewhere in this study, and it is an ideal cultural motif for synthesizing, in one urban microspace, the features of life in contemporary Mexico City.

In the case of Ripstein's film, it is an individual family that is involved, and so the diversity of urban types is less an issue in this case. Nevertheless, the sense of the film is to portray, through the Gabriel Lima family, one version of the paranoia born of the complexities of confronting modern life. There is very much a sense in the film of a portrait, through this one family, of a crisis in contemporary Mexican life; and, indeed, the film was made only a few years after the 1968 Tlatelolco massacre that shook confidence in the special destiny of Mexico to the core (see the analysis of Jorge Fons's *Rojo amanecer* elsewhere in this study). Concomitantly, it is a paranoia, one that is explored in a large segment of the fiction of the period, one that has to do with the sense of the futility of modern life, a futility that in Mexico replaces the now spent capital of postrevolutionary fervor that was such a unique hallmark of Mexican collective life during the half century between the end of the 1910 revolution and the events in the Plaza de las Tres Culturas (Tlatelolco). Whether it is a deception born of the failures of modernism, disillusionment with the ruling Institutional Revolutionary Party (which had become a veritable plutocracy), or the inevitable tensions of the emergence of Mexico City as the paradigm of the Latin American megalopolis, the sort of malaise captured in Ripstein's film is a palpable element of Mexican urban culture during the final decades of the twentieth century.

Yet the family portrayed in the film exemplifies the modernity of Mexico City in only a tangential way; indeed, the family exemplifies a feudal construction of patriarchal society (Berg's comments on the film come under the heading "Machismo's *Last Bunker*" [160–163]). Gabriel Lima (the irony of his name becomes quickly apparent) has imposed a lockdown on his wife and their three children (two girls and an older son). He is clearly the head of the family in as many authoritarian ways as possible, and he administers a very tight ship indeed. He supervises the entire economy of the family, making sure that everyone is productively engaged and wholly accountable to him. Transgressions are punished severely, including incarceration on a diet of bread and water. Lima routinely abuses his wife and children verbally and also by slapping, pummeling, kicking, and beating them with a belt, all in the name of keeping them pure, free from sin and free from the contaminations of the world. These literal representations of severe masculine authority are unsurprising and even reasonable manifestations of the sort of patriarchal authority Lima imposes on his family and in his household.

Lima's isolation of his family is the consequence of his conviction that the world is a very evil place and his commitment to protecting his family from that evil. Meanwhile, he devotes himself to the perfection of a potent form of rat poison. Both of these propositions are interrelated and are eloquent

FIGURE 9   Porvenir (Future) jailed in the dungeon of the father's castle.

signs of a particular way of reading Mexico City in the 1970s. It is well known that rats are one of the common features of city life, and, indeed, the rat is virtually an icon of the growth of the modern city. Although rats appear related to cities throughout history—the rats of the bubonic plague, the rats of the folkloric Pied Piper of Hamlin—the modern urban rat is an index of the exponential growth of cities in recent centuries, an index of the prosperity of the city (the directly proportional relationship between prosperity and rat-infested garbage), and an index of the problems of infrastructure that the city is never able to address completely or adequately: problems of waste disposal, problems of plumbing, problems of overcrowding, problems of structural decay, problems of eradication through public health. Thus, in one dimension, the rats that Lima proposes to exterminate (and the implication is that they are a hardier breed of rats, impervious to earlier and weaker forms of poison) are a direct evidence of the enormous growth of the city as a consequence of the postrevoluntionary programs of modernization/modernity.

The issue of the rats that demand elimination—and one could suppose that the ramshackle dwelling inhabited by the Lima family is a particularly potent nest for the proliferation of rats—is directly related to the evil of the city. That is, the rats symbolize the underdefined but nevertheless virulently felt sense of danger in the urban landscape, and this leads Lima to his imposition of a convent-like reclusion on the members of his family. One can speculate on the degree to which Mexico City had become a very dangerous landscape by the 1970s. There is evidence that Mexico City was a dangerous place during the colonial period and the early days of the republic, but the decades following the revolution undoubtedly brought an urbane tranquillity to the city such that personal security was not much of a problem during this period, nor, therefore, anything of a presence in the cultural production: in all of the delinquency modeled in Luis Buñuel's 1950 *Los olvidados,* none is the consequence of street violence as it is now customarily understood. One might question the sense of urban dangers expressed by American tourists as tourism to Mexico began to develop extensively in the period following World War II, but it is worth noting that the almost hysterical record regarding the violence of Mexico City could be interpreted to mean that it is a relatively recent phenomenon rather than a long-standing and integral part of Mexico City culture. If the latter were so, it is unlikely that there would now be so much emphasis devoted to it. It is important to note that the period of the film, the early 1970s, corresponds to the beginning of massive internal migration in Mexico,[2] toward cities like the Distrito Federal, Guadalajara, Monterrey, in the quest for the employment promised by the industrialization that was a key to the modernization of the country; many sectors of the hoards of internal migrants were made up of the sub-hoards of the unemployed and the underemployed, for whom crime was one of the only means of survival.

Yet the accelerated growth that Mexico City experienced beginning in the 1960s, which was a period of intense modernization, unquestionably brought with it significant structural changes in the city, mass migration from the provinces toward the all-embracing, all-providing megalopolis, and an increase in violent crime. Lima is obsessed with erecting a barrier between his family and what he considers to be the depredations of the world. Rather than assisting them in self-empowerment and equipping them to defend themselves against the dangers of the world, Lima engages in an effort to keep them away from the world and, concomitantly, to keep the world away from them. This reclusion has lasted eighteen years, which means that it dates from the time Lima married Beatriz; Beatriz notes that they moved to the house when the older girl, Utopía, was only a few months old. Thus, in effect, all three were raised, so to speak, in captivity, and there is no indication of or reference to any other family for either parent.

The sort of reclusion that Lima imposes and Ripstein investigates is radical by any standard, beginning with the fact that it is difficult to imagine that there is no other human being who impinges on the lives of these five individuals. Individual recluses are a fact of human society, and one is always hearing about individuals who have, for a variety of reasons, withdrawn virtually completely from human commerce to shut themselves away in some sort of hermetic domain, such as a seedy apartment. But it is difficult to envision for an entire family the sort of radical reclusion that Lima imposes. Although Ripstein's film is based on a true story, one that circulated in various other cultural forms before he made it into a movie, it is perhaps more profitable to see it less as a real-life story and more as a fictional allegory in which the verisimilar circumstances that would put into question the possibility of such a radical reclusion—beginning with the fact that there must be some other family out there that wonders what has happened to these two adults and whatever children they might have had or the fact that at some point they might need to seek medical treatment (one also asks whether Beatriz gave birth to her children alone, without any professional assistance)—are allowed to recede and remain uninterrogated in favor of enhancing the allegorical meaning the story might have.

Ripstein, in a series of comments to the camera, placed at the beginning of the video release (exact date undetermined), asserts that *El castillo de la pureza* exemplifies the failure of utopian thinking. Ripstein does not specify exactly what he understands by utopian thinking, nor does he elaborate on what might be the precise utopian dimensions of Lima's undertaking: his wife, Beatriz, does note that he is a "creador de utopías, de lugares que no existen."[3] We do know from statements Lima makes, sometimes in private to his wife, sometimes as part of the school lessons he provides to his children, that he has a bleak view of mankind, which he compares with vermin. Additionally, Lima subscribes to an Old Testament understanding of the inherent corruption of woman. He constantly accuses his wife of having a shady past and of fantasizing erotically about other men. He says he married her out of pity and that the human weaknesses of their children, particularly the initial manifestations of sexual desire in the son and the elder daughter, are the consequence of his wife's moral failings: she has taught them to defy him and to engage in the corruption of the body. His hysteria over sexuality reaches its apogee when he discovers the two older children engaging in heavy petting, and it is noteworthy that while he beats and kicks his son, he saves the bulk of his white fury for his daughter, cornering her and beating her savagely with his belt. When he is unsuccessful in attempting to seduce the daughter of a storekeeper (played by the very young María Rojo), he responds to her rejection by claiming to her mother that she attempted to seduce him, enjoying the vicarious pleasure of knowing that the mother will beat her daughter for her licentiousness.

In general, Lima's relationship to sexuality appears to be confused, and Ripstein's film—perhaps to its credit—does not undertake to interpret it. Rather, it limits itself to showing his need for sex, whether with his wife, with the shopkeeper's daughter, or with a prostitute, while at the same time showing his aversion to female sexuality, as seen in his treatment of his wife, his daughter's pubescent needs, and the shopkeeper's daughter: when he propositions her, he holds a handkerchief over his nose and mouth, as though fearing contamination from her. Lima and Beatriz sleep in different rooms, and part of her wifely responsibility is to coddle him and to rock him to sleep, as though he were her baby rather than her husband. I would like to speculate that Ripstein felt no need to do much psychoanalytical probing of Lima's sexuality, confining himself to a few choice fragmentary representations and counting on the rather narrowly defined heterosexism and machismo of traditional Mexican culture to build the case for seeing through Lima's troubled sexuality a key to his hysterical fanaticism toward social life.[4]

Lima's utopian mind-set is particularly evident in his obsession with producing rat poison and perfecting his product. Some of his customers, operators of the small general stores that still proliferated in the central core of Mexico in the 1950s of the real-life events or in the 1970s when the film was made, have chosen to carry new mass-produced products rather than the homemade, artisanal product Lima has to offer (and herein lies a commercial cameo of the modernizing transformations occurring at that time in Mexico City), and this only serves to affirm Lima's conviction that his unnamed enemies are out to destroy his business. Lima, in addition to having an almost fanatical obsession with the rat population in the city (and, although the decaying house he is living in requires propping up, his wife and children are repeatedly seen engaged in acts of personal hygiene and house cleaning), sees rats as symbols of mankind; and there is the constant insinuation throughout the film that he may kill his family with rat poison—as much to punish them for their moral weakness as to protect them from the corruption of the world—and perhaps even the insinuation of the hope that they may poison him. When the children are not engaged in doing their lessons (which include a heavy dose of indoctrination regarding the perfidy of mankind and moralizing injunctions regarding the sort of personal nobility Lima intends to pass on to them) or confined each to his or her own cage in the basement, they work in Lima's laboratory preparing the rat poison. Each one of the children has a specific task (note the names): Porvenir mixes the poison; Utopía,[5] the elder daughter, prepares the packages for retail sale; and little Voluntad (who is her father's ally) stamps the packages. This is a cottage business in its purest form, and its representation in the film is integral to Ripstein's interpretive use of Lima.

Lima is the only member of the family who moves in the outside world. He goes forth on a daily basis with a suitcase to place his product in the dozens of stores in the downtown core. If the Lima household is starkly convent-like in its isolation from the world of Mexico City, Lima moves among the teeming masses in the streets, on the sidewalks, in the parks—in short, the immense urban conglomeration that is present-day Mexico City. Although the film does not show any incidents out on the street of human perfidy that would serve to confirm Lima's interpretation of the human species—and herein lies perhaps a missed rhetorical opportunity—the disjunction between the solitude of the ancient structure and the vortex of people out on the street is effective in underscoring the radical reclusion that Lima imposes on his family. Moreover, there is a subsidiary contrast between the crowded nature of life in modern-day Mexico City (see, for example, the confined spaces of the general stores, the hole-in-the-wall restaurants where people eat standing up on the sidewalk, the tiny cubicle of the prostitute) and the spacious layout of the tumble-down mansion the family of five occupies. This sort of contrast is typical in suggesting the remove from the real world of the well-to-do, where living space is one explicit correlative of wealth. But here it functions to mark the division between the world and a family that is otherwise a part of the city's vast masses. To be sure, Lima is an engineer, has a small business, and is an educated and bookish man, but the despair of his existence is the futile attempt to separate himself from the masses he so vehemently despises.

The film turns to a heavy-handed irony in its portrayal of the collapse of Lima's utopia. Utopía, aching for a life outside the walls of her confinement and fearful for her life after her last beating and her father's threat to kill them all, throws a note over the ledge of the roof terrace, but it is trampled under foot by passersby and washed away in the rain. However, on one of his rounds, Lima is stopped by a police inspector, who demands to see his license for selling a dangerous product. Lima has left it at home and asks the inspector and his accompanying officer to follow him home to get it.

Yet Lima thinks that the two are really agents of his enemies, and once they are inside of his home he first attempts to assault them, but then takes his own family hostage in the incoherent effort to drive the police from his home (Beatriz, in turn, believes that the police are there as a consequence of the note that Utopía has thrown over the ledge of the roof). Lima deliberately sets the room on fire, the police call for assistance, the fire is put out, and Lima is dragged off, presumably to the mental ward. There are two concluding moments to the film. The first is the camera's blurred stare at the whirling red lights of a patrol car: a stop to the madness of Lima's utopia, the imposition of law and order on his violent authority, and the intrusion of the hated outside world into the sanctity of his mad haven. If such an ending might serve to suggest the arrival of sanity and safety for Lima's wife and their three children, the second ending disrupts such a convenient resolution. After Lima has been hauled off by the police, his family returns to their now seriously fire-damaged home, and the mother's gaze becomes fixated, then blurred on the rusty cans that constitute her husband's primitive door-alarm system. The horror of his utopia has suddenly disappeared, but after eighteen years of reclusion, how will she and her family fend in the outside world? Will the patriarchal authority of that world, which has asserted itself in Lima's arrest, offer anything better than the nightmare of life within the family walls? (I take note at this point of Ayala Blanco's opinion that the film is outrageously trite in setting up a situation to prove the obvious: "Incólume, la figura del padre seguía rigiendo sobre la familia mexicana" [*Búsqueda del cine mexicano* 117].)[6]

Mexico City is virtually absent from the film, and it is in this way that it is dramatically present as a hidden and unknown text. There are two dominant metonymies of the city that are present throughout the film. One is the fact that it is constantly raining (in this way the film is reminiscent of Lewis Milestone's 1932 film *Rain,* based on Somerset Maugham's eponymous short story, and Curtis Burnhardt's 1953 remake, *Miss Sadie Thompson*). Heavy rain is one of Mexico City's trademarks. One supposes Ripstein uses rain in the film to suggest the oppressive environment of the Lima household. Since they live in a decaying nineteenth-century mansion, the ground floor is an open patio, with rooms opening out onto it along the four sides, and on the second floor, rooms open out onto a gallery/corridor reached by a sweeping staircase. This open patio, among other uses, was a porte cochere (the front door of the house is in reality a dual door system: there is a large double door that opens to allow for the entrance of a carriage or, later, a car, and there is a smaller door set within the larger door, one that may be either single- or double-leaved in construction, that allows for the

FIGURE 10.   The disabled car as a refuge from the "purity" of the father's castle.

passage of persons). Part of the patio, in fact, is dominated by an apparently broken-down car from the 1930s or 1940s; it is in the backseat of this car that Lima discovers Utopía and Porvenir engaged in heavy petting); throughout the film the abandoned vehicle is one objective correlative of the severance with the outside world or, alternatively, of the way in which an article of the outside world has been immobilized in the utopian space of Lima's universe.

The incessant rain in the film, however, can be read in ways other than indicating the oppressive environment of the characters. The nature of rain in Mexico City brings with it specific public-health problems, and it is almost certain that the rat population and that of other vermin in the city is the result of the breeding conditions produced by so much rain. In this way, then, the ever-present rain in the city, as incorporated into the film, is a correlative of Lima's central obsession. Although the city does not enter the household with the rain, the rain is a dimension of life in the city that cannot be closed out of the otherwise overly protected household: it is interesting to observe that one of the children's entertainments is to play in the rain and often to assume immobile poses under the downpour, as though they were cement statues.

And too, incessant rain contributes to the decay of buildings, particularly the acid rain that has come with the appalling smog conditions Mexico City has experienced as part of the project of modernity in the past fifty years—giving falsity to the claim of the city to be the region "where the air is clear" (hence, the title of Carlos Fuentes's 1958 novel of that very name, which is the first great Mexican novel of modern urban Mexico City, written at the height of the mid-century modernization of the city). Although, on the one hand, the decay of the Lima household, represented by the crisscrossed beams that have been added to shore up parts of the structure, contributes to the foreshadowing of the collapse of Lima's utopia, it also signals the particular problem of structural integrity in the city as a consequence of environmental conditions. (Ripstein might well also have mined one of the other major hallmarks of the Mexican capital, earthquakes; and indeed, some of the structural problems of the old mansion may have been caused as much by earthquakes as by humidity-induced rot, pollution, and the inability to provide routine maintenance.)

The other metonymic detail that portrays the incorporation into the household of the outside world in the film is in the form of the bureaucracy of Mexican life. One could argue that Mexican life is highly bureaucratized irrespective of the size and complexity of the city: Byzantine bureaucracy in Latin America is a reflex of the Luso-Hispanic colonial legacy. Undoubtedly, this is true to a certain extent. However, bureaucracy is also the consequence of the project of modernity and the need to control and regulate aspects of life in order to ensure the particular bourgeois values that sustain modernity: in another sense, one could argue that modern bureaucracy is sedimented on top of premodern bureaucracies in a society, such as that of Mexico, that has gone through many different stages of national identity, and each successive bureaucracy serves to support the interest of a particular identity; with each new identity, older bureaucracies are absorbed into the new one without ever completely disappearing or being superseded. In the case of Ripstein's film, bureaucracy is present in the person of the inspector who has to approve the permit for the continued manufacture of the rat poison, the police agent who demands to see the permit, and the police officers who take Lima away. Clearly, all three of these incursions of Mexico City bureaucracy into Lima's utopia are significant ones, since they lead progressively to its destruction and yet another level of desolation for the family. The fact that Lima must move between the city and his refuge in order to market his rat poison means that, despite his intentions, he brings the city with him into his utopian universe. This is particularly notable in the case of his visit to the prostitute: he returns home, insults his wife with the news that he has just been with another woman, and then proceeds virtually to rape her. Thus, Lima contributes directly to bringing the harsh realities of life in the street into the refuge he believes he is maintaining.

The title of Ripstein's film comes from Octavio Paz, and it, too, serves to bridge the two spaces of the film, the refuge and the city, and in so doing underscores the way in which such a separation is an impossible one. On the one hand, the title suggests Lima's ideal, to create a realm of spiritual and moral purity in the Augustinian City of God that is the fortress of his home. Yet, by the implacable logic of semiotic meaning, his putatively godly city cannot exist without its binary opposite, which is the degraded City of Man whose material reality he wishes to stop at his front door. Indeed, one of the most striking scenes in the film is when he takes the garbage out, leaving the door ajar, only to suddenly see that his two older children have followed him out to the street, chasing after the younger daughter, Voluntad, whose impulsive exit after their father they think puts her in danger. Their looks of wonder upon beholding the world beyond are interrupted only by their father's hysterical command to them to get back inside. The fortress of the world is greater than his utopia; and an ironic reading of Ripstein's title is that, in the end, it is the very real material of that fortress—in this case, the realities of Mexico City and the human life it sustains—as much as it is repugnant to Gabriel Lima, that will prevail.[7]

Todo el poder (All the Power)

Films are about seeing. We take this seeing for granted, and we customarily expect the camera to go into places for us where we could not go in our real lives, or where we would not go for one reason or another. We may want this seeing to be intensely realistic, intensely fantastic or magical, or intensely dangerous: I underscore intensely here in order to capture the function of film to engross our interest and attention in the hyperrealism that is something like a ground zero of filmmaking. The way in which we take this privileged seeing for granted translates into how we rarely question in an explicit fashion what the limits or parameters may be on seeing with the camera. Fernando Sariñana's 1999 *Todo el poder,* by contrast, is a film that engages a metafilmic dimension of filmmaking in order to examine the ways in which the seeing of the media routinely becomes automated: we assume that what we are seeing—what we are being given to see—is the whole story and nothing but the story. We rarely wonder what is going on outside the frame of reference or wonder whether that frame of reference has been staged; and even though we understand that all media coverage is edited in some way, it takes a special effort of consciousness to attempt to gauge the way in which the process of editing, in a revival of the New Critical belief that form is content, is what is being shown and narrated. Spectators may subscribe to a degree of commitment to the idea that the media are not to be trusted, but it is quite something else to contemplate the proposition that the creation of a mediated reality is what the media are about and not the transmission of a reality of independent existence that is somehow already there before the cultural production of the media event.

In *Todo el poder,* there is an apparent narrative to be told, that of life in assault-ridden contemporary Mexico City: people are held up on the street, they are held up in their cars, they are held up on the subway, they are robbed almost literally naked in restaurants, their vehicles are stolen, they are kidnapped for ransom (as a consequence, providing round-the-clock bodyguards is a growing service industry in Mexico); and in all of this, the authorities charged with maintaining law and order—despite solemn protestations to the media that they are doing their job and that you, the criminal, will be brought to justice—are, in fact, if not always the perpetrators of assault, complicitous with it. Such complicity extends from the average policeman to officers to police chiefs and to the government ministers who oversee them. The wolves are guarding the hen house, and in a city topping twenty million people, there is always plenty to steal: if you no longer have a watch or a wallet because they have already been stolen, then just hope you still have your shirt, pants, and shoes to give them, because they will find something else to take.

Gabriel is a freelance documentary filmmaker who is mostly unemployed: when he is offered the position of director for the public-relations campaign of the Comisión Nacional para el Control del Crimen Organizado, he turns it down because he thinks it is a disingenuous smoke screen; he certainly has grounds to believe so, since the commission is headed by the notoriously corrupt politician and ex-congressman Julián Luna. Gabriel has contacts with a news group at what is apparently a large television network, one that specializes in covering the vagaries of megalopolitan life. Early in the film, Gabriel is seen interviewing a cross-section of individuals on the problems of crime in the city, and during the course of his interviews, he and the film crew are assaulted by masked bandits. One of the consequences of this assault is that, although the camera is jostled and knocked from the hands of the individuals handling it, the assault is captured live. The result is that through the film we see a media coverage of a social issue, and then we see that actual social issue take place through the camera of the film and before the camera of the television coverage, only to be reduplicated, in turn, by the latter camera in which the movie screen and the television screen become duplicating mirrors in a rhetorical affirmation of the totalizing aspect of armed violence in the city.

Inspired by the randomness of the assault and the way in which it is one enactment of an ongoing, repeated pattern of life in the city, Gabriel gets the idea to roam the city with a small video camera that can be concealed. This camera will capture the variety and scope of assaults to which the ordinary citizen is exposed; and the simple fact is that Gabriel himself is assaulted three times himself in the same day, once as part of the assault on the film crew, once as he is riding the subway, and once in the restaurant where he has gone to meet with his colleagues at the station. When the police arrive at the restaurant, he learns that his ex-wife's Jeep Grand Cherokee, which he is using in part without her authorization, is stolen.

All of this is the setting for a series of events in which various forms of assault take place involving Gabriel directly or witnessed by him. His pica-resque peregrinations are intersected by his relations with his young daughter, who is a pawn in the war of personality still being fought by her divorced parents. Gabriel also becomes involved with a young woman who is interviewed for an on-screen broadcaster's position and, although she is rejected, becomes his lover and, eventually, his collaborator in a scheme to expose police complicity with urban criminals. They carry out a successful sting operation, his lover enjoys herself, his colleagues are excited, and his ex-wife is even civil; his daughter hopes to see them back together; and the spectator is entertained by the neat execution of this minor example of urban comedy. In the end, the plot of the film is not particularly interesting nor well executed. It is repetitive and slapdash and does not aspire to more than an example of clever entertainment, one in which, in one of the country's most venerable cultural traditions, Mexicans laugh at their own misfortunes: in one scene, one of the thieves dons a Salinas de Gortari mask. Bichir is a bit too cute as the protagonist of his own film (that is, when he films himself), and the chicanery of the police is a bit too transparent: it is highly unlikely that it has anything to show jaded *defeños* about the treacheries of life in their city or that it shows non-*defeños* anything they don't already believe about life in the nation's capital.

FIGURE 11   Incorporation of the sweep of Mexico City in *Todo el poder*.

However, *Todo el poder* is not without interest for purposes of this project. The film opens with a deliberately artificial view of the monstrosity of Mexico City's urban sprawl. The camera careens just off the ground in what is meant to be an eagle's view of the city. Its flight is dramatically accelerated, as if to underscore the territory it must traverse, even in a single straight line, because of the immensity of the city (I choose to make reference to the view of an eagle here because of the eagle as a founding symbol of the Aztec Tenochtitlán, the pre-Columbian kernel of what is today Mexico City). As the camera reaches a high-rise office building, into which it seems like it is about to crash, its flight decelerates to a more conventional pace, only then to zoom in on the reporter interviewing urban assault victims. There are several other moments in the film when similar panoramic shots make use of alterations in a non-foregrounded pace. For example, the dense and complex movement of the city's traffic along the central arteries that crisscross the downtown area (anchored at the famous intersection of La Reforma and Insurgentes) is portrayed through speeded-up images that underscore how the movement constitutes an urban raging river. Additionally, when things heat up in terms of the victims pursuing their protectors— i.e., Gabriel and associates pursuing the police—various views of traffic jams, traffic congestions, and bumper-car driving contribute to the image of the city as a sea of four-wheel monsters. None of this is particularly excit-ing or original, but it does contribute to the growing inventory of cine-matographic images of the enormity of Mexico City daily life.

Where there is some originality of treatment is in the image of Gabriel's ex-wife's black Grand Cherokee. The vehicle's very name is ironic, not only because downtown Mexico, where Gabriel lives (his apartment is a lovely example of buildings done in the 1940s with the first big urban growth of the city), is hardly suburban, but because the van, on the road and parked, takes up the room of several of the smaller cars that are the ideal sort of transportation around town. As luxury vehicles, they are pretentious sym-bols of economic power—and, as a consequence, they are highly prized by thieves and car jackers. Tere, whose prosperity is as evident as Gabriel's marginality, lends her ex-husband the vehicle when she drops their daugh-ter off for her weekly visit to her father because he has to take her to a grad-uation party. After his ex-wife upbraids him for the irresponsibility of his life, he gets his daughter to agree to stay home while he goes off to a social engagement at a restaurant; it is there he is assaulted and the Grand Chero-kee is stolen.

The Cherokee is shown on several occasions traversing the city. After it is stolen, Gabriel sees it on the street, thanks to its highly visible profile. He has the woman he has just met follow it in her car to what appears to be a warehouse/garage. He then goes to the police, who try to brush him off. But after he insists, they pretend they have found his car and turn it over to him. Suspecting that there is more to this than meets the eye, Gabriel sets out to find out about the warehouse, and he discovers that it is a chop shop run by associates of the police. This provides for a number of plot elements, in-cluding an attempt to take pictures within the shop by sending his lover dis-guised as a fainting nun, who uses his video camera to take pictures while the man who answered her knock on the door goes for a glass of water: even urban thieves in modern Mexico still respect the agents of the Virgin of Guadalupe. But the man smells a rat, and when Gabriel returns with an as-sault team disguised as the police, with a view toward doing an exposé, the warehouse is abandoned. Much of this is a bit slapstick, but the point in re-counting it is to underscore how the black Cherokee anchors a series of events that refer to the functioning of violence in contemporary Mexico City and constitute one more proof of the precariousness of personal and prop-erty security. Furthermore, in Gabriel's approach to the problem of recov-ering the Cherokee and then going after the thieves, there is an element of the ingenuity of ordinary citizens in protecting themselves against the daily indignities of a life of perpetual insecurity, risk, and violence.

Another slapstick dimension of the film concerns the police officer assigned to the assault on the restaurant. Comandante Eleuterio Quijano prefers the nickname Elvis. With his tall and lanky frame, his sideburns, and his flashy clothes, he is a Mexican impersonator of the American rock star. This dimension serves to underscore the lack of seriousness of the Mexican police command, not so much because of the dimension of Americanization involved in imitating Elvis, although this is a common theme with reference to the culture of Mexico City; rather, Quijano's credibility as an honest policeman is diminished by his greater attention to the creation of an Elvis persona. He is constantly humming or singing the words of Elvis's songs in a mumbled and garbled way; he is constantly checking his slicked-back hair; he is constantly smoothing down his hotshot clothes; and he is constantly coming on to women in ways that cause them to react to him as a slimeball. As the central figure of police authority in the film, Quijano stands out not only because of his unconventional clothing and general appearance, but also because his constant lechery summarizes the way in which the police are concerned about things other than providing security and enforcing the law. Gabriel and his lover, Sofía, however, turn this detail of Quijano's personality to their own advantage when she sets out to seduce him in order to keep him distracted from the sting operation Gabriel and his associates have staged against the minister by kidnapping his wife in order to force the release of their television colleague, who has himself been kidnapped to pressure the news team into backing off from criticizing the violence in the city, the inability of the police to do anything about it, and the complicity of the police with the very criminals against whom they are supposed to protect.

Sariñana's characterization of the Mexico City police through the figure of Quijano is not an entirely unproblematic one, nor is it particularly original. There is a long tradition of novel and film, drawn from film noir and refined by modes of exposé and denunciatory culture (see Curtis Hanson's neo-noir *LA Confidential* [1997]), that has underscored, to the detriment of the citizenry, the synergy of the tandem relationship between the growth of urban crime and police corruption, and one could make many different structural relationships between the two. In the case of *Todo el poder*, the police have so much power not only because of the statutory power granted them to enforce public security, but because of the way in which their corruption produces violent transgressions of public security: the police not only fail to provide security, but their corruption serves to increase violence in an exponential fashion. Moreover, this corruption is often masked as ineptness. When Gabriel goes to Quijano to insist that the latter recover his vehicle for him from the garage to which he followed it, Quijano becomes violent with him for having insinuated that the police are uninterested or inept, even though that is what Gabriel has done without intending it; he will only later discover that they are involved in the operation of the chop shop.

Of course, it is hardly an original observation, and not a very daring proof, to dwell on the corruption of the police in large metropolitan areas. Yet it is done so with some cleverness here because it is executed through the synecdoche of the automobile, the overwhelmingly present icon of an urban area like Mexico City. *Todo el poder* dwells on the iconicity of the automobile, from the accelerated images of the swirling streams of traffic in the city to the high interpersonal stakes involved with Tere's Jeep Grand Cherokee, to the representation of police corruption in terms of involvement in a theft ring and the violence necessary to protect the operation of that ring. Tere's Grand Cherokee is strikingly dominant as a symbol of her economic power and of the irresponsibility she attributes to her ex-husband. But it is also strikingly dominant as a token in the operation of the theft ring, which meets the question of the supply and demand for vehicles in a metropolitan area like Mexico City, where a car is absolutely necessary as both a status symbol and a mode of transportation, while at the same time also serving to index the ills of the city: the monstrous traffic jams (Does one have a luxury vehicle to get around town in style or to have someplace comfortable to sit while being stuck in traffic?), the constant threat of traffic accidents, the lack of adequate parking, the assaults on drivers and their cars, and the theft of high-priced vehicles and their subsequent alteration and resale as an integral part of the economy of the city.

Todo el poder points toward a fundamental understanding of megalopolitan culture, one in which there is little autonomy and power for the individual; nor is it so much that power is concentrated in the hands of a few individuals, the owners of the land and the air, and everyone else functions to enrich them; rather, power lies in the structural circumstances of the city, whereby in the end everyone is a cog and a victim in a vast economy that functions without controls and without any one individual able to grasp it. In this sense, Sariñana's film provides an image of late capitalism as accessible through a specific set of events in late-twentieth-century Mexico City. Of course, there are specific victims, like Gabriel, and, of course, there are specific points of convergence of political and economic power in the person of the minister, and, of course, there are specific agents of that power in the form of Quijano and, perhaps, Gabriel's ex-wife, who appears to endorse the "system" and decries her ex-husband's insistence on attempting to stand critically outside of it. But Quijano is less brought to justice than he is strategically made a victim of the system he services; this could also be said to be the case of the minister, when his wife is kidnapped by Gabriel and his colleagues in order to force the release of their fellow journalist. But nothing in the system changes: police corruption is not done away with or even dented, and the minister will continue to enjoy his temporary access to governmental power but will in time be replaced by someone else. And when Gabriel and his colleagues traverse the streets of Mexico City in the final sequence of the film, flushed with the victory of their operation, it is only to become, once again, a part of the hypercharged urban landscape that lies beyond anyone's grasp or control.

An interesting symbol of the loss of urbanity in the city lies in the person of Doña Cleofas (note the quirky traditional name), the manager of the apartment house in which Gabriel lives, paying rent only now and then. Doña Cleofas is nicely played by the character actress Carmen Salinas, who does essentially a reprise of her role as the rundown hotel owner-manager Doña Ti in *Danzón*, which I analyze elsewhere in this study. Doña Cleofas plays a "real" human being, alongside the posturing and pandering types Gabriel runs into in general in his undertaking to film the violence that is Mexico City and specifically in his attempt to outwit the police and the string of events that derive from the theft of his ex-wife's vehicle. Gabriel jokes with her and joshes her as he might his mother or a beloved aunt or grandmother, hugging and kissing her; she reacts demurely in a game of affection that is not present in Gabriel's relations with anyone else in the film. Of course, he flatters her to keep her from insisting on his paying the rent he owes her (the real irony is that Tere owns the building), but it is a bit of human theater that would be out of place in any of the other spaces in which Gabriel moves.

Such traditional domestic warmth (reinforced by the fact that the apartment building belongs to a long gone Mexico City in which provincial manners like those of Doña Cleofas's were a norm that no longer exists) is in stark contrast to the harsh manners, brusque and rude dialogue, and usually brutish interpersonal relations that dominate survival in the postmodern megalopolis. Therefore, it is an important detail when Doña Cleofas is caught in the domino effect of an act of police violence against Gabriel, an act Quijano uses to punish him for his challenge to the latter's efficaciousness and honesty. Gabriel is picked up on the street, shoved to the floor of a vehicle, roughed up and insulted, and then thrown out of the moving vehicle in front of his apartment building. His camera is damaged, in an eloquent indication of the impudence of his filmic undertaking, and in being thrown from the car he collides with Doña Cleofas, who is once again (against all odds at maintaining cleanliness) sweeping the sidewalk in front of her building. Thus, she is, in a translative fashion, a victim of the violence against Gabriel, an endangered bystander in the savagery of the city.

So what, then, do we see through the act of filmed seeing in Gabriel's undertaking in the streets of Mexico City? *Todo el poder* offers a cleverly reduplicated image of the chaos of the city as synthesized in a series of incidents structured around vehicular traffic and organized robbery and assault, not as specifically relating to vehicles, since other forms of theft and assault are involved, but intersecting significantly, in the sense that the necessity of transportation in the megalopolis provides both the opportunity, in the form of expensive vehicles, and the demand, customers for the products of reduced price generated by the chop shops. Gabriel's condition as a bystander is significant for the sense of the film, for it is as a bystander that he becomes involved in the robbery of his ex-wife's car and in the series of events that ensue. His acts of photography are, therefore, not a project that is specifically framed by a deliberate narrative (as is Sariñana's film) but depend, rather, on the randomness of events in which he becomes involved.

This randomness, in turn, serves to underscore the arbitrariness and, more importantly, the non-teleological nature of life in the megalopolis: random acts take place, and the power is that of the random system and not of any clearly defined social or political system. The latter serves the former rather than being its determining agent. Repeatedly, throughout the film, we see Gabriel hastily whipping out his camera, frantically attempting to focus on something he wishes to capture while at the same time trying to hide the camera to avoid being caught in the act of filming, only to hope that he has captured on film that on which he has focused. Gabriel does, of course, record some strategic material, and he does experience some sort of triumph in getting his ex-wife's Grand Cherokee back and in rescuing his colleague from the kidnappers. But as we see Gabriel and his associates racing through the night-time streets of the urban monster in the closing sequence of the film, there is no reason to believe that these accomplishments have any real meaning, since the next day life in Mexico City starts all over again with essentially nothing changed.[8]

Lolo

The penultimate scene of Francisco Athié's *Lolo* (1992) has the protagonist, Dolores Chimal, running away from his Mexico City neighborhood, ac-

FIGURE 12   The urban bus as a vehicle of escape from a hostile social reality.

companied by Sonia, who is devoted to saving him from the violence of their lives, a violence that especially affects young men. As the bus they have boarded—she has had to help him on board because he has been seriously beaten by a gang for what they believe to be his betrayal—pulls away in a cloud of dust and belching exhaust fumes, which swirl around the shacks and improvised, half-finished dwellings of the neighborhood, the camera focuses on an idealized image of the Valle de Anáhuac (the indigenous name of the valley in which the Mexican capital is located) that decorates the back of the bus, serving as a sun screen. Whatever fate holds in store for Lolo and Sonia, it is certainly not going to be the opportunity to attain to that idealized image, and there is little reason to believe that where they will end up will be any better than the hard-scrabble colonia they are fleeing. Unquestionably, it will not be to any place that provides any greater measure of economic security, personal protection, or social well-being.

Lolo is something of a revision of Luis Buñuel's *Los olvidados*, a film the Spaniard made in the 1950s with the support of the Mexican government, only to find that its supporters and movie goers were outraged at his suggestion that life in the society that had been remade by the 1910 Mexican Revolution was both a dead end for children and a jungle in which they were routinely exploited, abused, forgotten, and, ultimately, discarded as so much urban trash. By contrast, Athié's film hardly raised any eyebrows: the dimensions of despair for individuals like Lolo (who is actually eighteen years old, and therefore more a young adult than a child) have outstripped Buñuel's most intransigent pessimism; and the elimination of these children, as takes place in many forms in this film and not just, as Buñuel's film, in one cathartic finale, is, if not official policy, at least a practice tolerated and even pursued by some agents of the State.

Athié presents Lolo's life as a *via crucis,* and Roberto Sosa's body and his representation of the Lolo character are not without Christological dimensions—at least, in the sense that he is an Everyman for a sector of Mexican youths, and his persecution by the circumstances of his society is not without an exemplary meaning, constituting as it does a partial mosaic of the odds for survival faced by Lolo and youths like him in Mexico City at the end of the millennium. I have noted that Athié provides something like an update of *Los olvidados;* and were one to be interested in a comparative analysis, it would be possible to point to specific examples of intertextuality between the two films, from the harried single mother who abuses her son (as much as, by contrast, she seems genuinely affectionate toward him) to the injustices of the workplace, the violent code of conduct of the gang, the arbitrariness of the justice system, and, most strikingly, the juxtaposition between lives of social and economic marginality and the modernity of the city.

I am not specifically interested here in demonstrating the intertextual structure of Athié's film vis-à-vis Buñuel's: the parallels are neither surprising nor unexpected given the demographic development of Mexico City during the almost fifty years since *Los olvidados* and current concerns regarding youth violence in the Mexican capital. But what is notable about the two movies is the presence of a remote and almost ethereal Mexico City in which the lives of these young people are alternatively submerged and juxtaposed. In Buñuel's film, the lasting image is the construction of the buildings that will proclaim Mexico's entrance into modernity, a project of considerable concern for the Mexican government, which was, by midcentury, anxious to set aside the antagonism with the United States provoked and exploited by the 1910 revolution and now willing to participate in the new postwar global economic order that would confirm Mexico's singular importance in Latin America as a partner with the United States.

This new positioning was important to Mexico, especially in the context

FIGURE 13   Utilization of the nightscape of Mexico City in *Lolo*.

of the new power arrangements that were emerging in Latin America as a consequence of the war, which is why Buñuel's suggestion that all was not rosy with Mexican society, despite the beneficent programs of the institutionalized revolutionary government, was greeted with considerable outrage. *Lolo*, too, was made at a time in which Mexico was jockeying for a place in the new world order of neoliberalism that Reaganism brought to Latin America in the 1980s. Mexico's adaptation to this regime (through its participation in NAFTA) has not been as successful as it has been in Brazil or in the Southern Cone, but it has had a profound impact on the local economy, whether as seen in the precarious nature of industrial employment (local industries have been hard hit by the import economy supported by neoliberalism) or in the way in which a pharmacy is a preferred target of robbery: drug prices have soared in a complex pattern of fewer government subsidies, foreign controls over production patents, and the demand created by American tourists seeking what are still lower prices than in the United States. Yet the purpose of the robbery is not to obtain the pharmaceutical products as medicine, but rather as a source of drugs for themselves and others to whom they sell them on the streets.

By the time in which *Lolo* takes place, Mexico is now a megalopolis, whose inner core is pretty much an exemplum of liberal modernity. As opposed to the image of the city under construction in Buñuel's film, there are two dominant images of the cityscape in Athié's film. One is the vast sprawl of the pollution-shrouded city at dawn: the sun, rather than penetrating the smog, only serves to highlight it and make even more ghostly the skyscrapers that iconize the economic progress that is far, far out of the reach of Lolo and his generation. The other dominant image is the nightscape of the city, which is seen on several occasions from atop the hill where the colonia inhabited by Lolo appears to be (the film credits acknowledge the north central Delegación de Cuauhtémoc). Mexico City stretches out below the rise in, as the bolero says, a blanket of stars. Such an image is immediately invested with romantic or sentimental notions, but there is nothing romantic or sentimental about the foreground of the sequences in which the image appears. The setting is a vacant lot where the gang (a *pandilla* or *grupo de chavos banda,* literally a "youngsters' band," that is, an outsider gang) assembles to drink and to conduct other rites of solidarity; more on their presence in the film below.

The point here is that the backdrop of the twinkling lights of the city is one of destitution, danger, and categorical marginality: this is unquestionably Mexico City as slum and its inhabitants as social outcasts, with a distance between their grubby lot and the splendors of the city light years away from each other. Of course, they are part of the city, and the city presents many islands of abject poverty, in many cases in the shadow of the icons of urban modernity. However, the social realities of Mexico City as a whole are not the issue here. Rather it is the semiotic composition created by Athié's film, the us-versus-them mentality the gang cannot help but promote in its sense of alienation from whatever the city has to offer in terms of established wealth and power, survival and community.

The disjunction between those who profit from whatever Mexico City is as a site of prosperity and those who are its excrescent socioeconomic misery could be triangulated from any position within the city, and the fact that Athié chooses to handle it in this fashion, from the vantage point of a peripheral barrio (neighborhood), is only one way of effecting such a representation. The result has the effect of an inverse rhetoric: the king of the hill is the outcast gang, who disport themselves as though they were lording it over the wretches below, when it is, of course, the other way around; one might also note that the pockets of greatest illumination are likely to be the largest commercial and tourist centers and not other, equally bleak, neighborhoods, whose precarious illumination can hardly compete with the international-quality lighting of the centers of power. Furthermore, the light available to the *chavos* is that of a primeval bonfire, a circumstance that underscores their condition as outcasts from modern society.

One of the auditory features associated with the megalopolis is noise, the cacophony that overshadows all personal and interpersonal communication. This noise is sustained and unremitting, shifting perhaps in intensity according to the time of day or shifting in tone and pitch with climactic conditions and the varying interdependence of sources of noise as they play off of each other. However, this dimension of urban experience is not primarily present in *Lolo*. Although some miscellaneous noises are to be heard that can be attributed to specific sources, such as the wail of an ambulance or the roar of a city bus pulling away, paradigmatic urban noise is not a part of the texture of Athié's film. Yet another sort of noise is. It is a surreal noise, that of clanging gates, screeching machines, buildings that seem to howl like monsters, and an assortment of sounds that it is difficult to attribute to sources as trivial as car brakes, police sirens, or domestic appliances. This background cacophony is not the concert of big city noises that are to some degree comforting, because they tell us that the city is working and that the infrastructure is "turned on." One will recall those grade-B science fiction movies of the 1950s or early 1960s, when the camera would pan across a cityscape that was absolutely devoid of human movement and, what was more eery, absolutely devoid of any of the sounds that make up the hustle and bustle of the city. Such a configuration—hustle and bustle—and its Spanish equivalents (*ir y venir, vaivén, ajetreo y bullicio*) are somehow comforting, perhaps because of their morphological equilibrium or symmetry, and the sense is that the city is alive in a positive way.

But the sounds in *Lolo* are not comforting: they are not the auditory icons of a city alive and they are not the sounds that, for anyone in the city, are almost there because of their familiar, no matter how high-decibel, nature. Rather, these are the sounds of disarray, of psychological and physical torment, of destructive forces and their impending doom for the unprotected. And as Athié's film makes clear, no one is protected: some are only a little more protected than others, but all are subject to the law of maximum social danger. This danger comes in the form of random violence, and part of its threat is the degree to which it is impossible to adequately protect oneself against it. It comes in the form of the arbitrary exercise of authority, such that the function of the police is to counter violence with violence, not as a form of either protection or retribution, but in order to maintain a sem-

blance of the balance of power between the individual and the State, with
the apparent hope that most will accept that the power of the State is greater
and therefore yield to the State rather than joining the so-called "criminal"
elements that are alleged to provoke the force of the State in the first place.
And danger comes also in the form of social rebellion that generates a confrontational cross fire between the individual and the State or between different groups of individuals, which produces a violence to which third parties (innocent bystanders) are suddenly and defenselessly exposed. It is,
nevertheless, undeniable that the chavos impose some measure of moral authority in the face of the random violence of the State, and it is this authority that makes them attractive: Lolo's sister Olimpia is a member of the gang
that appears in the film, and her mother asserts, "Prefiero tener una hija
muerta que ratera,"[9] presumably in the sense that Olimpia, although she
may die as a gang member, will die with a measure of dignity lacking for the
petty thief, which is what, ironically, her son ends up becoming.

The plot of *Lolo* is fragmentary and unfolds in such a way that it represents metonymically circumstances that characterize the forms of danger
mentioned more than it affords a tight narrative logic. By this I mean that
what happens is less of consequence than the signs of unchecked and
uncheckable danger it signals. For this reason, the story line is quite spare.
Lolo attempts to contribute to the maintenance of his mother's husbandless
home by working in a steel mill for poverty wages. When he complains to
his supervisor about how meager his salary is, the next time he picks up his
pay envelope (and complains to the paymaster about all of the deductions),
he is robbed and beaten senseless for attempting to withhold the money
from his assailants. After five days in the hospital, he returns to work to find
that he has been fired for unexcused absence; it is difficult not to believe that
the holdup was the design of the supervisor, since labor laws in Mexico require a concrete reason for dismissal. Indeed, Lolo's supervisor attempts to
get him to think in terms of bettering himself through the educational programs available to him in the system, instead of grousing about his poor
pay. However, when Lolo chooses to be a troublemaker rather than to participate in the system, the decision is made to get rid of him. This is the first
of a series of dead-end choices for Lolo, and the beating he receives as part
of the probably put-up robbery is only one of a series of such beatings that
will graphically punctuate his subsequent choices.

After his mother kicks him out, Lolo goes to work for an individual
identified only as El Alambrista, presumably a neighborhood electrician
whose work is less that of a skilled craftsman and more that of someone

who is skilled in finding ways of illegally tapping into power lines. El Alambrista has a street organ, and Lolo tries to make a living for himself in that fashion. One evening, he sits down to rest against the gate to the house of Doña Luz, the neighborhood cutthroat moneylender (she charges 50 percent interest per month, up front) and finds that it is open. He pushes his way in, finds her money chest, and is interrupted by her sister Martha, whose head he smashes in with a crystal vase.

The only evidence against Lolo is his red tennis shoes, a pre-Christmas gift from his sister Olimpia. While the police think that El Alambrista must have been the intruder because of the abandoned street organ, Lolo trades his tennis shoes with Bobo, who is mentally deficient. However, his cousin's husband, Marcelino, who is a neighborhood cop, sees Lolo in the area of Doña Luz's house and surmises he may have been the thief. He follows him and discovers him digging up the moneylender's roll of bills he has hidden in the vacant lot where the gang hides out. Marcelino confronts his relative and, in the name of family solidarity, tells him to get out of the neighborhood, but not without first driving him around the neighborhood in the police car so that he will lose face before the gang. Marcelino, after telling Lolo the sort of treatment El Alambrista is receiving in jail and what awaits Lolo if he is arrested, also threatens him with the repeat of his own story: get out or be drafted into the police force, a chilling reminder of how the police fight juvenile delinquency by forcibly recruiting new officers from among the very delinquents they pursue. The gang members, whom Marcelino has informed about Lolo's responsibility for the death of the moneylender's sister, and who believe in turn that he is responsible for El Alambrista being arrested and tortured by the police for the crime he, Lolo, has committed, confront him, calling him a *culaid* (*culero* [fag] blended with Kool-Aid, apparently a derogatory trope), beat him with a chain attached to a lead pipe (called a *chacos*), and leave him for dead. This is the fourth beating Lolo receives in the film: when he is robbed of his pay, when he goes to the movies with Sonia, when he is seen with Marcelino in the police cruiser, and when the gang finds out he is Martha's murderer. As one beating follows another, there is very much a sense for Lolo, and for the spectator, that life in the urban jungle has its own terrible and implacable logic.

Lolo makes his way to Sonia's, tells her that Martha's death was an accident, as he only wanted to get his mother's watch back for her birthday, and she agrees to escape with him; but first she prostitutes herself with the aid of her hooker sister in order to have enough money to pay for their flight. She has made Lolo swear that he is not deceiving her, but as he passes

Bobo's hovel, tended by Bobo's Sara García–like sainted mother, Lolo asks for his forgiveness under his breath. Marcelino makes good on his promise to free the electrician, but of course there must be some sacrificial victim, and that victim will be Bobo.

The film opens with a scene that is repeated at the end of the story, and in this sense the narrative of the film is the elaboration of that opening scene: we see Marcelino "discovering" Bobo's body hanging from a beam in the jail; he is still wearing the red sneakers. Other police are called in; the press arrives to take photos; case closed. The result is that there are two intersected narratives in *Lolo,* and the quality of their intersection speaks to the issues of random violence and gross personal insecurity that constitute the image of the life of marginalized individuals in Mexico City, an image Athié wishes to propound. The first narrative constitutes the actual events of Lolo's life as we see them; a subnarrative within this one involves the crime that he commits and his attempt to flee from it. These two hierarchized narratives are driven by circumstances of life in the megalopolis, both in the sense of the dead-end opportunities that are available to Lolo and in the inevitability of crime as a consequence of that dead end. It is startling to see the grim inevitability of Lolo's life, especially in the context of the variegated forms of existence in Mexico City, even when seen only in terms of the segment represented by his neighborhood. That is to say, in the context of a city of twenty million people, while one would not fall into the simplism of believing that there is adequate opportunity for everyone, it might at least be possible to contemplate some network of adequate means of survival for most individuals.

Of course, this is what neoliberalism provides specifically and a conservative-reactionary political ideology provides in general: it is sufficient to be able-bodied, energetic, and willing to work, and there will be some way for the individual not only to survive but to get ahead. While this message is sold in multiple and overdetermined forms in urban society — beginning, for example, with advertising, which depends on the facile and false relationship between forms of consumerism and forms of social and economic triumph — it is important to note that Athié is careful to include no such allusions in his film. That is, there is no invasion of political slogans into the universe of the film, no presence of commercial products beyond the simple there-ness of the basic necessities of life, and, most significantly, there is no presence of TV in the movie.

Now, this is really a quite significant detail, since TV is the cultural medium that has now managed to reach into every nook and cranny of Latin

American society, to places where, previously, neither print culture, nor radio, nor filmmaking had penetrated. It is customary for there to be TV sets in the common room of lower- and lower-middle-class families (i.e., the combined living room, dining room, kitchen, and, often, sleeping area, as is the case in Lolo's mother's home, where privacy is nonexistent and where the mother makes love with the electrician in front of her presumably sleeping son), and is customary for the TV to be turned on throughout the entire day, with individuals stopping to view a fragment of a program, conducting the business of life (such as cooking, eating, sewing) while watching TV, or using the viewing of a TV program as the stuff of phatic conversation, either while viewing a program or after having viewed one. TV programming literally brings the world into these humble dwellings: since this fact is well known, I will not expand on it here.

But suffice it to say that part of the world that is brought into each household is a sense of the city as a vast arena of life, and while some messages, such as those of news programs, may focus on the corruption and violence of the city, the majority underscore the aforementioned ideology of opportunity, whether in the form of soap operas built around upper-middle-class ideals incarnate in actresses with blue eyes and blonde hair or in the form of advertising (which virtually overwhelms programming proper, such that it is, in effect, integral to the programming presented as separate from and supported financially by it) built around the same ideals. Perhaps I am exaggerating here the class uniformity of the images of television, but the point is that no matter what the class images of television might be in a subtler register than the one I am providing, they exceed those of the individuals whose lives are represented in Athié's film. Significantly, the only time there is an image of the TV—and then, only fleetingly—is when Lolo and Sonia pass by Bobo's apartment: he and his mother are watching TV, and Lolo murmurs his request to Bobo to forgive him for his betrayal.

The absence in *Lolo* of the image of television, which is certainly very much present in the other films analyzed in this study dealing with lower- and lower-middle-class families, serves to underscore, I would propose, the categorical lack of opportunities for Lolo: his world is so bereft of any possibility of transcendence that not even the disingenuous messages of television are present to him as a model. It is important to note that Lolo's cultural consumption appears to consist of *fotonovelas* (comic book–type narratives, in cheap newsprint format, built around still photographs rather than drawn figures); he always asks for police and detective fiction. This is a very traditional cultural medium in Mexico, especially in marginal neighborhoods, and Lolo's cousin Juliana, the one married to the police officer, runs a stand in which she sells food and such magazines, which Lolo always promises to pay for later.

Thus runs the narrative of Lolo's precarious economic circumstances, his assault, his loss of the only more or less formal job he is ever likely to have, his struggle to make some income on the street as an organ grinder, and, eventually, his turn—more by accident than design—toward crime, including murder. The simple fact is that there can be nothing surprising about the evolution of this narrative, neither Lolo's continued failures nor his ending up caught in a series of circumstances that bring him to the attention of his cousin-in-law as a criminal and force him to flee the neighborhood. And it is not unreasonable to expect that all that can await Lolo anywhere he goes is more crime, just as there is every reason to expect that Sonia, now that she has been initiated into the seemingly easy money of prostitution, will find further prostitution as her only means of survival. It is a moot point whether Lolo's and Sonia's neighborhood is a synthesis of all of Mexico City: whether they go to another neighborhood like theirs, or to the central core of tourism, or to another city in Mexico, or even across the border into the United States, the "urban training" they have received will lead them only to crime and prostitution and probably to early and violent deaths.

At one point, Lolo's mother says to him, after he has killed the money-lender's sister, that she hopes he will always remain attractive and honest. The spectator knows he is a murderer, and we subsequently see him betray Bobo after he has already betrayed El Alambrista (it might also be noted at this point that he has some ulterior motive for betraying this man, since he has seen him having sex with his mother). El Alambrista may be eventually let go, but only after being brutally tortured; and we subsequently see him beaten by the *chavos banda,* as the harbinger of many other beatings and, most likely, a final fatal one that he is likely to end up receiving. Ironically, his mother says this to him after Lolo has been beaten by the assailant that robs him, and his face bears the traces of other previous beatings. Indeed, the beatings Lolo has already received before the film begins, the beatings he receives during the film, and the beatings he is likely to receive in his life beyond the context of the film are the most specific traces of marginal urban life, and the all pervasive cacophonous sounds throughout the film can certainly be viewed as the abstract sound track of those beatings.

The second narrative represented in *Lolo* is the counternarrative organized first by Lolo and then by police officer Marcelino to cover the tracks of the murder Lolo commits. In this narrative, it really doesn't matter who the murderer is: it is first the electrician by default and then it is Bobo by arrangement. The important fact is that it is not Lolo. Why this counternarrative is of any significance—beyond the fact that it demonstrates the ease with which the official system of justice is able to rearrange the truth to fit someone's convenience (in this case, as a gesture of family solidarity, which is something of a redemptive opportunity for Marcelino)—is that it both drains Lolo's life of the events that give it meaning as a verifiable example of lived urban experience and at the same time provides the basis for a projected series of experiences. What I mean by this is that, in the first place, by arranging for Lolo not to have been the murderer—and, certainly, in terms of the official discourse that ultimately controls everyone's life, this fictional reality supersedes any "real" reality—there is a discontinuity with the complete sense of dead-end despair provided by the narrative of the film: Lolo will simply be seen by his neighbors to have disappeared, thereby depriving them of knowledge about Lolo that the spectator has, knowledge that, in a grim and dreadful way, gives a fuller meaning to his life as iconic within the socioeconomic domain of the Mexico City portrayed by the film. But yet, this arranged fictional reality will give another dimension to Lolo's life: that of what it is likely to be, and this reinforces in the imaginative projections of the spectator the inevitability of what his life has been to date. Yet another reading of the film might be able to see here the possibility for a new and life-saving beginning for Lolo and Sonia, away from the baggage of their lives in the neighborhood.

The discontinuity between these two narrative levels does not itself make a point about the sort of urban life led by Lolo and others like him. That is, the film is not a meditation on ways of narrating lived human experience in a metatextual sort of way, nor is it really about police corruption and the way in which official systems have their resources for reinventing reality for higher cynical or politically expedient reasons. Rather, the gaps between the two narratives compel the spectator to focus in on those aspects of Lolo's life that are the subject of the dual narratives—the murder he commits and how a life, and death, of criminal violence will now be all that is open to him. In this sense, the dual narratives serve as a form of rhetorical emphasis for the particular interpretation of current urban life on the margins of Mexico City.

I want to close by returning to the image of the chavos banda. They are represented in the film by a theater group called La Banda, a group that apparently has specialized in such representations. These bands, which have been represented in several important cultural productions (see especially Oxman's *La leyenda escandinava*), constitute the fringes of Mexican marginal society. They are, on the one hand, the product of the forces of alienation produced by the neighborhoods of the sort represented in *Lolo*, neighborhoods that are the reverse image of the closely knit and interdependent societies captured in Fons's *El Callejón de los Milagros*. By creating a self-image that proposes to be radically different from the accepted norms of Mexican society—attention is called in the film to the iconicity of the colored tennis shoes, but there are also the visible signs of dress, hairstyles, body language, and, as an overarching phenomenon, verbal language—there is the feeling of having stepped away from or outside of established society. However, it is clear that this cannot be the case. It is clear in the way in which one of the members of the gang is killed in the robbery of the pharmacy, and it is clear in the way in which the police know who they are and where they are, and the best they can hope for is a cat-and-mouse game with the authorities. When his cousin-in-law drives Lolo around in the cruiser so that the gang members can see that he is under the domain of police power, they go after Lolo and almost beat him to death. But that changes nothing for them, since the presence and the power of the police in the neighborhood remain just as they always were. The banda is one of the most interesting aspects of the film, not only because it represents an undeniable and intriguingly frightening aspect of Mexican society, but because of the display tactics of its members. Their entire persona is a challenge to Mexican society's conventionality, which maintains gender, class, and social roles in such a way as to naturalize the dynamics of Mexican society: things are as they are because that's the way they should be, and conformity serves to reinforce the fiction of naturalness of such arrangements. By challenging convention and by expropriating and attacking the sites of conventionality, such as businesses and the streets, and by staking a claim to alternative spaces, such as abandoned buildings and vacant lots, the gang's members are enacting a defiance to an urban system that is a dead end to individuals like Lolo. Although the film does little to go beyond establishing it as a given, the banda's defiance of institutional authority configures, in the culture of the barrio, a new moral center: in the absence of the father (Lolo and Olimpia's mother is a paradigmatic single parent, struggling to make ends meet, barely able to keep her family together), the banda is quite literally a substitute paterfamilias for Olimpia and, through her, almost so for Lolo. The fact that circumstances keep Lolo bound to the established system (the no-win situation in which Marcelino places him) means that neither the traditional family nor the banda are any longer options for him, which is why he has no choice but to flee the barrio. *Lolo* does not find the opportunity to do the ideological work necessary to confirm the legitimacy of the banda as a father substitute, but yet it is there as a significant dimension of the film. Yet in the end, the banda serves Athié as little more than yet another way of highlighting rhetorically his interpretation of life for young adults—and, indeed, for all individuals—in contemporary Mexico City.

THREE   # Mapping Gender

The representation of gender is an integral part of contemporary Latin American cultural production, and film is no exception (there are two studies concerning the representation of women in Mexican filmmaking, but both limit themselves to the so-called golden age of the 1940s and 1950s: Hershfield and Tuñón). In the case of Mexican filmmaking, María Novaro's *Danzón* (1991), although it is not without rivals, is perhaps the most successful text by a woman director to explore women's history and women's life in contemporary Mexico. Starring María Rojo, whose exceptionally fine work is featured in three other films examined in this study (*Rojo amanecer, La tarea, De noche vienes, Esmeralda,* not to mention her early bit part in *El castillo de la pureza*), *Danzón* is unique in focusing on the life of a middle-aged single mother and on how she gives that life meaning through the popular-culture genre of autochthonous ballroom dancing and its major related musical form, the Caribbean bolero. The film departs significantly from a soap-opera model as regards plot resolution, with the result that the spectator is obliged to make sense of major narrative details, such as cross-generational sexual relations and female sexual independence, in an analytical way that would be foreclosed if conventional plot expectations were fulfilled. In playing out the central characters' erotic history against the backdrop of popular Mexico City culture, urban space assumes a notably feminized dimension.

Jaime Humberto Hermosillo's *De noche vienes, Esmeralda* (1997) centers on a woman who has already discovered the secret to survival in the urban landscape: multiple marriages that provide her, if not with multiple resources for economic security, at least with multiple reserves of emotional fulfillment, and in this sense, her sexual history is an objective correlative of the complex multiplicity of the Mexican capital. But those multiple marriages are illegal, and Esmeralda's attempts to explain the rationale for her marital transgressions provide the opportunity for a woman to account explicitly, with the direct address the recording camera allows, for how she negotiates the alienation of megalopolitan living.

This final feature-length film for María Rojo (the last one in which she has acted) to be examined in this study presents yet another view of Mexico City women, in this case, of a middle-class professional woman whose sexual agency synecdochically marks her control over her personal life and the security of her position within urban life. In the four films of this study in which she is the star, María Rojo represents four very different classes of Mexican women: in *Rojo amanecer,* she is the conventional stay-at-home housewife, the partner of a mid-level government bureaucrat living in state-sponsored housing; in *Danzón,* while she is still at the bottom end of the middle class, she has the independence afforded her by a secure, if not very interesting, office job and the opportunity to engage in a project of self-discovery; in *De noche vienes Esmeralda,* her character is also toward the lower end of the spectrum of the middle class, but yet also with a secure job and a project of independent identity very much in place; finally, in *La tarea* (1990), her character is solidly middle class and very much able to assert a measure of personal independence, particularly in her relationship to her matrimonial partner.

María Novaro's *Lola* (1991) is not a counterpart to *Lolo,* although the star of the latter does have a small role in *Lola.* Like women in other films examined here, Lola is a single mother, but the film provides a different vision from that of the struggle for survival in the metropolis. Lola comes from a middle-class background, and she has chosen to alienate herself from her own family to indulge the adventure of living on her own and the highly precarious attempt to establish her own way in the world as against the bourgeois comforts of her mother's home. The result is a sort of self-imposed entrapment in the complications of urban survival, and a primary focus is on Lola's little daughter, Ana, whose progressive abandonment is an index of her mother's inability to free herself from the game she has chosen to play. Yet Novaro does propose a form of self-awareness for Lola and the possibility that, outside of the cheap thrills of urban life, she might assume the responsibilities of her motherhood. The idea of an extra-urban liberation rather than a progressive consumption by the city ends up modeling for Mexican society the need to imagine a reversal of the enormous allure of urban life, a much different proposal than the failed attempt to find refuge within the city proposed by *El castillo de la pureza* or the possibilities for renewal in the shifting urban spaces of *De noche vienes, Esmeralda* or *Lolo*.

The final film to be analyzed, Sabina Berman and Isabelle Tardán's *Entre Pancho Villa y una mujer desnuda* (1995), also involves a sophisticated urban woman, a business woman to boot. Yet Gina is seriously confused about the sexual options open to her, and part of her not inconsiderable conflict comes from the dissension between traditional views of Mexican machismo (the Pancho Villa figure) and the nonchalant attitudes of her contemporary male counterparts. An important dimension of Sabina Berman and Isabelle Tardán's film lies in the ways in which it is possible to perceive a dead end to Gina's sexual turmoils and her inability to confront alternative erotic agendas afforded by the city. Thus, there is a curious contradiction within the film: on the one hand, it portrays Gina's strenuous defiance of the all-consuming allure of conventional macho recognition, by means of which the woman is putatively afforded full validation by virtue of the gaze and the attentions of the masculine prototype; while, on the other hand, Gina is never able to turn her defiance of this model and the obvious inadequacies of the men in her life (which are humorously juxtaposed to the iconic paradigm of Pancho Villa) into any viable alternative for her psychosexual needs. By modeling what are undoubtedly the confused alternatives for modern sexually liberated women in Mexico City, the Berman-Tardán film cedes to some future Mexican feminist film the assignment of portraying possibilities of emotional transcendency for women on their own in the urban landscape.

The juxtaposition of *Lola* and *Entre Pancho Villa y una mujer desnuda* is particularly significant, since Gina is materially successful thanks to effectively pursuing options that Lola has chosen to repudiate by separating herself from her mother's bourgeois values. Yet, where *Lola* ultimately ends on a tenuously positive note thanks to the possibility of liberation from deadening urban realities, *Entre Pancho Villa y una mujer desnuda* shows how Gina, no matter how successful she might be in the privileged spaces of her ultra-modern metropolis, still remains cornered (literally, in the final sequence of the film) by macho aggression.

Danzón

María Rojo is one of the most famous actresses in Mexico at the moment (she has also served as a *diputada* and played an important role in promot-

FIGURE 14   The all-female space of telephone operators.

ing laws affecting the film industry). She played the role of the mother in *Rojo amanecer,* and she has played the leading female role in some of the most important films to come out of Mexico in recent decades. Now, as a middle-aged woman, she is able to play parts that have important feminist dimensions relating to the breaking of stereotypes of feminine beauty. Although a woman with very attractive features—audiences most often remember the brilliance of her smile—Rojo goes against the grain of both the standards of young beauty in Western society as a whole and the idea of the younger the better for women stars (the Lolita syndrome). Also, in a country such as Mexico, where the demographic pyramid is dominated by a vast base of individuals under the age of twenty-one, Rojo calls attention to the possibility of a beautiful and interesting woman who is older than the dominant norm in Mexican society and, therefore, in the erotic imagery found in advertising and the like.

In María Novaro's *Danzón* (1991), María Rojo's character, Julia, has a daughter who is a paradigmatic representative of Mexico's youth culture. The mother obtains a job for her with the Mexican telephone company where she works in downtown Mexico City, and although Perla has no conflicts with her mother or her coworkers, Julia is continually appalled at the level of cultural taste her daughter has. Perla reads movie magazines, listens to American music, wears American youth fashions, and shows little interest in her mother's identification with traditional Mexican culture. In this sense, Novaro introduces through the figure of Perla an implicit criticism of the Americanization of Mexico—long an issue with leftists and cultural nationalists of various political persuasions—and of the multinationalism that is part of the process of late capitalism in the country. Despite the difficulties Mexico has had in participating fully in the neoliberal economic projects that have become the order of the day throughout Latin America, the superficial trappings, especially in major population centers, of import products and their copies are considerably in evidence.

Danzón is eminently a feminist text, perhaps one of the best feminist films produced in Latin America to date. To a great degree, its feminism derives from Julia's condition as a middle-aged woman who is determined to satisfy her own personal needs. Julia lives to dance *danzón,* a form of ballroom dancing that came into Mexico in the nineteenth century from the Caribbean, where it had originated as the Creole aristocracy's adaptation of the French cotillion dance (see López's analysis of Latin dance in film, including his extensive comments on Novaro's film; the relationship between dance and melodrama in the film is discussed by Tierney). In Mexico, danzón is strictly a form of lower-middle-class culture. Julia has, apparently, danced danzón since she was a child, and the walls of her modest home are decorated with pictures and diplomas of her many triumphs. Danced in a *salón* with an orchestra (there are tables and a bar service for those who just like to watch the dance or for dancers to rest between numbers), danzón also involves prize competitions, and the most serious dancers usually have a fixed partner; and it is clear that the relationship with this partner has all of the intensity of an intimate relationship, without being conventionally sexual—that is, Julia and her partner are not lovers. Julia dances with Carmelo, an older man from Veracruz. Carmelo is a distinguished and reserved mulatto, whose trademark is his white Panama hat. He is a dignified dancer, courtly in his interaction with his partner, and the glow on Julia's face as she dances with him underscores the intensity of their relationship.

When Carmelo fails to appear one evening to dance with Julia—it seems they dance together several times a week—she is devastated and tries to find him. But it becomes clear that she really knows little about his personal life. In a delightful scene, she unsuccessfully seeks him out in a traditional Mexican restaurant in the city's center where she believes he works. The restaurant is across the street from the studios of KWX, one of the oldest radio stations in Mexico and virtually the pioneer in the broadcasting of Mexican popular music. Since Julia knows that Carmelo is from Veracruz, and having overheard that he has perhaps returned there in order to escape being charged by the police for theft, she decides to travel to Veracruz, a city on Mexico's Caribbean coast, where danzón entered Mexican culture; it is, moreover, a city much more tied to traditional Mexican culture than Mexico City, which, because of its position as the nation's capital, is more exposed to the influence of late capitalist consumerism.

Julia does not find Carmelo in Veracruz. But she does find other things that contribute to her sense of erotic self-identity. First of all, she meets the gay transvestite performer Susy (played by the famous drag star Tito Vasconcelos). From him she learns not only respect for sexual dissidence, but also greater ease for her own female sexuality and her beauty as a woman. Although she resists Susy's attempts to give her a more flamboyant image, Julia and Susy develop a deep and loving personal relationship that provides, as an important dimension of the film, a very delightful image of the sympathy that often develops between gays and women, especially women with deep emotional commitments; concomitantly, this brings with it an implied legitimation of both gay sensibility and the role of transvestite performance in Mexican popular culture. Julia also develops a loving relationship with Doña Ti (played by Carmen Salinas, whom the Mexican audience will recognize as a famous singer of boleros from the 1950s and 1960s), the owner of the port-area hotel frequented by prostitutes. Doña Ti has six children by six men and lives alone, and her stories help Julia to understand how important it is for a woman to shed romantic notions of eternal love in the company of men. When Doña Ti is later rude to Susy (she does not know that Susy and Julia are friends), it is a blatant example of homophobia directed against the effeminate and/or feminized man. Yet perhaps her reaction not only is conventional homophobia, but also includes a reaction to the way in which Susy's cross-dressing is part of one gay narrative about achieving the romantic love Doña Ti rejects.

The other experience Julia has in Veracruz is with Rubén, a tugboat operator. Julia spies him when she goes to the port authority looking for a Greek ship she thinks Carmelo may have shipped out on as a cook to escape the police. She is frustrated again in her search for Carmelo, but she meets Rubén, who personifies for her a certain type of feral masculinity, with his picaresque smile, his longish hair, and his lithe and sensuous body. However, the affair does not last long. In the first place, Rubén can't dance danzón and doesn't seem to be much interested in doing so. But Julia does bed him, and in one scene she contemplates his (almost) naked sleeping body in what must be a highly innovative and daring scene in Mexican film-making: the concession to the female gaze of the right to eroticize the male body (curiously, although she speaks of Julia's gaze vis-à-vis Rubén's body, López does not mention this scene). However, Rubén shows up one day with his hair cut, and suddenly he becomes for Julia a young kid not much older than her daughter. Novaro's film is full of ironic twists, and yet another one is that it is Julia who abandons Rubén when she decides to return to Mexico City. The pained look of desolation on Rubén's face is a reprise of all the faces of female protagonists in Mexican films who have ever been abandoned by, as the bolero would say, perfidious men. Wiser as to the romantic and sentimental situation of women and reinforced in her own erotic self-image by Susy's attentions and Rubén's lovemaking, Julia returns to Mexico City.

In Mexico City, after vaunting her new image to her daughter and her women friends, Julia returns to the dance floor of the salón, and the film concludes with her dancing in Carmelo's arms. It is never explained where Carmelo went and why he disappeared, and it is evident that Julia does not care or need to know. They are back together again, dancing, and that is enough for her. This frustration of the soap-opera's narrative need to tie everything up in terms of an acceptable plot formula is Novaro's final surprise twist, and it opens the film up, just as it is ending, as regards the nature of Julia and Carmelo's relationship. Certainly, there is a sexual relationship, despite the fact that any erotic feeling between them is limited to what they enact on the dance floor, even though Julia's beatific smile would intend to indicate how she experiences intense pleasure in Carmelo's arms. Perhaps class difference between the two of them is minimal, and for the social class to which they belong, Carmelo's condition as a mulatto is hardly of any particular significance. Carmelo is, however, quite a bit older than Julia, and in the context of the overwhelming youth culture of Mexico, Julia, who has already shown herself to be scandalous in her relationship with Rubén, may be viewed as equally outrageous in confining her sexual life in the end to the danzón and to an older man as a partner about whom she knows very little, about whom she has no need to know anything more than his outstanding quality as a dance partner, no matter how mysterious his comings and goings may be.

In these details Novaro may not be making a strident feminist declaration of how the conventional heterosexist romance narrative may be defied.

Indeed, there are those who could argue that Julia's commitment to the danzón is a form of romantic reinscription for women, particularly given the lyrics of the love-story musical themes that are its backdrop. I think this would be an incorrect assessment, however, because it is obvious that Julia's erotic paradigm is one that she has chosen, and one that is very much at odds with any interest in having a typical romantic involvement with a man, as prescribed by the heterosexist norm in which women on their own and alone are an affront to social decency. However, perhaps the most effective cultural texts are those that subtly undermine social norms, as here the woman makes use of her body according to her own personal program of fulfillment; perhaps this is what makes Novaro's film so strikingly attractive.

I would like now at this point to focus a bit more on the question of the relationship of the film to the depiction of urban images. The danzón, as a dance style, and the public space it creates are of considerable importance in this regard. It is significant to note that, in the juxtaposition between Veracruz and Mexico City, the danzón, which entered Mexico through the port city of Veracruz, is enacted in open and very public spaces in Veracruz, making passersby, in general, spectators to the dancers and the dance, with all of its rituals in clothing, footwear, and intersexual relations (nowhere in the film, except when Julia attempts to teach Susy to dance the danzón and they negotiate over sex roles, is there any suggestion of the possibility of same-sex dancing, whether in public or in private; there is one case in which a grandmother dances with her young granddaughter, but this is hardly a queering of the dance). The principal sites we see in which danzón is performed in Veracruz are the Parque Zamora, the city's central park, and several restaurants where Julia observes customers (including children) dancing: in both cases there is a direct representation of the multigenerational aspect of the danzón and a particularly effective use of elderly dancers, something that is also noticeable in the main salons of the segments featured in Mexico City. It is in one of these Veracruz restaurants, an open-air one on the beach front, that Julia discovers that her young lover cannot dance danzón, and this is the beginning of the separation between the two of them. Julia simply cannot conceive of life without dancing danzón, and it is clear that the sexuality of this dance is more important to her than conventional genital sex.

In Mexico City, however, the nature of urban life makes danzón a semi-enclosed spectacle. The majority of Julia's life takes place in the Salón Colonia, featured in the opening scenes of the film. It is here where she dances with Carmelo; and if after his disappearance she goes to other places, it is in the hopes of seeing him and/or to escape a place where she cannot bear to be without him. The Salón Colonia is typical of these spaces in Mexico, and it is iconic of the venues of popular culture in the city: the Salón México is the most famous of these cabarets, as featured in Emilio Fernández's 1949 film, *Salón México,* starring Marga López; María Rojo starred in a bad remake of the film in 1995 by José Luis García Agraz, and she was a partner in restoring the original Salón México, located north of the Parque de la Alameda in downtown Mexico. The remodeled Salón México appears in Sabina Berman and Isabelle Tardán's film version of Sabina Berman's play, *Entre Pancho Villa y una mujer desnuda* (1995).

The Salón Colonia is typical in that it is a large barn of a space, generally in disrepair, and located in a marginal neighborhood, as we can see when Julia and her friends leave the dance hall at the end of the evening. Such an establishment is, therefore, semipublic, in the sense that it is a public convenience while at the same time limited to those who pay to use it—unlike in the Parque Zamora or even the open-air restaurant, passersby do not enjoy access to what goes on inside, although it is not uncommon to see passersby peering in through the entrance portals to participate vicariously in the spectacle of the patrons.

The point here is the degree to which dance halls like the Salón Colonia constitute an integral part of the urban landscape. To be sure, they are part of the strips of public conveniences that punctuate the streets of the city: bars, restaurants, drug stores, clothing outlets, appliance and hardware stores, and the like. One can tell a lot about the priorities and possibilities of urban households by scrutinizing the wares of these establishments, both what they hold and what they do not (that is, what is not offered for sale). Although cities like Mexico City continue to have bazaars and markets— groupings of stalls within an enclosed or relatively open space—that cater, alternatively, to the lower economic classes and the tourists, the strip establishments represent aspirations to the middle class: they sell products that are often identified by brand names, and they engage in various forms of advertising to get the goods sold. This latter marketing, as primitive as it may be, lies at the lower end of organized capitalism, by contrast to the immediate need fulfillment of bazaars and markets.

It is for this reason that the dance hall points toward the modern urban organization of modern cultural production. For Julia, it is a refuge from home and work (and the fact that work takes place for her as a woman outside the home is certainly an element of modern society). It is not that either of these two realms is unsatisfactory for her: she enjoys an excellent personal relationship with her fellow workers, with some of whom she goes to the dance halls, and her daughter not only lives with her, but also works with Julia at the telephone company. It is never explained in the film why Julia is a single parent, but one must assume that her home symbolizes, for her, abandonment as a woman: its solitude (the fact that her daughter belongs to a different generation and, therefore, has other tastes and interests is made quite clear) bespeaks the way in which she does not participate in the scheme of the heterosexual couple, a scheme that is modeled, promoted, and reinforced at every turn by official and popular culture. In this sense, the single woman—no matter for what reasons she is single—is a sexual outlaw, because her singleness, which may be overtly displayed in numerous ways, such as the lack of a wedding band or strategic references in conversation to her husband or partner, to her "man," constitutes a defiance of heteronormativity, which, in effect, requires that everyone be paired: even nuns wear wedding bands as brides of Christ, and female whores are presumed to be handled by male pimps. The exceptions to heteronormativity, either by circumstance or as the consequence of gender nonconformity (always relatively visible in Mexico City, especially male-to-female dispositions), and the queering of compulsory heterosexuality (the increasingly visible gay and lesbian community) are of course all over the place (there is even now a *Ferrari Guides' Gay Mexico* [Black] tourist guide). But they are always trumped by the overdetermination of heteronormativity, which is why the film can assume that the spectators share with Julia the cuteness of little boys and girls paired off as nascent danzón partners.

Thus, the dance hall for Julia is both a source of pleasure and the public manifestation of gender compliance. When Carmelo disappears, her franticness is unquestionably a sense of the loss of personal sexual fulfillment, in whatever the ways in which dancing with Carmelo make her happy as a woman in the arms of a man. But that franticness is also over the disappearance of what provides her with public, and therefore personal, recognition of complying with the demands of compulsory heterosexuality. The men who offer to dance with her when she is left partnerless, the Russian sailor who comes on to her no sooner than she begins to roam Veracruz looking for Carmelo, and Rubén, the young tugboat captain with whom she subsequently has a fling, are all unsatisfactory options because they cannot give her what she gets from Carmelo, which is as much his public persona as an acceptably masculine partner as the sexual joy of dancing with him, such that the two are one and the same thing and define each other mutually.

FIGURE 15   The female gaze at the (almost) nude male body.

Carmelo's quintessential masculinity is what explains why Julia is concerned with, but yet seduced by, the transgression of Rubén's long hair, and
then equally concerned with, and ultimately repelled by, his short haircut
because he then becomes less of a man because he looks too much like a boy
the same age as her daughter, to whom she has assigned an age half of what
it really is. Rubén's charms are not lost on Julia nor, presumably, on view-
ers of the films, and Novaro has Víctor Carpinteiro play his alternatively
wild-man and boyish allures to the hilt. The camera details the extent of
Julia's erotic gaze: at first it is shyly embarrassed, but in their last night
together it is frankly and unabashedly intense; and the way in which she
focuses avidly on his exposed and tanned flanks as he lies sleeping is all the
sexier because the draping of his buttocks with the white sheet, ruffled
gently by the overhead fan, becomes a euphemism for how in real life, beyond the compliance by Novaro's camera with some measure of decency,
she would be relishing his fully naked body.
    Novaro has Julia's gaze suggest the importance of male buttocks in the
female erotic gaze, which is confirmed by how, at the end of the film, Susy,
who never knows of Julia and Rubén's affair, is given a really very humor-

ously played opportunity to become distracted by Rubén's derriere, clothed in tight and rain-soaked pants: Susy, as a transvestite, reduplicates the "truly" feminine gaze at Rubén's body, while, as a queer, suggesting the gaze of the queer spectator in a way that overdetermines Rubén's erotic masculinity. Yet for Julia, Rubén's masculinity is not enough, which is why she abandons him, returns to Mexico City, returns to the Salón Colonia, and recovers Carmelo, the only man who can adequately fulfill her need for a display partner. Carmelo, who virtually never speaks during the film, is all things masculine to Julia: he makes her feel like a woman (that is, fulfills her sexually: never mind that his fulfillment does not comply with conventional ideas of sexual performance) because he is such a gentleman (as her friend Silvia finds it necessary to point out to *her* dancing partner) and such a fine dancing partner, and because she is able to display this to her friends and the world (indeed, in this sense, Silvia's comment to her partner is a confirmation of Julia's good fortune).

Therefore, in the importance of the dance hall as a refuge from home and work is the importance of making the right sort of public display about one's sexuality, about one's gender fulfillment. Julia becomes impossible when Carmelo disappears, and one of their fellow employees asks her daughter what is wrong with her mother. Perla makes some sort of general comment about her mother being upset because her man has disappeared. It is noteworthy that this exchange takes place on the public street, where both women, reinforcing the transparently public nature of sexuality in Mexico City, ignore the sexual comments of a bum who watches them go by. It is obvious in all this that Carmelo is not "just" a dance partner, but that he fulfills a very large role in making Julia feel like a woman and allowing her to display broadly—at least in the many dance venues in which she and Carmelo appear—the legitimacy of her heterosexuality.

Certainly, much of what I have said to this point hinges on how dance is sexual and how the danzón in particular is an enactment of compulsory heterosexuality. I cannot examine in detail here the boleros featured in the film (some as background music and some as themes for dancing), but they are traditional popular songs of lost love and romantic suffering. One of the several slyly humorous moments in the film is when Julia goes to the port of Veracruz after hearing that perhaps Carmelo, who is a cook by profession, has signed on one of the ships: ship after ship has either the name of a bolero, a phrase from a bolero, or something evocative of a bolero. Even Rubén's tugboat participates in yet another display of the discourse of compulsory heterosexuality, as it is called *Me Ves y Sufres (You See Me and Suffer)*. Although the bolero certainly has a homoerotic dimension to it

(I have written elsewhere about how this emerges in Luis Rafael Sánchez's 1988 novel, *La importancia de llamarse Daniel Santos [The Importance of Having the Name Daniel Santos]*; Santos was a renowned Puerto Rican bolero singer, and Sánchez explores the polyeroticism of his artistic persona [see Foster, "Luis Rafael Sánchez"; see also Quiroga]), it is not allowed to be evident in this film, as I have already stated. Thus, to whatever degree dancing in couples is an erotic enactment, and, therefore, ballroom or dance hall dancing is a particularly public display of that enactment, dancing to the bolero as it is traditionally understood is categorically an enactment of heterosexuality.

One might be hard pressed to decide if compulsory heterosexuality is more obligatorily enacted publicly in the urban megalopolis than it is in traditional towns and villages, or even in a large yet still very provincial city like Guadalajara. I suspect that in Guadalajara (which has its own measure of queer visibility, but mostly at night and only in limited public spaces)—and, therefore, in traditional towns and villages—there are few alternatives to being heterosexual, at least in public, which means most of the time, since our lives are essentially public in the sense that they are played out before others most of the time. In the case of Mexico City, not only are there more opportunities to be non-heterosexual or queer in public, but, in the end, few care; they are so busy surviving in the urban monster. This is why Carlos Monsiváis can, so brilliantly, note that the policing of social uniformity is impossible when "el pensamiento más excéntrico es compartido por millones. Somos tantos que a quién le importa si otros piensan igual o distinto" (*Los rituales del caos* 112).[1] Under these circumstances, the injunction to manifest publicly the fulfillment of compulsory heterosexuality (or any other social mandate, such as allegiance to the Virgin de Guadalupe or to the Mexican flag) is perceived on an entirely personal and subjective level. I use the word "perceived" advisedly, since the injunction is not likely to be enunciated in so many words and the subject is not likely to understand it to exist in so many words: hegemonic ideologies are unconsciously internalized, and even if one subsequently becomes consciously aware of them and subjects them to deconstructive analysis, they are first and foremost already and ever there. The very nature of ideological formations is that one can only decide not to be subject to their powerful hegemony through an arduous process of analysis and detachment, which is why it is not really surprising that all individuals comply with many internally contradictory ideological formations usually without ever being troubled by those internal contradictions or even perceiving them.

Thus, Julia's decision to live by the law of danzón (she tells Silvia at one point that danzón is the most important thing in the world) is only partially a consciously taken one. It is more that she finds in danzón, given the circumstances of her life, a most efficient vehicle to express her heterosexuality as a woman, and not that she in any way decides that she is going to abide by the imperatives of that heterosexuality. Thus, she may be exceptionally and exemplarily tolerant of Susy, but, after all, Susy is only reenacting the heterosexual binary in his transvestism, which is grounded in the fact that he really senses himself to be a woman (which Julia recognizes by carefully addressing a note to him with grammatically feminine markers). And when there is negotiation between Julia and Susy over sexual roles, it is still based on the heterosexual binary, never on a reassessment of the sense of the gender binary. Finally, although by the end of the film, after her experience in Veracruz, Julia may have decided to break with some of the gender obsequiousness (i.e., after lecturing to her daughter and Susy about the obligatory modesty of the female gaze, she now looks Carmelo squarely in the eye while dancing with him), there is still, nevertheless, the reaffirmation of the gender configurations of heteronormativity; and Julia feels herself, in the end, fully reintegrated into the proper sexuality and, therefore, the properly fulfilled womanliness of her world, as exemplified by her well-heralded return to the dance hall and, immediately thereupon, to Carmelo's arms.

A movie such as *Danzón,* about the gender odyssey of a woman like Julia, could really have taken place in any of the other city spaces that provide the opportunity for public enactment of structures of social compliances. However, the world of the dance hall, the bolero, and the danzón provides overlapping configurations that Novaro's film makes use of in a notably efficient and superbly artful manner. Julia undergoes a series of self-discoveries in her trip to Veracruz and then back to Mexico City. One clever detail of the film occurs when she is going to meet Rubén on the docks of the port and there is an ice-cream vendor whose product is called Anagnórisis. Julia does undergo an anagnorisis in her experiences with Rubén and Susy, and it is that process that enables her to return to a more secure life as a woman in Mexico City.

De noche vienes, Esmeralda (Esmeralda, You Come by Night)

Jaime Humberto Hermosillo's *De noche vienes, Esmeralda* (1997) is perhaps the crowning achievement of his career as a director; certainly, it has had a profound effect on it, as it led to his losing his position as a professor of film studies at the Universidad de Guadalajara, where, despite his long list of controversial film credits, he had served for two decades. However, the new conservative forces in that city and in the university can be credited with accurately interpreting, if only through ham-fisted censure, the way in which *De noche* is, undeniably, Hermosillo's queerest film to date. I have written extensively elsewhere regarding the gay utopia provided by Hermosillo's most famous film, *Doña Herlinda y su hijo* (1986), and the way in which the gay utopia it figures can only be achieved through a substantial queering of the patriarchal family (Foster, "Queering the Patriarchy"). But perhaps because the facade of the sacred Mexican family is maintained in this film, including respect for properly heteronormative procreation, *Doña Herlinda* passed safely into Mexican film history without any substantive scandal.

Not that *De noche,* once released, produced much of an uproar. Indeed, it seems not to have made much of a splash in Mexico or Latin America, despite the quality of the artists involved in its making or the fact that it is based on a short story by Elena Poniatowska (see Moorhead's analysis of this text). Nevertheless, as I shall argue, it is easily the queerest film made to date in Mexico, and it is very much a masterwork of Hermosillo's career as a director (see the review by Sen). Following faithfully the outlines of Poniatowska's story, the film is a series of flashbacks that enact Esmeralda's telling of her polyandrous matrimonial career. Esmeralda is a registered nurse who, because of the long and changing hours she is required to work, is able to juggle multiple domestic situations. At the beginning of the film, she awakes from spending the night with one of her husbands and, insisting that she must go off to work, rushes to her father's house—her home base—to change into a well-used wedding gown that will serve her for the church wedding to husband number five. However, the man whose bed she has just abandoned, the most conventionally macho of the lot, has discovered her marriages to other men, and he petitions an order for her arrest for violation of the laws against bigamy.

Esmeralda is arrested at the altar, with the police appearing in a parody of the formula "Is there anyone present who knows why this man and this woman . . ." Hauled before a prosecuting judge, who will take testimony from her as part of the preliminary investigation (i.e., to determine if there is the basis for a criminal trial), in conformance with Mexican judicial practices, Esmeralda reveals that she is much more than a mere bigamist: she has previously married four other men, and she has so far been successful in being the happily married, if rather harriedly employed, wife to all of them. As she tells the judge about each one of her marriages, with court personnel and passersby hanging on every word of her account, the film provides an enactment of her narrative, such that the audience, on both levels, meets each of her husbands and perceives the way in which she interacts with each of them.

The core of the film's queerness, therefore, lies with the challenge to a heteronormative patriarchy in the degree to which a woman is able to pursue a personal objective of multiple marriages. Like most Latin American societies, Mexico is characterized by an unofficial acceptance of masculine philandering and even, at least in the megalopolitan capital in which the film takes place, some rights for modern women to have sexual experiences outside the matrimonial bedroom. But the idea of a woman maintaining relations not just with five men, but with five "legally" wedded husbands stretches the codes of social convention beyond credulity (religious practice seems only to be evoked in the film as a way of rhetorically highlighting the outrageousness of Esmeralda's five marriages, since even for the cosmopolitan secularism of professional and official Mexico City, the defiance of the church cannot but contribute to the general sense of outrage the plot provokes in a first instance).

The measure of conventional outrage that the film works with is evoked on two levels; the degree to which the film is successful in queering the patriarchy, such that outrage is dispelled, both for the immediate audience of Esmeralda's declarations and the audience of the film, involves the creation of a counterdiscourse that closes the film. Whether or not this closure is ideologically convincing and rhetorically effective is a matter that will be taken up below. The two levels on which conventional outrage is elaborated concern the reaction of the official legal system, in the person of the persecuting judge, and the manner in which Esmeralda tells her story (the way in which Esmeralda's telling is a form of feminist self-empowerment is treated by Moorhead). The severe and dour judge, Lic. Víctor Solorio, is played by a stock character actor, Claudio Obregón, who is able to infuse his character with all of the drab and pompous majesty of the law. This is the law that depends for its proper function less on the necessary blindness with which it must apply itself to a diverse humanity and more on the blindness with which errant individuals are obliged to accept the intrusions of the law into the microdramas of their lives.

The outrage of the judge cannot last, and its dispersion or dispellment in the course of the film leaves as its trace the inevitability of the majesty of the law not being taken seriously by those who may, nevertheless, be forced to experience its arbitrary inequities. Hermosillo in this sense does not have much of a challenge for the semiotics of *De noche,* and in a slapstick evocation of Cantinflesque comedies, the law is easily shown to have little point to make in the regulation of human affairs. The angry spouse who originally brought the charge against Esmeralda quickly regrets his rashness and withdraws his protest, but, of course, the law, always impelled by its own officious momentum, moves forward on its own; and while the outrage of the judge—and, therefore, presumably, of society—is dispelled at the end of the film, Esmeralda, in perhaps a suggestion of the way in which social convention cannot simply be laughed away, is still facing formal charges; the judge, however, promises to work for her release. More on this below.

Hermosillo reduplicates the expected reaction of his film by surrounding the judicial inquiry into Esmeralda's transgression with a sympathetic audience, one that extends, in receding layers, from the court officials assigned to Solorio's jurisdiction to circumstantial functionaries and citizens in general who are passersby and happenstance listeners to Esmeralda's account because they, too, have been caught up in the implacable machinations of the Mexican legal system and are on the scene in order to attend to their own charges and cases. This assorted "common Mexican" spectatorship represents the spectators of the film, and there is every reason to believe that few will have any meaningful investment in the integrity of law, not at least as it is embodied in the bombastic demeanor of Solorio. Therefore, of much greater interest will be the way in which Esmeralda's account effects a change in Solorio's opinion: such a change, because he is the embodiment of the law, if only on a very minor, first-instance court level, will point hopefully toward successive modifications of opinion throughout Mexican society, since her case is, in effect, a direct challenge to the overarching patriarchal superstructure.

The second aspect of outrage over Esmeralda's account is her own personal stance toward it and the way in which she expounds it. Esmeralda is played by superstar María Rojo, and Rojo is in full command of the role she plays. Esmeralda is simply incapable of understanding all the fuss that is being made over her. She appears before the judge magnificently turned out— not flamboyantly, but nevertheless dressed to kill, in a way that asserts total comfort with her femininity and with the decisions she has made to control her life, her body, and, most significantly, her sexuality. She never loses her smile and is always the consummate professional (one recalls that nursing emerges in postrevolutionary Mexico as one of the sacrosanct professions, and while things have changed a lot in Mexico since the days of the forging

FIGURE 16.   One of Esmeralda's engaging smiles directed at the prosecuting judge. Note the Marilyn Monroe pose, and note also the presence of the image of Sor Juana Inés de la Cruz, the foremother of Mexican feminism.

of modern Mexico, nursing continues to remain a viable profession for many women in that country). Esmeralda's smile is accentuated by a quizzical look, as if the discourse articulated by Solorio were virtually incomprehensible to her; this stance of incomprehension is the corollary to Solorio's outrage, because he, likewise, finds Esmeralda's discourse of personal erotic freedom absolutely incomprehensible: I would propose that Hermosillo's directorial voice, guiding the position of the spectators, is as outraged at Solorio's pompous fulminations as it is amused by Esmeralda's quizzical attitude, creating thereby a third-position discourse in which it becomes possible to entertain critically the validity of the scandalous propositions regarding matrimony being made by Esmeralda in her responses to the investigating judge's inquiries. Indeed, evoking the root word of "quizzical," Esmeralda's stance toward Solorio is implicitly to quiz him on the validity of the interrogation to which he submits her. Even when she does not ask him "Why?" seeking a way of understanding the basis of his questions to her, her look, her facial attitude, and, indeed, her entire body language are a challenge to the comprehensibility of his juridical discourse directed at her.

Esmeralda's genteel stance, alternating between bemused amazement over why she is being interrogated and irony over the bases of that interrogation, is supplemented by the internal audience of the film. Both Lucita, the stenographer who is taking down her statements, and Solorio's male assistant (whose own personal life—there is the hint that he is gay—is implicated in Esmeralda's story) themselves insinuate objections to the judge's questioning and on separate occasions speak privately with Esmeralda about her account. In fact, one of the most entertaining sequences in the film is the "woman's room" conversation between Esmeralda and Lucita, played by Martha Navarro, in the rest room, where they retire for a smoke, a private conversation about women's lives, and an exchange of shoes: Lucita's admiration for Esmeralda's clothes is a material corollary of the way in which she supports Esmeralda in direct defiance of the system she represents as the hearing's stenographer; she would, literally, like to be in her shoes. Additionally, other court employees and passersby react with surprise, repudiation, and outright indignation at the course of Solorio's interrogation, all of which provide additional opportunities within the social discourse of the film for the spectator to assess critically both Esmeralda's account and the nature of the juridical discourse that calls it forth.

During her account, Esmeralda answers many of the judge's questions in a manner that enhances this critical space. Perhaps her most entertaining answer—which is not meant to be funny, but rather to state a moral position—comes when she is asked why she married so many men. Esmeralda answers with the full force of a woman's convictions in the face of the uncomprehending male dolt, to the effect that she is an honorable woman and is unable to go to bed with a man to whom she is not married. This answer, which depends for its validity on adherence to the moral principle of no sex outside matrimony, is hilarious because of the way in which it is contradicted by the principal motivation of the judge's question, which has to do with the violation not against the taboo of extramarital sex, but against the taboo of multiple marriages, which implies multiple sexual partners. Certainly, for most Mexican urban sophisticates, there is little taboo against extramarital sex and hardly (the risk of sexually transmitted diseases aside) against multiple sexual partners. For Solorio, an agent of the patriarchal system, polyandry is a violation of the law; but why might it be for the urban sophisticate who is witness, within the film narrative or as a spectator of Hermosillo's film, to that account? (I acknowledge that I am assuming here a certain kind of spectator for a film by Jaime Humberto Hermosillo.)

Perhaps it principally lies in the attitude of why be married in the first place? Why collaborate with the patriarchal system, as represented paradigmatically by a church wedding, when one's life is that of a modern professional and when one is a woman who is concerned about exercising her rights to the sort of independent life made possible by professionalism? And why does anything come to the attention of the legal system, much less to that of such a preposterous agent of the patriarchy as Solorio shows himself to be? It is the insouciant innocence (which surely comes accompanied by a measure of strategic disingenuousness) of Esmeralda with regard to these matters that makes her most engaging to both the internal and external witnesses to her account. And, too, it must be observed that Esmeralda serves to create a homosocial bond between her husbands, all of whom get along very nicely at her birthday party (note, however, that they all only meet each other after she has been detained). Indeed, one of them is, in fact, bisexual (or does he not have sex with his wife?), and he lives more continuously with his same-sex lover than he does with the once-a-week Esmeralda.

On a micronarrative level, the way in which Esmeralda's account is enacted by the cuts to her interactions with her spouses is particularly effective because of the way in which the cuts confirm the emotion and intention of her interaction with each of them. There is a purity or nobility about the intense devotion Esmeralda has for each of her husbands, and this distances her erotic life from that of the promiscuous woman. Hermosillo runs the risk of investing in a rhetoric that would appear to disclaim the validity of promiscuous eroticism, rather a serious risk for an openly gay cultural producer. The inquiry into the legitimacy of the heterosexist denunciation of female promiscuity (not including the exceptions the patriarchy has always been able to tolerate as part of the sentimental education of the macho, as exemplified by the official toleration of prostitution) has been an integral part of the gay movement in the West; and the legitimation of promiscuity, admittedly much more an issue for gay males than for lesbians, has been frequently viewed as integral to the repossession of one's body, wresting it from the control of the patriarchal sexual economy. Whether or not sexual promiscuity is fundamental to unsupervised sexual fulfillment is less an issue than is the need to bear witness to a defiance of that economy and whatever ideological bases drive it and allow it to define the erotic parameters of the lived sexual experience of the individual.

Hermosillo, to be sure, both promotes promiscuity and circumscribes it—sanitizes it for a mainstream audience—in *De noche*. Perhaps it is particularly transgressive that he uses a female character to promote the proposition of the legitimacy of multiple sexual partners. The representation of the sex hunt of the gay male (see its defense by the Chicano author John Rechy in *The Sexual Outlaw*) might have been too obvious and too off-putting for the sort of audience to which Hermosillo has been able to aspire with the use in so many films of an actress like María Rojo; and, indeed, filming Poniatowska's story enables him to promote one version of multiple sexual partnering without evoking Rechy's image of erotic outlawry that could have come with a film on gay male sexuality. Certainly, the beatific way in which Esmeralda evokes her multiple husbands contributes to the sanitization of sexuality and makes the basic proposition at issue, the legitimation of promiscuity (there is no way of knowing exactly *how many* Esmeralda intends to end up with, although five or six would seem to work best in juggling a conventional work week—with Sundays always reserved for her father), much more palatable to a broad moviegoing audience, as opposed to the more circumscribed audience of gay films. This is an important decision, despite the deleterious impact that it appears to have had on Hermosillo's university career, since one reasonable commitment of the subaltern filmmaker is, precisely, to model alternative experiences for society at large rather than to continue to validate the rights of subaltern groups. In fact, Hermosillo appears to have accomplished both goals with *Doña Herlinda*, since not only is there a model, as controversial as it may be even for gay culture, for meeting the erotic needs of two male lovers within the highly homophobic setting of a Mexican city such as Guadalajara, but also it presents a model, as even more controversial as that may be for patriarchal culture, of the collaboration in the execution of the first model by those who would seem to be disadvantaged by accepting gay relationships (indeed, even, virtually, a gay marriage), such as one's mother, one's wife, and, eventually, one's children (one will recall that the wife of one of the gay partners has the first labor pains for the birth of their first son exactly at the same time as we see him being fucked by the other partner).

Hermosillo's modeling in this case centers on heterosexual matrimony, albeit it is polyandrous. Yet one can wonder if this might be even more transgressive, more outrageous, than focusing on what many might well feel to be a minority group of gay sexual partners (whether that may be an erroneous assumption in a society in which a lot of homoerotic sexuality that is not defined as gay takes place is another matter). That is, Esmeralda appears in every regard to be a conventional woman, and Hermosillo's film may well depend on the Everywoman–Every Mexican Woman persona of María

Rojo to promote, at least initially, audience identification with or assimilation into the normalcy of Esmeralda as the embodiment of an acceptable modern femininity.

What is problematical is the way in which this turns out not to be true, and it is not true in at least three dimensions. The first is the very fact that Esmeralda practices polyandry. This may be a logical outcome of the sexual liberation of women in contemporary Mexico City, and/or it may be a disastrous consequence of that liberation: women defy the patriarchal hierarchy by attaining too much agency in their own lives, and that agency, by its very existence, is the occasion for social disruption, with disastrous consequences for all concerned (see Alberto Isaac's revision of this formula in his 1994 film, *Mujeres insumisas;* also of note is Jaime Humberto Hermosillo's examination, in his 1978 *Amor libre,* of the heterosexual revolution in Mexico City). Most immediately, it means incarceration and possible criminal prosecution for Esmeralda for breaking the law regarding the contract of marriage. It also involves the demeaning of the ideology of masculine control, an ideology that the patriarchy seeks to infuse in every male social subject: the ones who don't get it right, or for whom the processes of encoding of the patriarchy don't go right, are those who end up being assigned to the social control group known as sexual deviants; these are a social control group to the extent that they point out what the macho must be via a demonstration of stark oppositional differentiation. This is the case with the judge's male assistant: the degree to which he is less than outraged over Esmeralda's conduct and the degree to which he appears to identify with Esmeralda's sexual gaze are important indicators of his potential sexual deviance within the realm of the sober patriarchy that his supervisor struggles to maintain.

The second dimension of Esmeralda as a problematical heterosexual woman lies with her fully sexualized gaze. While it is true that, with the emergence of the modern urban woman of Mexico City, the woman now has considerable latitude as sexual instigator (see, below, my comments on *La tarea*) and while, moreover, it is true that Esmeralda is a practicing nurse for whom the male body holds, at least clinically, no secrets, that does not necessarily translate into the ability to pursue personal sexual *jouissance*. While Esmeralda's full sexual relations with her various husbands are alluded to in several moments in the film—the opening scene shows her displaying her nude body as she dresses to her teasingly almost nude husband after they have spent the night together—the definitive confirmation comes in a scene in which Solorio's accusations that she is an unrepentant tramp translate into a scene of table dancing in which Esmeralda explores, with her hands, her face, and her tongue, the body of a male member of this Mexican performing community, found as much in ladies-only venues as in gay male clubs. There are two delightful aspects of this scene. One is the complete involvement of Esmeralda in the exploration of the table dancer's body, front and back, top to bottom, and dimensions in between, such that her commitment to erotic fulfillment is left nowhere in doubt. The other involves the tracking, by the camera and through the camera by the spectator, of the gaze of the judge, stenographer, assistant, and bystanders as they collaborate with Esmeralda in the appreciation of the table dancer's body. In part, they appreciate Esmeralda's sexual involvement with the dancer; in part, they collaborate with Esmeralda in appreciating the dancer's body, and nowhere is the sexuality of Solorio's male assistant more ambiguous than at this moment.

The third dimension of the problematical nature of Esmeralda as a model of patriarchal heterosexuality comes with the fact that one of her husbands is, in the manner of the son in *Doña Herlinda,* also engaged in a matrimonial relationship with another man. When it is his turn to receive Esmeralda, we see that he and his partner live in conventional domestic bliss, that they have a lovely meal prepared for Esmeralda as though she were an honored guest rather than the "legal" wife of one of them, and that, when they all retire for the night, it is Esmeralda who goes off alone to get a good night's sleep, happy in the knowledge that the two men, as we see confirmed in a subsequent explicit scene, will make passionate love in the bedroom next door. This indiscriminate mixing, on Esmeralda's part, of gay and straight husbands is yet another occasion for Solorio's outrage, while providing yet another occasion for the spectator's critical assessment of the magnanimous nature of Esmeralda's matrimonial project.

The degree to which Esmeralda is generous with her affections is borne out in the relationship that evolves between her and Solorio, and this, perhaps more than anything else, will serve to model for the spectator the legitimacy of the beneficent effect of her pansexuality (also, it is noted that she marries one man on his deathbed as a favor to him). Solorio ends up so enamored of Esmeralda's person that he not only visits her in jail, but acquiesces in allowing for her various husbands to visit her, including the man who appears to be the first among equals, the opera singer Antonio Rossellini, played in a marvelous cameo appearance by Pedro Armendáriz Jr.—

this, incidentally, adds a tangential legitimacy to Hermosillo's image of pan-sexuality, since the Armendáriz film dynasty exemplifies the traditional image of the Mexican heterosexist macho. But even more, Solario undertakes to organize a picnic in the courtyard of the jail to celebrate Esmeralda's birthday, and all of her husbands, the court staff, and various peripheral characters of the film are invited to this celebratory event. Much more than a celebration of Esmeralda's birthday, it is a celebration of an extended human family united by their love and admiration for a woman whose spirit of giving through joyful sexuality is a model for those who are fortunate to become involved with her.

The confirmation of the effect that Esmeralda has on those around her is borne out by the final scene of the film. Esmeralda has teased out of Solorio the fact that he has always been dissatisfied with his inability to fully express himself in life, that he has always harbored the secret desire to be a dancer like Fred Astaire or Gene Kelly. At the end of the film, it begins to rain as Solorio leaves the jail after having paid a visit to Esmeralda. Casting his umbrella in the garbage, Solorio begins to dance to the music of the rain, and his routine of Mexico City in the rain bespeaks his conversion to Esmeralda's philosophy of life. Of course, the fact that she seems to have agreed to marry him when she gets out of jail is undoubtedly a stimulus to his joyful footwork; and this triumphant display of Esmeralda's success, once again, in queering the patriarchy hardly needs the spectator to recall that Solorio's mentor, Gene Kelly, was himself often gay-marked,[2] too gay to be contained by the sober conventionalism that Solorio has gone a long way toward shedding as he releases himself from the heteronormative law he is sworn to uphold.

It would be unfair to conclude without referring to an aspect of Hermosillo's film that is a brilliant added dimension of critical commentary, and this is the participation in the film by Tito Vasconcelos, the Mexico City drag artist who came to international attention for his role as a tutor in feminine sexual independence for María Rojo as Julia in María Novaro's 1991 film *Danzón*. Vasconcelos plays at least a half dozen bit parts in *De noche*, both as a man and as a woman. The crisscrossing of the film by his presence in these roles, a sort of presence where, obviously, Tito Vasconcelos is always playing Tito Vasconcelos playing a bit part, adds a vein of queerness to the film that is like a recurring underlying refrain in a complex piece of music. It is this sort of attention to cinematographic details—essentially visual ones, since Vasconcelos's characters mostly do not speak in the film,

FIGURE 17   The judge has his chance to dance in the rain.

except for one appearance, in which a militant neighborhood matriarch demanding justice is represented—that makes Hermosillo such an eloquent commentator on Mexican sociosexual ideologies.[3]

La tarea (The Assignment)

Jaime Humberto Hermosillo's *La tarea* (1990) is one of his most ingenious productions. Starring María Rojo, who has made numerous films with him, including the masterpiece *De noche vienes, Esmeralda* (1997), *La tarea* is a further experiment of Hermosillo's, but in a comedic vein, of the grotesque and black humor of *Intimidades de un cuarto de baño (Intimacies in a Bathroom)* (1989), in which a single fixed camera transcribes the microdramas of domestic life in contemporary Mexico City.

In *Intimidades*, the characters are unaware of the camera's presence, as it is positioned behind the vanity mirror over the wash basin in a lower-middle-class urban household. As one of the prime domestic sites for the fulfillment of human needs, needs as diverse as human functions, the cleansing of the body and the preparation of the public facade of the body, the bathroom is a synecdoche within a synecdoche: if the household is a synecdoche of the trivial humiliations of urban life, the bathroom is the site of the extreme limit to which those humiliations can be carried; and the bathroom becomes, literally, a dead-end for the Mexican urbanite who electrocutes himself or herself in the shower stall, which is yet a further spatial synecdoche in that it is where one sheds the grime of the city and, with any kind of fortune, its pressures and tensions. *Intimidades* is built around a particularly acute form of voyeurism, as the essential voyeurism of film is reduplicated, with all of the psychosexual overtones of the bathroom, in that domestic sphere in which the body is most intimately and privately in contact with itself. Indeed, many Mexican films have been made about the intimacy of the boudoir, but one is hard put to recall any antecedents to Hermosillo's privileging of the bathroom in this film.

The semiotic of voyeurism is considerably compounded, however, in *La tarea;* and, in fact, the film uses very much of an exercise in metafilmmaking while at the same time continuing the general interest of Hermosillo's films in questions of contemporary urban sexuality in Mexico. The proposition of the film is simple: Virginia (Rojo) is taking a film course, and her assignment is to make a short film in a video format. She decides to make an erotic film, and she invites her ex-lover, Marcelo (Alonso), to come by and see her. She has hidden a video camera in a strategic location in her small apartment, and when Marcelo arrives, in full business uniform, including a briefcase, she proceeds to seduce him. Along the way, Marcelo discovers the camera, but, already enticed by Virginia's passionate come-on, he decides to go through with the project to help her out with her assignment; it is also very clear that he is enchanted with performing erotically in front of the camera, with or without Virginia in the picture.

However, along the way, the spectator, who may have been relishing Virginia's cinematographic ingenuity and her presumably feigned sexual aggression (which itself is a sly comment on the way in which all female sexuality with a man may be a feigned performance) and who may have also been relishing the enthusiasm with which Marcelo is exposing himself to the camera (making this film the first instance of full frontal nudity in Mexican filmmaking outside of underground pornography), discovers that the whole thing has been a put-on: Virginia and Marcelo are really María and José, husband and wife, and the tape has been made in order to supplement the family income. As we learn this, they are joined by their children coming home from school and/or play, and the holy Mexican family, heterosexual, married, and with children, is joyfully assembled as the film closes.

There are a host of urban issues that Hermosillo raises in this film, beginning with the way in which Mexican filmmaking not only now privileges urban life, but has become a privileged cultural genre for exploring urban life (see the considerable success of urban domestic geometry at work in Antonio Serrano's 1999 *Sexo, pudor y lágrimas*). Some of these include (1) the role of filmmaking in recording urban life and in providing a particularly urban interpretation of national life; (2) women as cultural producers; (3) the affirmation in modern Mexico City of the role of women as sexual agents; (4) the reconfiguration of male sexuality vis-à-vis women; (5) the reconfiguration of male sexuality as display; (6) the commercialization of sexuality; and (7) the blurring of the boundaries between sexual life as private intimacy and sexual life as display. I do not propose to treat all of these issues in detail or in turn, but they are significant aspects of the originality of *La tarea* and will guide the following discussion.

The particular genius of Hermosillo's filmmaking has more to it than simply the willingness to take on these issues that for many might be considered taboo or scandalous, such as gay male sexuality quite graphically depicted, as in *Doña Herlinda y su hijo;* the collapse of the myth of macho superiority and the suicide (still very much of a taboo in traditionally Catholic Mexican society, and illegal to boot) that results from the humiliation of confronting that collapse, as in the aforementioned *Intimidades;* or the insouciant polyandry whose depiction results in perhaps the most sexually queer film made to date in Latin America, *De noche vienes, Esmeralda.* Hermosillo has always enhanced his examination of the taboo by upping the ante of what many view as intrinsically scandalous by embedding it in or framing it with what is additionally scandalous. Thus, in *Intimidades* it is the wife of the failed macho who articulates, as a woman in charge of her life, the litany of the manly qualities necessary for survival in the jungle of urban life. In *Doña Herlinda,* what is at issue is not only the romantic involvement between two men, but the fact that one of them is married and that his wife is aware of his other erotic needs and is complicitous with them and that his well-to-do mother enthusiastically provides an alternative universe, in the context of Mexico's most traditionally Catholic city, Guadalajara, for them all—including the child that is born of one half of her son's erotic life—where they can live happily ever after together. In *De noche,* not only is Esmeralda married to five or six men at the same time, but one of her husbands is also, with Esmeralda's full knowledge and support, living sexually with another man, and Esmeralda sees nothing the matter with either this or any of her other erotic commitments—and, moreover, she is able to convince the dour judge, who wishes to try her for bigamy, of the virtue of such an arrangement, with the implication that he may well become the sixth of her husbands.

In *La tarea* what Hermosillo provides for the enhancement of the scandalous concerns the display of the male body. It has long been a principle of, at least, the feminist analysis of film that not only does film constitute a form of voyeurism in which women and women's bodies are the objects of scopic fixation (itself, certainly, a primary feminist postulate), but film imposes on the female spectator a male gaze that obliges her to be complicitous with the paradigmatic male gaze that is the very constitution of film viewing. Film is constituted by the male gaze to the extent that it is—especially in its Hollywood and commercial institutionalization, but also in the vast majority of so-called independent art films—a reinscription of the patriarchal interpretation of society in both its overwhelming sexism and its imposition and naturalization of compulsory heterosexuality. Such an imposition and naturalization is so monumental as to make it virtually impossible for the viewer, whether female or male and whether homosexual or of any other subaltern gender/sexuality not encompassed by and resolutely excluded by patriarchal heteronormativity, to entertain the possibility that things could be other than as they are depicted so hegemonically by film.

It is his forms of alternative configuration that make Hermosillo's interpretation of the issues he raises so interesting, and it is difficult to know, in the case of *La tarea,* if it is the audacity of the film student, Virginia, the complicity of the husband, José (as Virginia's ex-lover Marcelo), or the pornographic enterprise of José and his wife, María, that stands as the most outrageous proposition of the film.

Although María Rojo is undoubtedly the star of *La tarea,* as one of Mexico's most widely utilized film stars in the past two decades, it is difficult to underestimate the role played by José Alonso as Marcelo/José. Alonso enacts a quintessential macho businessman, as we see him as Marcelo and before we know that he is also José. Marcelo and Virginia have been lovers. Although their relationship has cooled, it is Virginia's clever idea to invite him back to her apartment and to have sex with him, but less because she wishes to reinitiate a relationship with him than because she wishes for him to be the unknowing star of the video she is about to make as a class project. It is never clear why Virginia thinks of Marcelo, whether it is a pretext to reinaugurate a relationship with him, whether it is a form of retaliation against him for whatever went wrong with their affair (that is, through the humiliation of finding out that she tricked him into performing for a secret camera), or whether, of all her boyfriends, she judged his body to be the most photogenic—which, given the general Mexican phobia about the display of the straight male Mexican body, beyond certain stereotyped parameters, constitutes another dimension of possible humiliation.

Alonso's body is well worth placing in the line of scopic vision, and in this regard Hermosillo reduplicates, presumably for critical purposes but also without suppressing its voyeuristic potential, the sort of gaze of the macho normally reserved for viewing women's bodies. Dressed as a conventional Mexican mid-level bureaucrat, he is pleasing enough. He has a degree of measured urbane masculinity that constitutes virtually a ground zero of compulsory heterosexuality, and it is as though Hermosillo cast him to represent a sort of thoroughly male urban Everyman, a figure of the translation of the ideals of Mexican manhood into the workaday business and commercial setting of the contemporary Mexican capital. The examination of varieties of Mexican masculinity in film has yet to be executed: part of the effect of the hegemony of compulsory heterosexuality in all filmmaking is to assume that there is little notable to be said about the straight male and that the male is only of particular interest for scrutiny, whether as the object of film discourse or the object of the critical analysis of that discourse, when he becomes problematical—that is, feminized, as the failed male segueing into being the queer male (on this topic in film, see Lehman). The sheer "normalcy" of Alonso's character, bemused at the pleasant surprise of having been invited back into Virginia's apartment (his masculinity surely must have been perceived to be irresistible after all), probably makes some spectators feel sorry for the way in which the "devious," and apparently rather scatterbrained, Virginia is about to trick him.

Yet spectators must never forget that they are viewing a film by Mexico's great gay filmmaker, and Hermosillo is not about to miss the chance to introduce an element of queering of the social structure into his film. This comes in four stages. The first involves Virginia's decision to make a secret video with her former lover. The degree to which the modern Mexico City woman is able to assume sexual agency may be highly problematical in terms of a feminist political agenda, but there is no question that it is very much a part of the order of the day in a society that has long been viewed as involved in an intractable subordination of women and the erasure of their overall social agency, including the negation of sexuality in any and all forms and its displacement into a desexualized, compulsory maternity that is the alleged natural destiny of women. This is not the place to attempt to review the historical facts of this negation of female sexuality in Mexico, nor to chart the factors that may be contributing to its substantial disappearance. There are unquestionably, at least from the point of view of the film record, significant images of the wages of sexual sin and the virtues of Marian chastity, that is understood not necessarily as virginity but as compliance with the reproductive imperative but without sexual fulfillment or as unerotic reproductive compliance as itself the full measure of sexual fulfillment: ironically for Mexican film history, La Doña, María Félix, the grande dame for almost fifty years of that history, did a splendid job in both of these paradigmatic roles (e.g., the virginal schoolmistress in *Río Escondido* [1948] and the courtesan in *La mujer de todas* [1946] or *Doña Diabla* [1950]).

Whatever the exact historical circumstances and social changes at work, the modern Mexico City woman, at least the one involved in the professions and in middle-class life in general, has achieved a level of social agency that is in marked contrast to the role of women as portrayed throughout Mexican filmmaking. Recent films like Alberto Issac's *Mujeres insumisas* (1995), Alfonso Cuarón's *Sólo con tu pareja* (1991), Sabina Berman and Isabelle Tardán's *Entre Pancho Villa y una mujer desnuda* (1995), and, once again, Hermosillo's *De noche vienes, Esmeralda* are part of an impressive inventory showing new directions for women's lives in Mexico. It was only in 1979 that Hermosillo made *María de mi corazón,* starring María Rojo and with José Alonso also, in which the protagonist is locked away in an insane asylum as the inevitable consequence of her nature as a strong and ingenious woman. *María de mi corazón* was something of a cult film in the early 1980s, when the emphasis continued to fall on the woman as victim, and it is significant that María Rojo was very soon after making films in which the woman is the protagonist of her own destiny, with or without men crying crocodile tears over having become the victims of feminist independence. Precisely, one of the secondarily scandalous dimensions of *De noche vienes, Esmeralda* is that is shows, in the person of the dour judge, how a woman's independence is also a man's independence from repression and stifling social convention.

Thus, when Virginia undertakes to make a video that will turn on the woman's seduction of a man; when that man is her former lover who has, with the pride of the beckoned macho, accepted her invitation to come over and see her again, an invitation that is inevitably also necessarily a sexual one; when she undertakes to seduce him in front of a hidden camera and to oblige him to display his masculine nudity to that camera, Hermosillo is successively taking female sexual agency farther and farther away from the model of passive, discreet, and chaste femininity, a model that women are, at least, expected to wear as their daily social mask.

There is a corollary that needs to be mentioned here; it provides an added resonance to the queerness of this situation when viewed from the position of conventional Mexican heterosexuality, and that is how Virginia and the audience simply take for granted her nudity and her participation in erotic display. That is what women have always done in film, no matter what the degree of limitations on explicit and graphic portrayal may have been. Whether it is the glimpse of a woman's stocking or the scopic convergence on the genitalia, women's bodies have been the center of heterosexual love-making as portrayed historically in film. That Virginia will undress and that she will be seen to be fully engaging in sex is simply the current explicitness of filmmaking, even in formerly very circumspect Mexico. But the presumption very much remains unquestionably that her body and its sexual history will dominate the film.

Indeed, the fact that she is the seductress, and the trickster, has little to contribute to modifying the assumption that when women become sexually aggressive, they will act as perfidious predators, but that only serves to lock the camera even more on the behavior of their bodies. If there is any queerness about this, it must come in the way in which the spectator is able to hold onto the idea that this is an Hermosillo film and, thus, the conventions of heterosexist filmmaking are hardly going to get rehearsed without something really scandalous happening.

That something scandalous comes with Marcelo's discovery of the hidden camera. One would assume that Marcelo would be outraged to discover that he has been invited back to Virginia's apartment to be used as part of a class project without his knowledge or consent, and even more so when he discovers that he is to be filmed in intimate situations with her. Of course, he is, but not for very long. Indeed, he is rather intrigued with the idea, and his transition to willing appreciation dispenses rather quickly with various subcategories of the Mexican macho version of the code of compulsory heterosexuality: the love tryst has been arranged by the woman, not by the man; the woman has staged an erotic performance without his permission (of course, men are tricked all the time by sexually aggressive women, but then they are not the sort of women with whom self-respecting machos involve themselves for long); and, moreover, that staging is being videotaped, an indirect violation of the prohibition against the display of masculine eroticism beyond the narrow range of permissible visual fetishes. However, at least one can say that Marcelo is being a good sport about it all and that his benevolence toward Virginia, while perhaps demonstrating a lapse on the part of the rigorously self-controlled macho, does indicate some measure of residual affection toward her as a person.

However, where the film begins to become particularly interesting—that is, where it begins to become exceptionally queer—is in the enthusiasm with which Marcelo assumes his part in Virginia's staged filming. Not only does Marcelo agree to strip (Alonso's body is quite nice, confirming the judiciousness of Virginia's presumed selection of Marcelo to star in her film project), but he undertakes to perform willingly for the camera. There are three violations of the taboo of the macho involved at this point, underscoring the queerness implicit in Marcelo's performance. Note that this antiheteronormative queerness is present, even though his performance is ostensibly before and for a woman with whom he will later have heterosexual sex. The first involves his willingness to display frontally his body for the camera. Alonso/Marcelo is very nicely endowed, so there is no reason for there to be any reticence in this regard. Yet this sort of display—and it is significant that Virginia is not present either to view, as does the camera, Marcelo's endowments or to admire them—is associated with gay porn, not with either conventional filmmaking or straight porn. While in conventional filmmaking there may be fleeting glimpses of male nudity, for reasons of "authenticity," one assumes, male nudity is not usually displayed unless either there is a homoerotic point being made or the still relatively taboo matter of the female gaze on the nude male body is under examination (as in the coy scene, in María Novaro's 1991 *Danzón,* in which the mature Julia, played by the omnipresent María Rojo, admires the partially nude body of her young lover); in straight porn, by contrast, all of the attention rests, of course, on the female body(ies) of the actress(es), although the male body may also be always phallocentrically in evidence. As is well known there is, statistically speaking, scant Chip 'n' Dale porn available for women, by contrast. To the extent that the female gaze is excluded from gay porn (less because of the matter of the display of the male body than because of the way in which erotic fetishes are handled, fetishes that may be significantly different for the male gazing homoerotically on the male body versus the female gazing heterosexually on the male body), the pose is simply quite different, which is why it is significant that Virginia is excluded from the scene in which Marcelo freezes in the display of his genitalia before the no longer hidden camera.[4] The principal point, however, is not that Hermosillo is repeating the reifying formulas of (gay) porn, although the scene works in part because of them and the way in which he can count on the audience's familiarity with them. Rather, the point is that this scene—and the so-called real-life setup it involves—is the opportunity for Marcelo to free himself from bourgeois, heterosexist taboos regarding the display of the male body;

concomitantly, it involves asking the audience to accept the legitimacy of this opportunity, especially when it involves a significant deviation from a Mexican–Latin American standard of proper masculine appearances. The fact that the film narrative will depart from such a criterion of appearances explains in part why Marcelo shows up in sober, picture-book business attire.

The next way in which Marcelo's display is queer confirms the difference between male display for a homoerotic male gaze and male display for a heterosexual female gaze: Marcelo turns halfway around and wiggles his nicely shaped derriere at the camera. The male posterior is symbolically, if not always really, the site of male homoeroticism as much as it is also of considerable fetishistic value for women in Mexican and other Latin American societies.[5] But the wiggle is paradigmatically a sexual come-on, and Marcelo's cheerful performance before the camera is, from the point of view of sober Mexican machismo, nothing short of outrageous. Marcelo's offering of his posterior might be taken as the site of his own homoerotic desire, and it is, thus, a scandalous display—or, at least, it was for a Mexican film made in the early 1990s. It is less scandalous today because of the enormous growth of the public sex industry in Mexico in the last decade, including what is available for women. The fact that Marcelo may undertake this performance in jest only makes it ambiguous, but no less suggestive: Marcelo may not be coming on to the male viewer, but Hermosillo cannot have helped but know that the straight male viewer would be shocked while the female or nonstraight male viewer would be bemused, interested, and perhaps even intrigued. The scene lasts but a few seconds, but it is an unabashed display that reminds us that this is, after all, an Hermosillo film, and that no viewer should be surprised at the disruption of heterosexist codes, no matter how briefly entertained.

Finally, Marcelo, in agreeing to perform in Virginia's film, proceeds to engage in sex with her. This rather long sequence, in which they make love in a hammock, with various contortions and changes of position, violates the conventions of straight filmmaking because the camera does not focus only on the body of the woman, much less on the conventionalized synecdoche of her face showing the transports of erotic pleasure in the hands of the expert macho performer. Quite the contrary: since the camera is fixed and the two adjourn to a space behind a sliding screen where the hammock is hung, we see the two bodies from a distance and barely see their faces. What we see instead is the full engagement of their bodies in the sexual act, including the acrobatics of the nude male body. Again, this is a display that is totally disconsonant with the decorum of a conventionally straight Mexican male sexuality.

Finally, Hermosillo engages our interest in the rupture of heterosexist conventions by the surprise ending of the film. After making love, Marcelo and Virginia, now dressed, sit down in front of the camera—is it still the video camera, or is it Hermosillo's camera? Although the framing is the same, it is not quite clear which camera is involved. All of a sudden, it emerges that Virginia and Marcelo are really María and José, a married couple who have made the video as a soft porn project to supplement their flagging domestic budget. That María appears to have been the instigator of this clever sideline is an ironic allusion to the resourcefulness of the modern urban woman who is also a resourceful instigator of sexual activity.

Although Hermosillo has played with the homosexual dimensions of Alonso's character in his willingness to perform, in his display of his nude body, and in his explicit evocation of gay sexuality, the film becomes queer on another level, that of the reconfiguration of the sacred Mexican family. While, on the one hand, the fact that it is a conventional family unit is underscored by the appearance of their two children (one boy and one girl, of course: the sexual binary must be preserved), the fact that their sex is not only not for the customarily sanctified procreational purpose, but for purposes of commercial pornography in order to save the family budget (this is, in the final analysis, the principal task—*la tarea*—to be performed) points toward a legitimation of a relationship between men and women as socially constituted couples, a legitimation that is hardly contemplated by the hegemonic patriarchy.

Hermosillo makes his point about the reconstitution of urban sexual politics, a point to the effect that traditional concepts of the relationships between men and women and the use of the body in these relationships make little sense in the urban reality that is contemporary Mexico City, through the device of three levels of filmmaking. In so doing, he is holding these relationships up for an analytical scrutiny that would not be possible within the naturalized realism of commercial filmmaking, where the camera is, rather than a lens for social commentary, a disappearing narrative framing that will always strive to give uncritical spectators the impression that they are seeing life in the process of being lived. The sort of analytical perspectives that Hermosillo achieves with his manipulation of the camera in order to promote a complex metacommentary about lived social experience must necessarily aggressively shatter the naturalized optics of the commercial product, and this he does via the process of reduplication that is so particularly evident in *La tarea*.

There are three levels of filmmaking in *La tarea*, and they do not easily nest themselves like Chinese boxes—that is, it is not merely a question of a film within a film within a film. Rather, juxtaposition rather than symmetrical nesting abets the need to examine the various levels in a critical fashion. Hermosillo's film, to be sure, constitutes an overall frame, and its development moves from the clever urban farce, the comedy of manners of the complex ways men and women get together and carry out relationships within the multiple, competing demands of life in the big city (there are thousands of American films in this category and probably hundreds of Mexican versions of them), to the scandalous proposition of engaging in soft porn as just one more way to make ends meet in the consumerist vortex of modern urban life. One survives as a producer by offering a consumer product (and pornography, like everything else in capitalism, becomes legitimate when it becomes a viable consumer product).

The second level of filmmaking is Virginia's class project, and as I have already stated, this is interesting, not only as a reference to film as a modern form of cultural production and one that now predominately takes place in the city and refers to urban life, but as, in many ways, an example of female initiative: the woman as student and cultural producer, the woman as active in the romantic relationship with a man, the woman as sexual agent, and the woman as socially independent, in the sense that she only feels the need to provide Marcelo with explanations when he discovers her trick. The fact that the film on this level detours into an intriguing performance by Marcelo is only incidental. Nevertheless, it does serve to suggest that, if Virginia is a thoroughly modern and liberated Mexico City woman, Marcelo has little need to continue as the sober Mexican macho, and he thus may entertain himself with a bit of questionably charged tease in front of the privileged eye of the camera arranged by this woman.

The third level of filmmaking is not within the second one and does not contain the second one. Rather, it is juxtaposed to it as a commentary in such a way that it both continues the second one and completes the first one, which is one way of understanding the ambiguity of whether the two protagonists are performing for Virginia's camera, for Hermosillo's camera, or for both at the same time. And this, in turn, leaves open the possibility of a fourth sort of receding-mirrors possibility: Virginia's film, with the cooperation of Marcelo, is about a married couple, María and José, who pretend to be a married couple making a soft porn video starring Virginia and her ex-lover Marcelo.

Where all of this constitutes a form of exceedingly self-reflective commentary on contemporary urban society in Mexico is in the way in which it opens up the social text to scrutiny on all sorts of grounds. No longer are the social roles promoted by patriarchal heteronormativity maintained, but they are subject to unstable alternative interpretations. It may be one thing for social roles to change—women may become more independent, men less macho—without disrupting patriarchal structures in any meaningful way; but what is disruptive is a circumstance in which assigned roles of instigator and recipient can no longer be sorted out in a way that maintains a distinction between them. It is this sort of disruption for which the queer aims, and if the queer is a fundamental ingredient of (post)modern urban culture, then it becomes the site or the practice whereby the urban culture critically reinvents itself in ways that challenge unexpected givens. The interchangeability between Virginia-María's and Marcelo-José's roles—or perhaps, between María-Virginia's and José-Marcelo's roles—and the way in which that interchangeability allows for the display of the nude male body, including a taboo-breaking suggestive display by the second partner in this pair, is proposed here to be an inevitable component of the queering made possible by the sort of contemporary Mexico City experience Hermosillo is interested in holding up for analysis in *La tarea*.

Lola

It is probably ill-advised to attempt to establish a hierarchy of which social groups are most disadvantaged by the many difficulties that plague cities in general and a Latin American megalopolis like Mexico City specifically. However, in terms of the specific demographics of the Mexican capital, single women must surely rank as particularly poorly situated since they are not able to attain much more than a wretched level of subsistence and, in many cases, not even that (see Sippl for an excellent analysis of *Lola*, in the context of filmmaking by women in Mexico and of the youth culture the film represents, as marked by a feminine inflection). Such women are drawn from many sources within Mexican society: middle-class women like the protagonist of María Novaro's *Lola*, who have descended in terms of their possibility for survival as a consequence of having become unwed mothers or, in a parallel circumstance, of ending up on their own without having secured any viable livelihood; women who have been left alone because of the violence of the city or because harsh economic realities have forced their husbands to emigrate to the United States in the hope that they will be able to either send for their family or, at least, send money to them; provincial women who are forced into the city because of their pregnancy or because there is simply not the possibility of feeding another mouth back in the countryside; or the women drawn from the city's vast lumpenproletariat whose own mothers or grandmothers may have come to the city decades ago in circumstances such as those described. For these women, there is some domestic service and similar menial employment; there is some factory work; there is street hawking; and, for those who cannot make it in these sectors, there is prostitution, which involves its own hierarchy of circumstances and opportunities.

However, the simple fact is that, it is difficult to envision for any of the women trapped in the lower depths of the Mexico City economic structure any measure of success and fulfillment; and the cultural production, in a wide array of narrative genres, returns again and again to this virtually inescapable reality. The theme of the lonely female prostitute, consumed by the urban monster, thanks to the abuse of her clients and her pimp, drugs, alcohol, and disease, is a staple of Western cultural production. One of the paradigmatic Mexican film texts on the theme of urban prostitution is Emilio Fernández's 1949 *Salón México;* reference might also be made to the various versions of Federico Gamboa's classic novel of prostitution, *Santa* (1903), including an early silent version by Luis Pereda in 1913 and Antonio Moreno's 1932 version, the first talky made in Mexico (see Gustavo García's essay on these films, "Melodrama: The Passion Machine," 153–162).

Lola (released in 1991) is of a whole with Novaro's other films in the sense that one of the interests of her production has been the lot of single women in Mexico City. In the case of *Danzón,* she deals with a lower-middle-class single mother whose steady employment allows her a certain measure of self-fulfillment, which she expresses in terms of the danzón. As I have underscored in my analysis of that film elsewhere in this study, danzón provides Julia with a basis of identification with Mexican culture and an anchor for her city life, which centers on the legendary danzón halls where she passes what she feels are the best and most meaningful hours of her life. *Lola,* however (like *El jardín de Edén [The Garden of Eden]* [1994]), deals with women—the former in Mexico City, the latter in the border megacity of Tijuana—whose roots may be with the lower middle class but whose circumstances have thrust them into the waters of bare-bones economic survival (Lola herself is from more of a middle-class family, although the point of the film turns in part on her descent into the casual labor class). In all three films, a single mother is involved, and in the two films since *Danzón,* marginality becomes the inevitable lot of these women, with the protagonist of *Lola* eventually ending up in compromising sexual situations, not so much because it is a more promising option for livelihood, but because it is all part of the life she has chosen to live.

The life Lola has chosen can hardly be characterized as anything other than that of a vagrant mother. Although she comes from what is apparently a modestly middle-class background, her relationship with a rock singer results in a child that she ends up raising alone. Eschewing any other form of employment that might be available to her, she becomes a street vendor and moves with a group of friends whose lives are best characterized as aimless. Lola, thus, represents an example of alienated urban youth, someone who is lost in the city and society not because of economic hardship but because of having no real purpose in life, no real sense of responsibility toward the decisions she makes, which include having a child to whom she pays minimal attention and to whom she provides decidedly precarious mothering: she leaves her alone, does not keep her or her clothes tidy, does not supervise her television, dumps her at her mother's when she gets tired of her, feeds her poorly (at one point, she has her drinking her beer), and in general treats her as a nuisance.

Lola more or less earns her living by working an open-air clothes stand where goods are sold on consignment. Street hawking, which is driven in large measure by the possibility of selling in mass at cut-rate prices, depends on the easy availability of goods, the chance that they are not available in other market venues (at least not for the same "reasonable" prices), and the likelihood that they continue to appeal to an urban market that wishes to consume, as best it can, such items, characteristically of inferior quality and shoddy manufacture. All of these are notably iffy propositions, and a street hawker like Lola is only one of thousands distributed among dozens, perhaps hundreds, of informal (i.e., unsanctioned) retail venues in the streets of major cities like Mexico and major provincial capitals like Guadalajara or Monterrey, with the result that the ability to procure the desired merchandise and to move it in a profitable fashion are often mere subcapitalist illusions for a vendor who has little overall understanding, by definition, of the functioning of urban retail economics.

Mexico City, thus, becomes overall, if only sporadically, the specific venue of the transactions of *la falluca*. The vast urban landscape is reinterpreted in terms of a crowded back street, or busy street (as is the case in the central core) perpendicular to a major thoroughfare, an eloquent index of the intensity of commercial traffic in a city in which the basic needs of millions must be met. Contrary to the image of major commercial installations, those that might provide a city as dynamic as the Mexican capital with pace-setting innovations, whether national or foreign or national interpretations of the foreign, the documentary substance of a film like *Lola* reduces the city to the narrow and cheap confines of the dimensions in which it is lived, not by its privileged glitterati, who are so prevalent in certain cultural products of the city, such as glossy magazines, television, and tourist-hungry guidebooks, but by women, their husbands/partners/lovers and their children, for whom the megalopolis poses a question of survival rather than the superavit of luxury and self-indulgence.

Lola provides little space for any urban reality other than the barest level of survival, whether that survival is defined primarily in terms of material comfort or spiritual transcendence. While it is true that Lola's mother is there in the background as a spokesperson for a certain level of bourgeois decency and respectability from which she is convinced that her daughter has deviated in her pursuit of a love affair with a national rock star, the film makes it clear both that that mother has nothing to do with the space in which Lola and her daughter (who is about seven or eight years old) find themselves and that her norms of bourgeois affirmation are alien to the world in which Lola and her daughter find themselves. In fact, it is quite clear that Lola is out on her own as a form of rebellion against her mother's bourgeois values and that her life is an attempt to have a good time outside the confines of those values and, most certainly, to discover, no matter how haltingly, a new set of values—which, in fact, she does by the end of the film.

There is much that can be said for and about the contours of that world. In the first place, the father of Lola's daughter is an aspiring rock star, and he chooses to abandon them for opportunities in the United States. This is not particularly surprising, given the possibilities of success within the parameters of cultural production in Mexico. However, it is used in the film to suggest the degree to which it is inevitable that Lola will be abandoned by the father of her child, by the man for whom she left a seemingly secure bourgeois home to insert herself into the dead-end opportunities for women to survive in Mexico City. In this case, it may be Mexico City at the end of the twentieth century, but a minimum of sociohistorical reflection will inevitably lead to the conclusion that Novaro is not describing contemporary urban demographics, but rather only a contemporary version of an abiding dynamic of Mexico City life, that of women who have, whether by design or by bad fortune, ended up on their own.

It is significant to note that Novaro's *Lola*, by contrast with a film like *Danzón,* is both essentially static and centerless. These are relative and impressionistic terms, so I would like to emphasize that what they place is a characterization of the film under consideration. Static refers to the absence of significant narrative development, in the sense that we attribute to narrative texts like film, the novel, or soap opera (to name only a few of the genres involved in narrative) a series of plot changes that demonstrably follow one from another in a conventionally agreed-upon framework of narrative exposition. Such narratives—and soap opera is particularly effective in meeting this challenge—seek dramatic reversals of fortune, along with equally dramatic rectifications of the plot drift, in terms of the institution of an acceptably positive denouement: the fabled happy ending that validates and legitimizes one category of narratives. Such validation and legitimation confirm the belief that social processes are not implacable, that the will of the individual must count for something, and that, in equal measure, "things are not as bad as they seem" and "there is a silver lining in every cloud."

Soap opera would be nothing if it were not for the grossly dramatic inversions and reversals that move the spectator from one episode to another, along with the equally dramatic rectifications of those inversions and reversals, rectifications that serve to reestablish the hegemonic ideology of the patriarchy that underwrites, on television and in barely transparent film productions, the most immediately consumed forms of cultural production. That such a production is classist, racist, heterosexist, and exclusively metropolitan is beyond question. That it is capable of closing off contestable cultural analysis, such that there can be no interpretation of human commerce other than the one pursued with intently superficial overdetermination, is perhaps less taken for granted, in view of an ethos that would promote the consumption of soap opera as a thin, but nevertheless essentially accurate, representation of a dominant lifestyle in the urban centers of the country.

This is not the place to engage in a microscopic analysis of the assumptions and presumptions of Mexican soap opera, nor of the degree to which specific texts engage in strategies that foreclose any interpretation of the assumptions of patriarchal and classist Mexico or promote an image of urban Mexican life that is fundamentally duplicitous as regards the majority of the population—if they are at all accurate in depicting the life of any independently verifiable social sector of the city (one wonders about the extent to which it benefits the super-rich to be misrepresented in such cultural productions, in order to effectively mystify the real dimensions of the privilege and power they exercise). Suffice it to propose that a film such as *Lola* derives its narrative effect from being a counter–soap opera, in the sense that the dimensions of Mexico City life represented both deny the transcendent signifiers of success against all social and economic obstacles, signifiers that make soap opera a false, disingenuous antidote to the harsh realities of urban life, and at the same time confirm an inevitable, implacable structure of denouement—the inevitable fall of the protagonist into, if not outright prostitution, then sexual abuse and exploitation (a signifier that itself remains essentially unanalyzed in the film)—that can in no way count on the sponsorship of the commercial interests of a sanitized metropolitan history: who would, after all, sponsor a soap opera (or a film built on the conventions of soap opera) that denied the promise of urban life that sponsors are specifically devoted to defending in order to sell their products?

In the end, what is static is not a filmic representation like *Lola,* but rather its intertext, a given interpretation of sociohistoric reality that demands/commands the existence of an immutably "positive" social reality, a contradiction of which is what stakes out the claim for the efficacy of Novaro's film. The inevitable near disintegration of Lola's life, therefore, is mostly a lamentable circumstance of her bad choices in her life and her rejection of the specific set of bourgeois values held by her mother. She has, perhaps unwittingly, opted for an urban dynamic that has multiple dimensions but unitary consequences: how else can the social record show women like Lola in the end?

The way in which *Lola* is, therefore, centerless does not have to do with any diminution in the central role played by the protagonist identified as Lola. Rather it signifies the multiply overdetermined ways in which Lola's life experiences are tokens for those of other women of her class: Lola's story is hardly unique and cannot therefore constitute the center of a putatively bourgeois cultural production like an art film. Aside from the way in which Lola's drearily paradigmatic story is a center for the film that confirms the way in which it is not a unique story but rather that of thousands and thousands of women caught up in the marginal economy of urban Mexico City, *Lola* can do little more than reiterate the details of that paradigmatic story: to do otherwise would be to singularize Lola's story in such a way that would invalidate the slice of urban reality being portrayed by the film.

To this extent, then, *Lola* is an ironic title for the film because the singularity of her name (no matter how resonant with the meaning of the more formal name Dolores) lies in the way in which it is hardly singular but rather points inevitably to how the actress is called upon to erase any singularity of character within the millions and millions of common fatalities of urban life.

This does not mean to say that *Lola* is lacking in discernible narrative texture. Although cast very much in a lento mode, the film explores Lola's relationship with her daughter, Ana: her inability to make ends meet and to provide her daughter with the sort of food a young Mexican child wants to eat (i.e., the low-quality food, often of American origin, pushed by television and billboard advertising) and her inability to provide her daughter with the sort of attention she feels she owes her as her only available parent (Ana expresses her anger at her absent father). Although mother and daughter have a loving relationship, Lola is much preoccupied with her economic situation, and her feelings of inadequacy and guilt are only intensified when she asks her mother (herself a woman on her own) to care for Ana, which in turn only makes Ana, despite the loving relationship she has with her grandmother, feel all the more abandoned. In the final analysis, these sequences of the film focus on the breakdown of a relationship of interpersonal, intergenerational affection viewed from one particular perspective of matriarchal feminism: the purported natural link between biological mothers and their children, particularly their daughters.

This, in turn, leaves the spectator to wonder what sort of adult Ana will become and what sort of mother she will turn out to be. In this context, Lola's forays into sexual adventure are grimly portrayed. As a young and attractive woman on her own, Lola is prey to a series of advances from the men with whom she works; and, at one point, when a group of them decide to drive off on a spree to Veracruz after their street fair has been closed down by the police, she knocks one man who has been persistent in pursuing her unconscious with a tequila bottle as an emphatic reinforcement of her unheeded rejection of his sexual advances. However, this rejection is hardly a consequence of Lola's interest in remaining faithful to her absent lover or to a criterion of sexual abstinence. Rather, it is the rejection of the availability to her of sex as the basis of any and every interpersonal relationship and perhaps even as a means of economic survival.

Thus, the grimmest scene in the film is when Lola and her daughter, Ana, are in the supermarket (itself an icon of a level of economic potential well outside of Lola's reach). When her daughter orders her to replace the conventional Mexican glass jar of honey for an American-style plastic bottle, in the form of a bear, because it is unbreakable, Lola slips the product into her purse, after apparently checking the prices and seeing that the latter packaging is far more expensive. This act of theft is observed by a store employee, and Lola and her daughter are hauled before the store manager: they lay out on his desk their respective shoplifted articles, all nonbasic foodstuffs that seem to underscore Lola's desire to provide her daughter with heavily advertised American-style candies and the like. When the store manager suggests to her that she is setting a bad example for her daughter, Lola in turn makes it clear to him that she is willing to trade her body for the merchandise. The following sequence involves cuts between the garage where Lola and the store manager are having sex and Ana sitting in front of a television eating candy and drinking artificially flavored soda pop.

Lola returns one night after an all-night adventure (it would seem with the store manager) and is accosted on the stairs of her apartment building by the man whom she will later bludgeon for his insistent advances, only to find that her daughter, who has spent the night on her own, has made a mess in the apartment, including leaving on a burner on the stove. In a fit of guilt, Lola carries her daughter in her arms across what seems to be a significant distance in the city to her mother's and asks her to take care of the little girl.

All of this constitutes less of a carefully interlocking narrative, as was the case in the fast-paced *Danzón,* and ends up being more of an impressionistic mosaic of the precarious circumstances and the ensuing despair of Lola over the aimlessness of her life. Although this mosaic is of importance in providing an account of the sort of life led in the city by probably millions of young women like Lola (that number may seem high, but the point of Novaro's film is to imply that Lola is only a token for a vast social reality), what is of collateral importance in the film is the itinerary of the city that emerges alongside Lola's story. Lola lives in a fairly common type of lower-middle-class apartment building in an area of the city close to the international airport (east northeast of the downtown). Her apartment building is not a slum, but it is bare bones in the amenities it provides, and it serves as a point of reference for the surrounding neighborhood, characterized by unfinished buildings, buildings damaged by wear or perhaps by the recurring earthquakes of the city (these cheaply built and poorly maintained concrete structures are particularly susceptible to the constant seismological activity of the central Mexican valley), or buildings that have fallen into one degree or another of decay and abandonment. We see rooftop areas for hanging clothing and for providing a sort of common outdoor patio, graced by a rusty set of swings for the children and mural of the 1985 earthquake painted by children (made in 1989, the film has constant allusions, perhaps meant to be taken ironically, to the 1985 earthquake, especially the government slogan seen throughout the film, "México sigue en pie").[6] We see rundown inner courtyards that constitute the ground zero of domestic space for the hundreds and hundreds of thousands of dwellings that make up housing in the city. We see buildings where shared common spaces such as stairwells be-

FIGURE 18   Lola carries her daughter through the early-morning streets of Mexico City.

come the meeting space in which forms of social life are negotiated, such as
an elaborate game of sexual seduction witnessed with disdain by Lola's
mother when she goes to visit her daughter. Actually, the scene is not without its charm, as it involves a very plain and fleshy middle-aged woman suc-
cumbing to the advances of a graying Lothario, decked out in the trappings
of the Mexican macho. This is the only scene of touching sexual seduction
in the film, and Lola's mother's disdain is more a rejection of the living space
her daughter has chosen to inhabit than a repudiation of sexuality as such
(notwithstanding the possibility of her classism being tinged with the older
person's jaded view of the game of romantic seduction).

   If the scene in the store manager's office is crucial to establishing the
humiliation of Lola at the hands of an economic system that ensures her misery and, therefore, her exploitation, the sequence in which she carries her
daughter in her arms to her mother's is equally eloquent. It is a veritable
Odyssey across the cityscape of the federal district in the weak morning
light. Lola traverses streets that seem endless, given the weight of her daughter and the duffel bag containing her clothes, as she passes before residential installations, a taxi stand, storefronts, abandoned buildings—in short,

an anthology of the drab landscape of the city. By choosing to evoke so insistently the shabbiness of lower-middle-class Mexico City neighborhoods (as opposed to what are directly identifiable as the slums of the city), Novaro provides an extensive objective correlative of the dead-end despair that can never be anything other than Lola's lot in the city.

When the street-vending installations of Lola and her friends are attacked by the police, a turning point in the film occurs, and there is a transition from grim social reality to a utopian opening that leaves the spectator wondering where Lola and Ana will go beyond the narrative frame of the film. The final sequences of the film are a direct repudiation of the urban reality of Mexico City as exemplified by Lola's irresponsible life. In larger terms, it is a semiotically lateral move that simply suppresses or eliminates the overwhelming presence of Mexico City. In terms of Novaro's filmmaking, it is important to underscore how Veracruz reappears in this film. It is not directly identified in the script, but rather is known to be the place of action from the closing credits. On a rustic beach frequented by locals, Lola finds a measure of peace that she has never known in Mexico City: the oppressiveness of the megalopolis is replaced by an Arcadian beach, and the camera dwells on images of individuals simply enjoying themselves in the water, including one long sequence focusing on an elderly gentleman who enthusiastically gives himself over to nudism. He is the only male figure in the entire film that the camera views with indulgence. Lola returns in the car to the city with her friends and fellow workers (with the head of the one she had bludgeoned in a helmet of bandages), but only to silently retrieve her daughter from under the perennial reproving look of her mother. But rather than return to their modest apartment, Lola and Ana set out for the same beach in Veracruz, and the film closes with the two of the them walking along the primitive shore (I stress primitive here, because, when the film was made in 1989, the beach had not yet been developed for international tourism, as have so many Mexican beaches on both the Pacific Ocean and the Caribbean, with Acapulco on the former and Cancún on the latter being symbols of the seaside tourism that is of considerable importance to the Mexican economy). This primitive shore is the antithesis to the fragmented city spaces that Lola and her daughter share, and it opens up, as I have stated, a utopian space in which they can alternatively recover and solidify the matriarchal bond between them.

Since this is a utopian space, there is no need to indicate how they will survive or even if they will remain in Veracruz. Perhaps Lola will return with her daughter to Mexico City to survive in earnest through the prostitution

FIGURE 19   The Veracruz beach as a utopian refuge from the streets of Mexico City.

of her body (and, perhaps in time, through the prostitution of her daughter's body). Or perhaps she will return to Mexico City and accept the benevolent relationship offered to her by Duende (played by the Roberto Sosa of *Lolo*), living on the margin, but with a measure of purpose that would enable her to be a better mother to Ana. Or perhaps they can remain in Veracruz and survive in a fashion that is no less marginal, but perhaps more tranquil, than employment on the streets of downtown Mexico City. Such details are quite impertinent to the final sense of Novaro's film, since what is directly at issue is a strategy of repudiation of the urban monster that threatens to destroy Lola; and in this sense, it is possible to escape from the labyrinth of the city. Novaro's film remains firmly utopian, not because it is impossible to escape from the city, but rather because no attempt is made to confirm the verisimilitude of the specific act of repudiation undertaken by Lola.

Yet the juxtaposition between the dirty realism of the majority of the film and the idyllic sequences of its conclusion, while it may not speak to socioanthropologically verifiable facts of Mexican life, particularly as embodied by women of Lola's social and economic class, stands as an eloquent cultural model that allows for the spectator of Novaro's film to question the degree to which anyone—and, specifically, a feminist like Lola—must remain irremediably trapped within the dysfunctional, dystopian space of the megalopolis.

Entre Pancho Villa y una mujer desnuda (Between Pancho Villa and a Naked Woman)

Based on her highly successful play, *Entre Villa y una mujer desnuda,*[7] Sabina Berman's 1995 film, *Entre Pancho Villa y una mujer desnuda* (note the full name in the movie's title for Pancho Villa), which Berman codirected with Isabelle Tardán, continues the development in Mexico of feminist filmmaking. The film is metatextual in the sense that the protagonist, Gina López (played by Diana Bracho, who as a child actor played Utopía in *El castillo de la pureza,* examined above), is helping her lover, Adrián Pineda (played by Arturo Ríos), in the preparation of a book on the famed populist army general and northern warlord of the 1910 Mexican Revolution, Pancho Villa, while at the same time attempting to straighten out their tempestuous relationship, a love of half-hearted constancy. She complicates the tempestuousness of their relationship by taking up with a younger lover, a sort of youth-culture type (more on this below). The film becomes metatextual in that the Pancho Villa of Adrián's book begins to appear to Adrián to offer him advice on how to hold and control Gina's love. This is metatextual in the sense that the appearances of Villa constitute an implied commentary on how Gina is undertaking to interpret him and what the Villa of national mythology (perhaps more so than professional historiography) has and has not to do with relationships between the sexes in contemporary Mexico City (the best treatment of Villa's role in Mexican history is Katz's *The Life and Times of Pancho Villa;* however see primarily Katz's photo book, *Imágenes de Pancho Villa*).

Gina is surrounded by three men: Pancho Villa, her business partner, Ismael (they own a maquiladora), and her vagrant lover, Adrián. All three constitute facets of Gina's erotic constitution. This is so in the sense that the film, rather than exploring a unitary personality for Gina, whether based on a conventional view of the faithful woman who is convinced of what sort of man will enable her best to fulfill her assigned social role or based on an image of a "modern" Mexican woman who is convinced of the legitimacy of her sexual liberty and, indeed, her erotic licentiousness, explores the profound internal contradictions of women who live enmeshed in contradictory social codes. It is not so much that contemporary urban life is more contradictory than either traditional urban life or nonurban life anywhere; rather, contemporary urban life, as seen in cultural productions like *Entre Pancho Villa y una mujer desnuda,* is particularly conscious of the contradictions of contemporary life and the need to explore them, such that the texture of meaning of these products becomes primarily the enactment of the substance of those contradictions.

In Gina's case, she is profoundly aware of her inability to find an acceptable erotic partner. The film opens with her watching a series of clips on Pancho Villa in a film archive, clips that are to serve as background for the book she is helping Adrián to write but that will also serve as the basis of the recurring images of her unconscious during her difficult and often both verbally and physically violent negotiations with the men in her life. The clips open with a sepia-toned northern Mexican desert landscape. As Pancho Villa comes riding in out of the distance, we hear a woman's growing sounds of ecstasy. These tones reach an orgasmic level as Pancho Villa rides into the camera in a clearly marked phallic way—phallic in his assertive masculinity, phallic in the symbol of his mighty horse (long recognized as a conventional evocation of masculine sexuality), and phallic in his energetic entrance into the vision of the spectator, which in the first instance is Gina herself. The fact that Gina has been totally possessed by this image is evident not only in the verbalization of her final orgasmic crescendo, but in the fact that when the camera zooms out, we see her collapsed in her seat, totally strung out from the experience. The man who has arranged for her to see the clips stares at her with a startled look that must duplicate that of many spectators of the Berman-Tardán film itself. Gina explains to her fellow viewer, and in turn to the audience of the outer film text, that Pancho Villa is for her the height in male sexiness.

Berman and Tardán parody Pancho Villa as an icon of traditional Mexican virility, and his iconicity is overdetermined both by the immediate trappings of the actor who incarnates him (Jesús Ochoa)—his strapping body, his mustache, his commanding look and martial bearing, his fetishistic military uniform—and by the hypermasculinity of the Mexican Revolution, whose triumph and subsequent official interpretations have long provided Mexico with a ground zero of patriarchal imperatives. In one sequence, which is something like a hyperparody of Pancho Villa as a superhero, he is berated by his mother for not settling down and getting married and giving her a traditional family and grandchildren she can hold and for the fact that he is always off running around the countryside. He responds haughtily that he has been off doing his patriotic duty, providing the fatherland with children. Her response is to smack him and refuse to give him her maternal benediction. The slogan "Haga patria: tenga hijos"[8] may ignore the teachings of the Catholic Church in terms of a stable and faithful family life, but it does underscore the macho's need to affirm his masculinity through the tangible proof of having as many children by as many women as possible, and this is what Gina finds particularly seductive.

The opening sequences of Pancho Villa are in sepia tones, but as the camera pulls back, we see Gina in, so to speak, living Technicolor; additionally, we see Villa against the primitive backdrop of the virtually untamed countryside, while Gina is clothed in the modernity of Mexico almost a hundred years later, sitting in a sophisticated screening room of a cinematographic archive. The juxtaposition between modern-day Mexico City and the marginal north of the days of the 1910 revolution is determined in a multiple manner, such that the film emphasizes the ironies of how Gina, as modern a woman as she may be (one immediately notes both the ultra-chic elegance of her clothes and her expensively sculptured haircut), is tied to a very conventional Mexican ideal of hypermasculinity. Throughout the film, even when Pancho Villa appears in the modern urban cityscape or when he is filmed against a rural backdrop in color in a way that evokes the glossy tourist images of traditional Mexico, Gina will struggle with the way in which her cosmopolitan feminine identity remains in part, and in a way that is very problematical to her, anchored in a set of fossilized sexual values that have allowed for Pancho Villa to transcend material history. Indeed, it is precisely this adherence to an ahistorical and, therefore, atopical concept of masculine sexuality that the film wishes to examine critically.

The disjunction between Pancho Villa as a traditional Mexican figure and Gina as an icon of the modern urban woman (even if not as modern as she might want to be) signals an important distinction in Mexican society between the metropolis and the provinces.[9] This disjunction existed in Pancho Villa's day, with the result that he was scorned and denigrated by the sophisticates centered in Mexico City and ultimately marginated by the metropolitan power structure following the end of the conflict, around 1920, as a throwback to the premodern Mexico that urbanites were at such pains to go beyond. Although the Mexican Revolution involved all sectors of Mexican society on all sides of the conflict, it was essentially—or essentially became in its triumph—about a project of modernity for Mexico. Thus, a certain iconicity for Pancho Villa as an authentic folk hero remained for the country as a whole (hence the importance of his widely scattered male seed for a machismo necessary to replenish a national population devastated by a decade of armed conflict). Yet the increasing urbanization and modernization of Mexico City could not, certainly for the sort of class represented by Gina and her associates, have more than a historic interest. It is for this reason that Gina's friends are at best bemused by her fascination for Villa's figure and her dithyrambic evocations of his masculinity. Whether her enchantment with Pancho Villa is a projection of her involvement with Adrián's project, because she is amorously involved with him, only compounds the irony of her sexual complexes: she claims at one point, "Cuánta virilidad, la metáfora perfecta de mi relación con Adrián. Llega a mi casa con toda su fuerza varonil . . . luego desaparece." [10] This is not to discount those manifestations, of which Gina's enthusiasm may be counted as one instance, of a certain morbid curiosity for the animal magnetism of Pancho Villa's masculinity, as evidenced in Martín Luis Guzmán's 1928 *El águila y la serpiente (The Eagle and the Serpent),* which is the chronicle of the experience of an urbane newspaper man as he witnessed, with a mixture of fascination and horror, Villa's conduct as a military leader.

As a consequence, Gina's interest in Pancho Villa involves as much an exception to the primacy of Americanized modernity as it is notably visible in the film as it does a return to a model of premodern Mexican masculinity (as a sign of that Americanized modernity, one of the key scenes in the film takes place in one of the sort of Denny's-style coffee shops that are a fixture of the capital). Of course, these dimensions are intimately related, because the one as much represents an exception to the primacy of the urban center in a country in which there is a virtually unstoppable demographic shift toward Mexico City and other major urban areas like Guadalajara and Monterrey; but also there is a questioning of various versions of urbane sexuality, from a bourgeois concept of the equality of the sexes to a feminist liberation grounded in sexual opportunism, from homosexual alternatives to compulsory heterosexuality to independent asexuality. Gina is in many regards a paradigmatically modern woman. She lives in a downtown apartment with nostalgic trappings of Mexican folklorism, trappings that are more trendy than traditional. She is a widowed mother and part of a business partnership, and she comes and goes as she pleases. In particular, she expresses herself fully, with none of the commitment to silence or measured expression associated with traditional Mexican female modesty.

Yet there is this dissatisfaction with modern sexuality, and this permits Gina to come virtually to orgasm at the sight of Pancho Villa in seventy-year-old film clips. In the process, this enthusiasm provides a circumstance of critique, one that is less an attack on feminism as such (with feminism here defined as an attention to the social and political rights of women) than it is an attack on a particular view of what it means to be a modern woman in contemporary Mexico City: Gina is not as liberated as she might appear to be, and how she addresses that incomplete liberation is one of the points of the film. In the process, Berman and Tardán cannot help but address specifics of the urban reality of Mexico City; and the way in which Pancho Villa emerges over and over again against the backdrop of the cityscape is as much an indication of the degree to which Mexico City's project of modernity remains in many regards unfulfilled (thus, Pancho Villa is the ghost of the repressed of that project of modernity) as it is a sign of how Mexico City has not—cannot pretend to have—separated itself from larger sociohistorical realities of the country as a whole, realities that are, therefore, as much a horizontal axis of the repressed as Pancho Villa's machismo is a vertical axis of it. This is borne out by the extent to which the *chilangos,* the citizens of Mexico City, live in disdainful separation from the rest of Mexico—even though Gina's maquiladora is in, of course, Chihuahua (specifically, Ciudad Juárez), Pancho Villa's state. Precisely, the provincial and rural migration toward the city is one of its most important defining characteristics. Berman and Tardán's film has few visible traces of how the spaces of Mexico City reveal over and over again the presence of this migratory influx. But the recurring image of Pancho Villa is there to mark it, as though he represented the invading hoards from the north (and, synecdochically, from other parts of the country), showing how the metropolis cannot separate itself from the sociopolitical and economic dynamics of the country as a whole. Indeed, the current business opportunities represented by the maquiladoras are yet another way in which prosperous Mexico City investors exploit the impoverished, underindustrialized north.

Gina's urban-centered apartment is not the only stage for her relationship with a phantom Pancho Villa, but it is where she is typing Adrián's monograph on him and it is where she receives the other men in her life who act both to fulfill her desire for an adequate sexual and personal relationship with a man and to embody in some contradictory way her complicated fantasy regarding the sort of masculinity represented by the revolutionary hero. We see the Mexico City skyline through the windows in Gina's living room and bedroom, and it is possible to speculate on whether the intrusion of Pancho Villa into her imagination, as the return of the repressed with respect to a prerevolutionary, rural Mexican social system, does not in some way point to the failure of the postrevolutionary society to build an adequately modern Mexico. Gina turns her radio console, a very 1940s or

1950s piece of furniture, on and off by kicking it, a detail that contrasts markedly with the trappings of modernity in the form of her clothes, the business offices where she goes, and the other typical spaces in which she moves. Gina's frustration with her amorous alternatives does not necessarily mean that Berman and Tardán are arguing for a return to the male sexuality offered by Pancho Villa: after all, his treatment as a buffoon at the hands of his mother undermines any significant remythologizing of his figure (concerning the battle of the sexes in Berman's film script, see Medina). But Gina's frustration can profitably be read as signaling all of the reasons women in contemporary Mexico City have to be dissatisfied with the alternatives offered them by a megalopolis created by and for male desire, whether sexual, commercial, or political.

It is for this reason that Gina is frustrated with the meager sexual and emotional attention Adrián has to offer her, although a certain amount of inertia allows him to continue to have access to her bed and body. Adrián is a likable and moderately handsome ne'er-do-well who has been the male protagonist of two failed marriages, including the one in which he currently finds himself. His wife, from whom he claims to be estranged, finds it necessary to communicate to him through Gina that he has not paid her any child support for the last month, which hardly encourages Gina, who has her own son to support. Adrián comes and goes in her life, showing up unannounced, disappearing for weeks on end, then calling by phone from an airplane to announce he'll be right there. When he is with her, it is in and out of the sack, because he has somewhere else he was supposed to have been hours before. When he arrives at her apartment, he has no time for the tea she wants to serve him from her elegant silver set, and he is already dressed to go before her orgasm has even cooled. In the sort of sexual explicitness characteristic of contemporary Mexican filmmaking, we very clearly are shown the sexual ardor of their coupling, and we are also shown the emptiness of Gina's postcoital embrace, as Adrián is checking his watch at the bedroom door.

This does not mean that Adrián is not an effective lover nor that he fails to provide Gina with some level of sexual satisfaction. Their erotic games have a certain charm: he likes to show up at her apartment door smoking a cigarette in the best manner of Humphrey Bogart. He casts the cigarette over his shoulder and storms her apartment to carry her off to the bedroom, ignoring her pleas to at least have a cup of tea. Understandably, Gina becomes fed up with Adrián: although he does respond to her sexually, his attention span is decidedly brief, and he makes it clear that she should not count on him as a viable life-partner. In fact, he underscores how he is not a very good candidate at all, given his track record with his previous wives, even though he does go through the motions of assuring Gina that his relationship with his wife is over and that he is only interested in her.

Adrián, whose profession is never specified (he is a leftist political activist as well as a sometime journalist and writer), is not without his own sexual adventurism, as demonstrated by his willingness to play the Humphrey Bogart role (which is, incidentally, another macho-drenched enactment that shows Gina's vulnerability for this sort of stereotyped erotic theatrics). There is an early scene in the movie, stressing the phallocentrism of Adrián's erotic discourse, in which he is returning by plane to Mexico City. He calls Gina on the plane's cell phone to tell her that he is on his ways to her arms. The phallic details of his whispered words are underscored by the image of the plane making its way through the clouds in a distinctly unsubtle reference to sexual intercourse. Adrián's sexual antics are a combination of traditional machismo (again, under the Humphrey Bogart disguise, but modernized: he wears an overcoat, but not the traditional trench coat and fedora of Bogart) and modern sexual technician. By the latter, I mean to draw a distinction between that and the sort of sexuality represented by Pancho Villa, a sexuality that assumes that women are always ready for a real man and that no sexual program or spectacle, beyond the direct sexual act itself, is required.

Adrián's willingness to collaborate, if only minimally, in sexual theatrics aligns him with the project of modernity, in the sense that there is a recognition of specific sexual subjectivity that requires a minimum of identification with and commitment to the psychological makeup of the other. Concomitantly, it also depends on the evocation of sexual narratives as found intertextually in songs, films, advertisements, and the like: the city provides a theatrical setting for the enactment of romance, of which walking through the street or the park hand in hand is only one highly conventional and highly readable metonymy; and modern urban life provides the textual elements for creating its discourse of romance, which is why it is so widely recognized that advertising, which is profoundly typical of the urban landscape, is based on a quasi-sexual seduction, makes use of overt and subliminal references to sexual fetish and response, and preponderantly sells products by aligning them with love and sex.

In the end, Adrián is rather a boring figure, and it is no wonder that Gina continually returns to Pancho Villa's sexuality. However, the film does not

FIGURE 20   Pancho Villa as macho standard-bearer and as mediator between Gina and Adrián.

simply propose a contrast between Pancho Villa's rough-and-ready sexuality and Adrián's shiftless urbanity (incidentally, a totally different feminist take from the one provided by *Entre Pancho Villa y una mujer desnuda* might stress the advantages to a woman of someone like Adrián: he makes good love, and then you can just wash him right out of your hair and move on with your life, knowing he will be back sometime but thankfully won't hang around long enough to clutter up the smallish dwelling space of a busy female urban sophisticate).

It is true that Adrián's negotiations over love and romance are interrupted by Pancho Villa's protestations that Adrián is going about it all wrong, and no wonder he cannot retain Gina's respect: women like to be bossed, and Adrián needs to be more aggressive and assertive, since real men are no-nonsense types whose pure animal sexuality, preferably accompanied by fetishistic projections like a horse, a gun, and some sweaty clothes, keeps women willing and waiting (a view that the film has already parodied in a reenactment of El Conde Lucanor's medieval exemplum, "El hombre que se casó con una mujer brava," [11] in which, after he kills the animals that refuse to obey his commands to be served, the haughty woman is suddenly compliant in order to escape a similar fate).

However, although Pancho Villa appears in the scenes between Gina and Adrián to counsel Adrián and it would appear that Gina cannot see or hear him, what Villa articulates to Adrián is precisely the sort of raw male Tarzan-like sexuality that caused Gina to swoon in the opening scene of the film. Adrián is willing to try Villa's advice, but he keeps getting it wrong, and Gina only grows more impatient with what comes off to her as male silliness. Each time Adrián says something that strikes Pancho Villa as an example of weak and ineffectual romantic love or each time he stumbles over the commanding speech of the firm and forthright male, Villa reacts as though being shot: he staggers back, moans in pain, writhes on the ground, and bucks in the air under the impact of the bullets of Adrián's betrayal of a proper masculinity, all with the sound effects of a heavy-duty pistol being discharged.

All of this provides for some riotously funny sequences, with a triangulation between Adrián's anguished ineptness, Villa's agonizing grimaces, and Gina's angry impatience. Although the audience of *Entre Pancho Villa y una mujer desnuda* can see the broadly played pantomime of Villa's slow death by gunfire, Gina is unable to see Villa, nor do any of the bystanders around them, not even when, inside a restaurant, Villa falls to the ground, knocking over furniture and a tray of crockery in the process. What adds to the fun of the whole matter is that Pancho Villa is attacked by gunfire: if a man's gun is one of the potent fetishes of his sexuality, it is as if the gun of masculine sexuality were being turned against the very embodiment of the latter.

The point is that, while the film, as a self-conscious cultural product, can engage in this expressionistic device to make evident the fact that the social and sexual parameters associated with Pancho Villa are still an issue in Mexico and in the relations between men and women, no matter how modern and sophisticated they may see themselves to be, these parameters are nevertheless part of the sedimented codes of Mexican social formation. These codes may emerge as part of reflective consciousness, and they may be directly articulated with varying degrees of explicitness or fragmentation in the ways in which one announces social positionings: this is why, although such an affiliation may be surprising to the man she is with, it is not incongruous for Gina to be able to verbalize her body's reaction to the image of Pancho Villa she is seeing on the movie screen. Diverse codes of social formation exist in precarious conjunction with each other, and this is what affords social subjects such notable complexity and often means that one's behavior is completely coherent: the way in which individuals around Gina tell her that she is not making much sense is the direct trace of this psychological reality.

Finally, there is Ismael. I do not know if this individual's specifically semitic name is a mark of Berman's own Jewishness, or if Jewishness is meant to be taken also as a critique of Mexico's project of modernity. I have spoken at length in my analysis of *Novia que te vea* of the problematical relationship of Jews to modern Mexico: Mexicans of Jewish extraction are undeniably direct benefactors and, indeed, major players in that country's project of modernity. But the loss of their ethnic specificity, at least in the public arena, such that Jewishness is not a visible marker in Mexico City's cultural production, has traditionally been the consequence of an imperative of assimilation to an overarching concept of modern Mexico, an imperative that is integral to that project.

Ismael is Gina's business associate. He is a young man in his mid- to late twenties, moderately nice looking in a more conventional Mexican mestizo fashion than Adrián's more cosmopolitan look. It is of particular importance that, in contrast to Adrián's suave Bogart look, Ismael sports a hippie persona: blue jeans, a black leather jacket, a ponytail, and an earring. When Ismael shows up at Gina's apartment unannounced just as Adrián is leaving, Adrián's initial burst of jealousy quickly fades as he fingers Ismael's earring. Not only does he feel he has the right to touch Ismael in a nonfriendly way, which in a traditional macho society such as in Mexico—or virtually anywhere else, for that matter—may be taken not only as a sign of the dominance of one male over another, but as a gesture that serves to feminize the other: "real" men do not get touched and take steps against those who attempt to touch them. Adrián asserts that Ismael is a homosexual and that "los homosexuales huelen a manzana." [12]

Ismael, however, does not react to Adrián's aggression with anything more than a slight grimace, and Adrián laughs him off as no threat to his masculinity and, therefore, to his presumed privilege with respect to Gina's affections and her body. Adrián may not satisfy Pancho Villa's norms of masculinity, but Ismael hardly satisfies Adrián's, and the result is that, while Gina may entertain herself in thinking that she wants an even more modern man, one with a sense of sensitivity and consideration for her femininity,

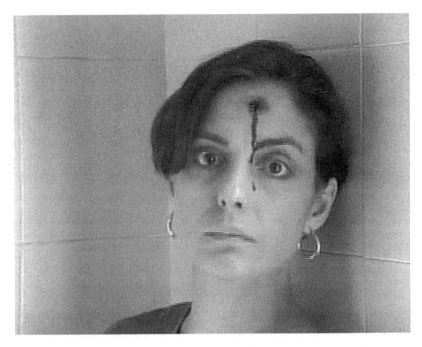

FIGURE 21   Gina "shot in the head" by the bullets of machismo.

Ismael is hardly an adequate substitute for what she has. If she dallies with him, it is to attract Adrián's attention, but there is hardly any contest in this regard.

At the end of *Entre Pancho Villa y una mujer desnuda*, there is no resolution for Gina's amorous predicament. She takes refuge from her situation in her bathroom, and Adrián, prompted by Pancho Villa once again, takes the latter's gun and shoots through the locked door. But there are two alternative endings, one, which takes place in Adrián's imagination, in which Gina is shot through the head, killed by all the testosterone-induced male hysterics raging around her. In the alternative sequence, which purportedly corresponds to "reality," we see Gina sitting on the lowered lid of the toilet, staring straight ahead, untouched by the bullet, but in a daze as to what she will do now.

The fact that the film ends in such a dead-end fashion no more suggests that love for women like Gina is a vain project than her predilection for Pancho Villa's swagger indicates that what women need is a return to raw male sexual power. Rather, given the way in which the film parodies virtually every sexual code, every sexual fetish it brings up, a properly understood feminist message is found in the way in which the contradictions in the romantic narratives that are available to the modern urban woman have little to offer her for the dignity and the integrity of her person, and the film implies the open question, Just what, then, is someone like Gina to do about her erotic and sentimental needs?

There is, of course, one answer that suggests itself, but it lies far beyond the horizons of this film, and that is the possibility of lesbian liaisons (among others, including a decision in favor of sexual abstinence). Sabina Berman is well known for the lesbian inflection of much of her writing, an inflection which alternates with broader queer perspectives, especially in her theater work, as in *Los suplicios del placer* (1994) and notably in one of the plays in this triptych, *El y ella,* in which a movable mustache is a shifting marker for the instability of sexual roles as well as their interchangeability (on queer issues in Berman's writing, see Costantino). I am not saying that Berman should have made a lesbian or queer film (even though the rejection of patriarchal heteronormativity in *Entre Pancho Villa y una mujer desnuda* in its three versions—four, if we count the dead father of Gina's child— is the whole point of the film), although, if she had, it would have joined a virtually nonexistent Mexican list of lesbian-marked films; see, however, the Argentine María Luisa Bemberg's 1990 film *Yo la peor de todas (I, the Worst of All)* on the reputedly lesbian seventeenth-century Mexican nun and intellectual Sor Juana Inés de la Cruz. At best, those familiar with Berman's cultural production in general can add to *Entre Pancho Villa y una mujer desnuda* the projection of a lesbian sequel as one way of understanding what might happen to Gina once she comes out of her daze and leaves the bathroom.

AFTERWORD

No selection of films can ever be adequately representative of a vast filmic production, and it is probable that not even an approach based on brief summary comments would be up to the task of charting all of the films that have been made in recent decades and refer, in one way or another, to Mexico City. However, the films that have been chosen for this study are representative in at least some significant ways: because they have attracted considerable national and international attention (*Danzón; El calle de los milagros; Frida, naturaleza viva*), because of the importance of the acting cast (such as the four films in which María Rojo has a prominent role: *Rojo amanecer; Danzón; De noche vienes, Esmeralda;* and *La tarea,* not to mention smaller roles in *El castillo de la pureza* and *El Callejón de los Milagros*), because of their uniqueness (*Rojo amanecer,* the one feature-length narrative film made on the Tlatelolco massacre; *Novia que te vea,* the first narrative film on Jewish society in Mexico; *Lolo,* for the presence of *chavos banda*), because of a particular modality they represent (*Mecánica nacional,* one of the first independent films to engage in Italian-style social comedy; *Sexo, pudor y lágrimas,* the intersection of television sitcoms and filmmaking), or because of the particular oeuvre of the director (María Novaro, with *Danzón* and *Lola,* significant for their different treatment of the theme of single mothers in Mexico City).

The Mexico City that is present in these films assumes different dimensions. In films such as *Lolo* and *Todo el poder,* the urban landscape is directly present, and the films concern survival within the distinctive parameters of that landscape. In *El castillo de la pureza* and *Rojo amanecer,* by contrast, there is little in the way of direct visual images of the city. Rather, the metropolis is brought into the domestic sphere in various ways that shape that sphere as a reaction to and, especially in the case of the former, a refuge from the weight of urban life. In the case of *Danzón, Mecánica nacional,* and *Entre Pancho Villa y una mujer desnuda,* the city is presented as highly metaphoric in terms of specific cultural representations: ballroom dancing, car racing, historical interpretation. Therefore, it is directly present while at the same time part of the psychological imagery of the characters as part of the way in which they situate their daily lives with respect to urban existence. A film like *El Callejón de los Milagros* uses a microcosm of the city to suggest the interpersonal dynamics that characterize urban life. Some films have been examined in terms of specific gender issues, such as single motherhood (*Danzón* and *Lola*), female sexuality and independence (*Frida, naturaleza viva; Lola; Danzón; Entre Pancho Villa y una mujer desnuda*), and political activism, while gender issues are also involved in a more diffuse way having to do with the features of specific social groups in the city, such as the bohemian world of *Frida, naturaleza viva,* the middle-class marriage in *La tarea* and *Sexo, pudor y lágrimas,* and the possibilities of queering heteronormativity (*Frida, naturaleza viva; Entre Pancho Villa y una mujer desnuda; La tarea; De noche vienes, Esmeralda*).

None of these films is about Mexico City as such; none really makes the city the protagonist in the sense of pursuing a social anthropological point of view about the city as it is lived out through individual and personal narratives. Of course, there are sociopolitical issues that are dealt with, and they are in the main immediately recognizable as matters that have some prominence in the collective social discourse of the country. Yet I have not wanted to focus on "agenda" films, and I have left documentary filmmaking for others to cover. My interest has, rather, been on the narrative film that has been a constant in the history of Mexican filmmaking, that is the main staple of what Mexican audiences see and want to see (for which reason, no claim is made that these are the very best films made in Mexico in recent decades), and that is the basis of international knowledge about Mexican filmmaking and Mexico through its films. Mexico City is a vast megalopolitan universe. It takes much more than film to adequately interpret it, which is why cultural production in the Distrito Federal is one of the most exciting and dynamic in the world, and it will take much more than this one handful of productions to understand comprehensively how it has been interpreted through film. Yet the sort of detailed analysis of specific and highly selective texts provided here is meant to stand as a model of how one can understand the importance of Latin American cities for filmmaking and of what some of the various representational strategies for narrating the story of the city through film might be.

There is, of course, no single sociocultural agenda that unifies these independent films, beyond the general goal of independent filmmaking to provide a sharply focused, critical interpretation of the parameters of historical experience. Nevertheless, what these films do have in common is that they celebrate, so to speak, the enormous importance of the growth of Mexico City and, more significantly, the enormous consciousness about it in contemporary Mexican life. As researchers such as Diane E. Davis have shown, Mexico City has, as has any national capital, a long history in the social life of the country. But two factors have coalesced to make Mexico City an acute presence in Mexican life beyond being only the sort of center of national life a capital customarily is. The first is the emergence of the city both as a megalopolis and as the city of greatest urban growth in the world. Jingoistically speaking, this might sound like a good thing because of the attention it brings to the city, but the critical situation that it has created for the infrastructure of the city, the almost insurmountable complexities relating to the delivery of basic services and the defense of the citizenry, and what this circumstance means for the balance of real and symbolic power between the capital and the rest of the country are hardly the stuff of chamber of commerce–like self-promotions. Films like *Todo el poder, Lola,* and *Lolo* are particularly eloquent in giving a sense of the precariousness of life in Mexico City and in echoing the themes that are part of the urban culture relating to the rigors of survival. This enormous increase in an awareness of Mexico City is what accounts for the concentration of films from the 1990s, and it also corresponds in general to an increase of print literature dealing with the dimensions of life in the city.

The other circumstance is the 1985 earthquake, which in its heavy devastation served as a loud alert to Mexicans concerning the precariousness of their urban life. In this sense, the earthquake was a rhetorical marker of the effects of megalopolitan growth; and references to it, such as certain iconographic features in *Lola,* serve as epiphenomena to underscore the acute sensitivity that the contemporary culture of the capital city has to the circumstances and quality of life it presents. The reader is referred to Alejandro González Iñárritu's stunning *Amores perros* (2000); although brought out subsequent to the completion of this study, it is the most implacable Mexican film made to date on the rigors of survival in the city: the closing image of an urban wasteland ringed by the horizon of ultramodern sky-scrapers is remarkably unsubtle, but it serves to confirm the central truth of the three interwoven stories the film has to tell. While the film contains within it a message of social redemption (otherwise, its narrative would be quite simply intolerable, something like a Buñuelesque version to the nth degree), it is unstinting in demonstrating how that negotiation must be worked out in the context of overwhelmingly destructive odds, as allego-rized in terms of the violence against the city's canine population, which are less figures of human beings than of companionable living and feeling be-ings whose lives are stark and unambiguous correlatives of those of human beings.

The point I have wanted to make throughout this study is how it is pos-sible to speak of an interpretation of the city through film. Certainly, a thor-oughgoing survey of over one hundred years of Mexican filmmaking will re-veal many images of the city and the many ways in which the city is interpreted through the lives of its inhabitants and vice versa: in this there is nothing particularly unique about this group of films. But what is unique, as I have affirmed repeatedly, is the particular prominence of an awareness of the city in recent decades, an awareness which makes it appropriate to in-quire how this prominence may also extend to filmic texts. Concomitantly, this study has had as its goal going beyond the unspoken assumption that the city is merely "there" and that, of course, it is merely there because the film has to take place somewhere, and why not in the urban center of the country. A proper response is that everything in a film (as in any other genre of cultural production) is merely just there, no matter how carefully it has been chosen by the director to be there: it becomes semiotically important as part of an interpretive project that undertakes to examine what role the city plays as part of the narrative. This role may be correlative, it may be contrapuntal, it may be ironic, or it may be synergetic. It may not even be immediately present, as in the case of films like *Rojo amanecer* or *La tarea,* which demonstrate how the city is present in more ways than the materially visible and how urban lives are imbricated with and circumscribed by urban realities in ways that have become naturalized such that they only become singularly meaningful when the critic begins to ask why they have assumed that particular configuration. Consequently, I am less concerned about what ways life in Mexico City may be unique, whether that uniqueness is in terms of the particular shape of the project of modernity in the city or the tensions between that project and harsh materialities that it often serves to mask or imagine away. Rather, my interest has been with how the very specific and very selective realities of Mexico City urban life, realities that are captured—by chance or as part of directorial-auteurial design (which is the case matters little from a semiotic point of view)—can be interpreted in such a way as to provide them with a significance they will not have when characters and story are viewed as floating free in a space that is denied meaning in itself, if only by omission or ignorance. Bachelard and others have taught us how to read space as invested with human meaning and how the meanings of human life interact with the space in which they occur. Bringing this important cultural perception to the analysis of a representative sample of contemporary Mexican filmmaking has been the principal concern of this study.

NOTES

1. Politics of the City

1. *Canoa* actually deals with the massacre of some students in the small town of Canoa as part of the hysteria against the alleged infiltration of student groups a month prior to Tlatelolco (September 15, 1968, to be precise). See Costa's useful discussion of the film in detail (100–108); it is the context of Tlatelolco and its consequences for Mexican cultural production that make it of interest for Cazals to record this incident.

2. But, as García and Coria assert with reference to Mexican filmmaking before the 1980s, "El sexo, al igual que la denuncia exacta de los horrores del régimen en turno, fueron prohibidos" [Sex, along with the precise denunciation of the horrors of the regime in power, was strictly prohibited] (66). Thus, "La hiperviolencia cinematográfica tuvo un génesis gradual en el echeverrismo, aumentó a partir del lopezportillato y pidió toda mesura durante del delamadridismo" [The hyperviolence of the movies developed gradually during the presidency of Luis Echeverría Álvarez, increased during that of José López Portillo, and went completely out of control during that of Miguel de La Madrid Hurtado] (66).

3. Gabriel Retes's *El bulto* (1991) concerns a man who awakens from a twenty-year coma that is the result of his being wounded in a massacre subsequent to Tlatelolco, the 1971 Jueves de Corpus violence, only to find a very different Mexico in which the massacre is a remote historical event.

4. Guillermo Bonfil Batalla observes: "El sistema escolar, los medios masivos de comunicación, la movilidad social, tanto en sentido horizontal, como vertical, así como muchas acciones de política gubernamental, empresarial, religiosa o partidaria, tienden en la mayoría de los estados nacionales a eliminar la diversidad cultural con algún propósito declarado o implícito: crear un mercado, reforzar la unidad nacional, realizar la justicia social o divina, alcanzar la democracia, etcétera" [The school system, news media communications, social mobility, both

horizontally and vertically, as well as many acts of governmental, business, religious, and political policy, have the propensity, in the majority of national states, to eliminate cultural diversity on the basis of a specific or implied goal: to create a market, to reinforce national unity, to achieve social or divine justice, to bring about democracy, or whatever] (10).

As a counterproposition, he continues: "Desmontar el andamiaje ideológico sustentoso de la visión cultural del sector dominante en nuestras sociedades, resulta entonces una tarea prioritaria para sanear el ambiente intelectual (en el sentido amplio, no restringido), construir una visión auténtica de nosotros mismos y conducir el debate sobre nuestro futuro a partir de concepciones e identificaciones más próximas a la realidad" [The deconstruction of the ideological apparatus that underpins the cultural vision of the dominant sector of our society ends up being, then, a priority task needed to sanitize the intellectual setting (in a broad and not limited sense) and to construct an authentic vision of ourselves, toward leading the debate regarding our future, beginning with concepts and identities closer to reality] (13).

5. Cimet quotes the famous Mexican-Jewish photographer Anita Brenner to the effect that "except to cultured Mexicans and foreigners, a Jew was either a 'Judas toy' or an 'evil spirit,' but not a person" (22). Cimet continues, "Being limited in number, Jews could escape prejudice. They remained mostly unnoticed" (22).

6. Now do you know what virtual reality is?

7. Where can I take a bath?

2. Human Geographies

1. One parenthetical detail: Alcoriza's film is titled *Mecánica nacional,* but my analysis focuses on the city rather than the nation. There are two ways to explain this: on the one hand, it is a set phrase, meaning something like "That's how things work here," and any advantage associated with using a set phrase would be lost if it were changed to something like *Mecánica municipal;* on the other hand—and this is one of my theses throughout this study—the nation has become the city and vice versa, to the extent that the weight of Mexico City is so enormous in Mexican sociocultural life that it is now a given assumption of Mexican life (at least as it is understood through and from the perspective of Mexico City) that what happens in the capital is a legitimate synecdoche of the country at large.

2. Montoya Arce asserts, "El Estado de México . . . aparece como un gran atractivo para la población de otras entidades donde no existen opciones para mejorar las condiciones materiales de vida de sus habitantes. Quienes pretenden cambiar su residencia hacia otro lugar buscan los centros de mayor acumulación de capital, de estímulo al crecimiento de las actividades económicas y la generación de puestas de trabajo; centros donde se eleva la oferta de empleo productivo y con ello se abren posibilidades ocupaciones" [The state of Mexico . . . is very attractive for the population of other entities where options do not exist for the improvement of the material conditions of life for their inhabitants. Those who would change their place of residence seek the center of the major accumulation of capital, the stimulation of economic activity, and the creation of jobs, centers where there is a promise of gainful employment, including job opportunities] (225–226).

3. He is a creator of utopias, of nonexistent places.

4. One of the other major contradictions in Lima is his imposition of vegetarianism within the home—he answers the daughter Voluntad's question regarding what meat tastes like by saying "horrible"—but then when he is out on the street he voraciously devours *dos tacos de carnitas*. In one scene, his wife finds him crouched in a corner jabbing himself with a pin and sucking his own blood.

5. At one point, Utopía appears to be identified as Sofía; this is perhaps more an acting error than a subtle shift in the script.

6. Absolutely unwavering, the father continues to rule over the Mexican family.

7. The title of Ripstein's movie is taken from Octavio Paz's essay on Marcel Duchamp, "El castillo de la pureza," in which, for Duchamp, *la pureté* is what remains when nothingness (*néant*) is banished. That is, the contradictions of the world are its purity, and not what one attains when one attempts to banish them, since what would remain would be nothingness.

8. A further important urban dimension of *Todo el poder* is the sound track, made up of music by well-known urban rock bands, and the film opens with "La tira" by the group Molotov. An important study that remains to be undertaken concerns the sound-track music of the films of this study as well as of contemporary Latin American films in general.

9. I prefer a dead daughter to a petty thief.

3. Mapping Gender

1. The most exotic idea is shared by millions. There are so many of us that no one even cares if you are of the same persuasion or not.

2. Hadleigh identifies him as "bisexual" (192), and his role with Frank Sinatra in *Anchors Aweigh* (1945) is often commented on in homosexual film contexts, such as Mark Rappaport's documentary film, *The Silver Screen: Color Me Lavender* (1998).

3. In cinematographic terms, there is one detail that bears underscoring, and this is the so-called magical realist effects of Esmeralda's declarations. Not only do her clothes change color throughout the course of her declarations (which presumably take place in a single sitting), but at one point the flowers of her dress begin to float off to fill the floor around her. In this way, the separation between her blithe persona and the sober social reality represented by the judicial process is underscored.

4. The fact that the female gaze may end up being excluded from the internal audience of the film may very well have to do with the fact that, although Hermosillo has not made films that can principally be described as examples of gay filmmaking, there is in his work an overarching gay perspective that requires analysis in terms of the way in which he sees women and how women's understanding of the male body is interpreted in his films.

5. The following is one of Carlos Monsiváis's entries in his catalog of sexual characteristics in contemporary Mexico City: "8. Alicia impresiona mucho a su profesora de literatura, la hace sentirse vieja. 'Yo me consideraba liberada,' le cuenta a unos amigos. 'Pero esta muchachita el otro día en clase, y sin que pudiera interrumpirla, catalogó treinta y dos variantes de traseros masculinos. Y si no se lo prohíbo

con las fuerzas que me quedaban, organiza allí mismo entre los chavos un concurso de las Mejores Nalgas" [8. Alicia makes a good impression on her literature professor, making her feel old. "I considered myself liberated," she told her friends. "But the other day in class, this kid—and I had no way to stop her—catalogued thirty-two kinds of male butts. And if I hadn't stopped her right there, with what little strength I had left, she would have organized among the boys right then and there a best cheeks contest] ("La hora del lobo" 164).

6. Mexico is still standing.

7. For an excellent analysis of the feminist and gender issues in the play, see Magnarelli. Her analysis, however, turns on a topic that appears only once in the play: the ritual of drinking tea together as an organizing principle for the display of sexual roles.

8. Be patriotic: have children.

9. I realize my statements about the modern urban Mexican woman may be somewhat tenuous, especially if one wishes for sociological proof of such assertions. However, in the first place, there is the cultural record of these films themselves—see especially, the sexual agency of someone like Julia in *Danzón,* the decision for gender independence of the protagonist of *Lola,* or the secure women's world attained by the two childhood friends as we see them at the end of *Novia que te vea.* Debra Castillo provides a far-ranging survey of women's issues in contemporary Mexican writing, a survey that stresses considerable liberationist successes, at least as viewed by women's fictional writing. Of special importance in understanding the discussion of feminist issues in Latin America for women of Gina's class are the two outstanding reviews *fem* (1976–date) and *Debate feminista* (1990–date), the former more popular in scope, the latter more intellectual and internationalist.

10. How much virility—the perfect metaphor of my relationship with Adrian. He shows up on the doorstep with all his manly strength . . . and then disappears.

11. The man who married a virago.

12. Homosexuals smell of apples.

FILMOGRAPHY

(Dates given refer to their release, not the year in which they were filmed.)

El Callejón de los Milagros. Dir. Jorge Fons. Script: Vicente Leñero. Alameda Films, 1995.

El castillo de la pureza. Dir. Arturo Ripstein. Script: José Emilio Pachecho and Arturo Ripstein. Estudios Churubusco Azteca, 1973.

Danzón. Dir. María Novaro. Script: María Novaro and Beatriz Novaro. Instituto Mexicano de Cinematografía, Macondo Cine Video, Fondo de Fomento a la Calidad Cinematográfica, Televisión Española, Tabasco Films, Gobierno del Estado de Veracruz, 1991.

De noche vienes, Esmeralda. Dir. Jaime Humberto Hermosillo. Script: Jaime Humberto Hermosillo. Consejo Nacional para la Cultura y las Artes, Instituto Mexicano de Cinematografía, Fondo de Fomento a la Calidad Cinematográfica, Resonancia Productora, Producciones Esmeralda, Monarca Productions, 1997.

Entre Pancho Villa y una mujer desnuda. Dir. Sabina Berman and Isabelle Tardán. Script: Sabina Berman. Televicine, 1995.

Frida, naturaleza viva. Dir. Paul Leduc. Script: José Joaquín Blanco. Clasa Films Mundiales, 1984.

Lola. Dir. María Novaro. Script: Beatriz Novaro and María Novaro. Conacite Dos, Cooperativa José Revueltas, Macondo Cine Video, and Televisión Española (TVE), 1991.

Lolo. Dir. Francisco Athié. Script: Francisco Athié. Centro de Capacitación Cinematográfica, IMCINE, and Estudios Churubusco Azteca, 1992.

Mecánica nacional. Dir. Luis Alcoriza. Script: Luis Alcoriza. Producciones Escorpión, 1971.

Novia que te vea. Dir. Guita Schyfter. Script: Hugo Hiriart. Producciones Arte Nuevo, 1993.

Rojo amanecer. Dir. Jorge Fons. Script: Guadalupe Ortega and Xavier Robles. Cinematografía Sol, 1989.

Sexo, pudor y lágrimas. Dir. Antonio Serrano. Script: Antonio Serrano. Producciones Titán, 1999.

La tarea. Dir. Jaime Humberto Hermosillo. Script: Jaime Humberto Hermosillo. Clasa Films Mundiales, 1990.

Todo el poder. Dir. Fernando Sariñana. Script: Enrique Rentería and Carolina Rivera. Altavista Films, 1999.

REFERENCES

Agustín, José. "Entrevista con Arturo Ripstein." *Cuadernos hispanoamericanos* 558 (1996): 83–94.

Álvarez Garín, Raúl. "Aclaración necesaria." *Nexos* 239 (November 1997): 73–74. Reply to González de Alba's comments in *Nexos* 238, followed by the latter's counterreply. Reply and counterreply bear the collective title "Dos aclaraciones."

Ayala Blanco, Jorge. *La aventura del cine mexicano en la época de oro y después.* Mexico City: Editorial Grijalbo, 1993.

———. *Búsqueda del cine mexicano (1968–1972).* Mexico City: Editorial Posada, 1986.

———. *La condición del cine mexicano (1973–1985).* Mexico City: Editorial Posada, 1986.

Bachelard, Gaston. *The Poetics of Space.* Translated by Maria Jolas. Boston: Beacon Press, 1994. Published originally as *Poétique de l'espace.* Paris: Presses Universitaires de France, 1967.

Bell, David, and Gill Valentine, eds. *Mapping Desire: Geographies of Sexualities.* London: Routledge, 1995.

Berg, Charles Ramírez. *Cinema of Solitude: A Critical Study of Mexican Film, 1967–1983.* Austin: University of Texas Press, 1992.

Black, Richard D. *Ferrari Guides' Gay Mexico.* 1st ed. Phoenix: Ferrari International Publishing, 1997.

Bokser de Liwerant, Judith, ed. *Imágenes de un encuentro: la presencia judía en México durante la primera mitad del siglo XX.* Mexico City: UNAM; Tribuna Israelita; Comité Central Israelita de México; Multibanco Mercantil, 1993.

Bonfil Batalla, Guillermo. *Pensar nuestra cultura.* Mexico City: Alianza Editorial, 1991.

Castillo, Debra. *Easy Women: Sex and Gender in Modern Mexican Fiction.* Minneapolis: University of Minnesota Press, 1998.

Cimet, Adina. *Ashkenazi Jews in Mexico: Ideologies in the Structuring of a Community.* Albany: State University of New York Press, 1997.

Colina, José de la, and Tomás Pérez Turrent. *Luis Buñuel: prohibido asomarse al interior.* Mexico City: Joaquín Mortiz/Planeta, 1986.

Cortina, Guadalupe. *Invenciones multitudinarias: escritoras judiamexicanas contemporáneas.* Newark, Del.: Juan de la Cuesta, 2000.

Costa, Paola. *La "apertura" cinematográfica: México 1970–1976.* Puebla: Universidad Autónoma de Puebla, 1988.

Costantino, Roselyn. "Sabina Berman." In *Latin American Writers on Gay and Lesbian Themes: A Bio-Critical Sourcebook,* edited by David William Foster, 59–63. Westport, Conn.: Greenwood Press, 1994.

Davis, Diane E. *Urban Leviathan: Mexico City in the Twentieth Century.* Philadelphia: Temple University Press, 1994.

Dealy, Glenn Caudill. *The Public Man: An Interpretation of Latin American and Other Catholic Countries.* Amherst: University of Massachusetts Press, 1977.

Elkin, Judith Laikin. *The Jews of Latin America.* Rev. ed. New York: Holmes & Meier, 1998.

Foster, David William. *Buenos Aires: Perspectives on the City and Cultural Production.* Gainesville: University Press of Florida, 1998.

———. *Contemporary Argentine Cinema.* Columbia: University of Missouri Press, 1992.

———. *Gender and Society in Contemporary Brazilian Cinema.* Austin: University of Texas Press, 1999.

———. "Latin American Documentary Narrative." *PMLA: Publications of the Modern Language Association of America* 99 (1984): 41–55.

———. "Luis Rafael Sánchez." In *Latin American Writers on Gay and Lesbian Themes: A Bio-Critical Sourcebook,* edited by David William Foster, 401–404. Westport, Conn.: Greenwood Press, 1994.

———. "Queering the Patriarchy in Hermosillo's *Doña Herlinda y su hijo.*" In *Sexual Textualities: Essays on Queer/ing Latin American Writing,* 64–72. Austin: University of Texas Press, 1997. Also in *Framing Latin American Cinema: Contemporary Critical Perspectives,* edited by Anne Marie Stock, 235–245. Minneapolis: University of Minnesota Press, 1997.

García, Gustavo. "Melodrama: The Passion Machine." In *Mexican Cinema,* edited by Paulo Antonio Paranaguá, translated by Ana M. López, 153–162. London: British Film Institute; Mexico City: IMCINE, 1995.

García, Gustavo, and José Felipe Coria. *Nuevo cine mexicano.* Mexico City: Editorial Clío Libros y Videos, 1997.

García, Gustavo, and Rafael Aviña. *Época de oro del cine mexicano.* Mexico City: Editorial Clío Libros y Videos, 1977.

García Arteaga, Ricardo. "El 'teatro light' y los nuevos productores en los noventa." Forthcoming.

García Riera, Emilio. *Historia documental del cine mexicano.* 18 vols. Mexico City: Ediciones Era, 1969–1976? Reprint, Guadalajara: Universidad de Guadalajara, 1992–1997.

González de Alba, Luis. "Para limpiar la memoria." *Nexos* 238 (October 1997):

45–49. See reply by Raúl Álvarez Garín, and González de Alba's counterreply, "A cada narrador sus palabras." *Nexos* 239 (November 1997): 74–75, 77.

Guillermoprieto, Alma. *The Heart That Bleeds: Latin America Now.* New York: Vintage Book, 1995, c. 1994.

Hadleigh, Boze. *Hollywood Gays.* New York: Barricade Books, 1996.

Hershfield, Joanne. *Mexican Cinema/Mexican Woman, 1940–1950.* Tucson: University of Arizona Press, 1996.

Howe, Irving. *World of Our Fathers.* New York: Harcourt Brace Jovanovich, 1976.

Katz, Friedrich. *Imágenes de Pancho Villa.* Mexico City: Ediciones Era/Conaculta-INAH, 1999.

———. *The Life and Times of Pancho Villa.* Stanford: Stanford University Press, 1998.

Krause, Corinne A. *Los judíos en México: una historia con énfasis especial en el período de 1857 a 1930.* Mexico City: Universidad Iberoamericana, Departamento de Historia, 1987.

Lehman, Peter. *Running Scared: Masculinity and the Representation of the Male Body.* Philadelphia: Temple University Press, 1993.

Lerner, Ira T. *Mexican Jewry in the Land of the Aztecs: A Guide.* 6th ed. Mexico City: Saul Lokier, Editor, 1973.

Lindauer, Margaret A. *Devouring Frida: The Art History and Popular Celebrity of Frida Kahlo.* Hanover, N.H.: University Press of New England, 1999.

Loaeza, Guadalupe. *Las reinas de Polanco.* Mexico City: Cal y Arena, 1989.

López, Ana M. "Of Rhythms and Borders." In *Everynight Life: Culture and Dance in Latin/o America,* edited by Celeste Fraser Delgado and José Esteban Muñoz. Durham: Duke University Press, 1997.

Lumsden, Ian. *Homosexualidad, sociedad y estado en México.* Mexico City: Solediciones; Ottawa: Canadian Gay Archives, 1991.

Luna, Andrés de. "The Labyrinths of History." In *Mexican Cinema,* edited by Paulo Antonio Paranaguá, translated by Ana M. López, 171–177. London: British Film Institute; Mexico City: IMCINE, 1995.

Maciel, David R. "Serpientes y escaleras: The Contemporary Cinema of Mexico, 1976–1994." In *New Latin American Cinema,* vol. 2, edited by Michael T. Martin, 94–120. Detroit: Wayne State University Press, 1997.

Magnarelli, Sharon. "Tea for Two: Performing History and Desire in Sabina Berman's *Entre Villa y una mujer desnuda." Latin American Theatre Review* 30, 1 (1996): 55–74.

Mahieu, José Agustín. "El período mexicano de Luis Buñuel." *Cuadernos hispanoamericanos* 358 (1980): 158–172.

Massey, Doreen. *Space, Place, and Gender.* Cambridge: Polity Press, 1994.

Medina, Manuel. "La batalla de los sexos: estrategias de desplazamiento en *Entre Pancho Villa y una mujer desnuda* de Sabina Berman." *Revista Fuentes Humanísticas* 4, 8 (1994): 107–111.

Mennell, D. Jan. "Memoria, *midrash* and metamórfosis en *Novia que te vea* de Guita Schyfter: un diálogo textual-visual." *Chasqui* 29, 1 (2000): 50–63.

Monsiváis, Carlos. "La hora del lobo: del sexo en la sociedad de masas." In *Los rituales del caos,* 163–165. Mexico City: Ediciones Era, 1995.

————. *Los rituales del caos.* Mexico City: Ediciones Era, 1995.

Montoya Arce, Jaciel. *Estado de México: población en movimiento: un análisis demográfico del período 1950–1980.* Mexico City: Universidad Autónoma del Estado de México, Centro de Investigación y Estudios Avanzados de Población, 1995.

Moorhead, Florencia. "Subversion with a Smile: Elena Poniatowska's *The Night Visitor.*" *Letras femeninas* 20, 1–2 (1994): 131–140.

Mora, Carl J. *Mexican Cinema: Reflections of a Society.* Rev. ed. Berkeley: University of California Press, 1989.

Mora, Juan Miguel de. *Tlatelolco 1968: por fin toda la verdad.* Mexico City: Editores Asociados, 1975.

Muñoz, Jorge. "Cine imperfecto y la reinscripción histórica en el film *Rojo amanecer* de Jorge Fons." *Romance Languages Annual* 7 (1995): 562–565.

Murray, Stephen O. *Latin American Male Homosexualities.* Albuquerque: University of New Mexico Press, 1995.

Nissán, Rosa. *Novia que te vea.* Mexico City: Planeta, 1992.

Noriega, Chon A., and Steven Ricci, eds. *The Mexican Cinema Project.* Los Angeles: UCLA Film and Television Archive, 1994.

Núñez Noriega, Guillermo. *Sexo entre varones: poder y resistencia en el campo sexual.* 2nd ed. Mexico City: Coordinación de Humanidades, Programa Universitario de Estudios de Género, Instituto de Investigaciones Sociales; Hermosillo: El Colegio de Sonora; Mexico City: Miguel Angel Porrúa Grupo Editorial, 1999.

Oxman, Nelson. *La leyenda escandinava.* Mexico City: Editorial Diana, 1989.

Paranaguá, Paulo Antonio, ed. *Mexican Cinema.* Translated by Ana M. López. London: British Film Institute; Mexico City: IMCINE, 1995.

Paz, Octavio. "El castillo de la pureza." In *Apariencia desnuda: la obra de Marcel Duchamp,* 13–103. Mexico City: Biblioteca Era, 1979.

Pérez Turrent, Tomás. "Crises and Renovations (1965–91)." In *Mexican Cinema,* edited by Paulo Antonio Paranaguá, translated by Ana M. López, 94–115. London: British Film Institute; Mexico City: IMCINE, 1995.

Pick, Zuzana M. "Identity and Representation: *Frida, naturaleza viva.*" In *The New Latin American Cinema: A Continental Project,* 89–96. Austin: University of Texas Press, 1993.

Pile, Steve. *The Body and the City: Psychoanalysis, Space, and Subjectivity.* London: Routledge, 1996.

Poniatowska, Elena. *Nada, nadie: las voces del temblor.* Mexico City: Ediciones Era, 1988.

————. *La noche de Tlatelolco.* Mexico City: Ediciones Era, 1971.

Quiroga, José. "Tears at the Nightclub." In *Tropics of Desire: Interventions from Queer Latino America,* 145–168. New York: New York University Press, 2000.

Ramírez, Luis Enrique. "'Y la nación se nos fue, joven, apenas con 30 siglos de resplandor.'" *La jornada,* Cultural Section (August 11, 1995): 29.

Rechy, John. *The Sexual Outlaw: A Documentary. A Non-Fiction Account, with Commentaries, of Three Days and Nights in the Sexual Underground.* New York: Grove Press, 1985, c. 1977.

Schaefer, Claudia. *Danger Zones: Homosexuality, National Identity, and Mexican*

Culture. Tucson: University of Arizona Press, 1996.

Schteingatt, Martha. "Mexico City." In *The Metropolis Era,* vol. 2, *Mega-Cities,* edited by Mattei Dogan and John D. Kasarda, 268–293. Newbury Park: Sage Publications, 1988.

Schütz, Jutta. *Insight Guides: Mexico City.* Boston: Houghton Mifflin; Singapore: APA Publications, 1994.

Sedgwick, Eve Kosofsky. *Epistemology of the Closet.* Berkeley: University of California Press, 1990.

Sen, Kanishka. Review of *De noche vienes, Esmeralda. Chasqui* 28, 2 (1999): 149–153.

Shields, Robert. *Places on the Margin: Alternative Geographies of Modernity.* New York: Routledge, 1991.

Sippl, Diane. "*Al cine de las mexicanas: Lola* in the Limelight." In *Redirecting the Gaze: Gender, Theory, and Cinema in the Third World,* edited by Diana Robin and Ira Jaffe, 33–66. Albany: State University of New York Press, 1999.

Soja, Edward. *Postmodern Geographies: The Reassertion of Space in Critical Social Theory.* London: Verso, 1989.

Stavans, Ilan. "Frida and Betina: Unparalleled Lives." In *The Riddle of Cantinflas: Essays on Hispanic Popular Culture,* 53–56. Albuquerque: University of New Mexico Press, 1998.

———. "Lost in Translation." In *King David's Harp: Autobiographical Essays by Jewish Latin American Writers,* edited by Ilan Stavans, 227–243. Albuquerque: University of New Mexico Press, 1999.

———. "The Riddle of Cantinflas." In *The Riddle of Cantinflas: Essays on Hispanic Popular Culture,* 31–52. Albuquerque: University of New Mexico Press, 1998.

Tierney, Dolores. "Silver Sling-Backs and Mexican Melodrama: *Salón México* and *Danzón.*" *Screen* 38, 4 (1997): 360–371.

Tuñón, Julia. *Mujeres de luz y sombra en el cine mexicano: la construcción de una imagen, 1939–1953.* Mexico City: El Colegio de México; Instituto Mexicano de Cinematografía, 1998.

Valdés, Mario J. "The Configuration of the Filmic Subject." *Semiotica* 112, 1–2 (1996): 141–154.

Ward, Peter M. "Mexico City." In *Encyclopedia of Latin American History and Culture,* vol. 4, edited by Barbara A. Tenenbaum, 38–42. New York: Charles Scribner's, 1996.

Wood, Michael. "Buñuel in Mexico." In *Mediating Two Worlds: Cinematic Encounters in the Americas,* edited by John King, Ana M. López, and Manuel Alvarado, 40–51. London: BFI Publishing, 1993.

Zamora, Martha. *Frida: el pincel de la angustia.* Mexico City: n.p., 1987. An abridged edition in English appeared as *Frida Kahlo: The Brush of Anguish.* Translated by Marilyn Sode Smith. San Francisco: Chronicle Books, 1990.

Zavarzadeh, Mas'ud. *Seeing Films Politically.* Albany: State University of New York Press, 1991.

Zolov, Eric. *Refried Elvis: The Rise of the Mexican Counterculture.* Berkeley: University of California Press, 1999.

INDEX